The Value Vector

Building Scalable Generative AI-Based Applications

Jaydeep Chakrabarty
Harinee Muralinath

Apress®

The Value Vector: Building Scalable Generative AI-Based Applications

Jaydeep Chakrabarty
Bengaluru, Karnataka, India

Harinee Muralinath
Bengaluru, Karnataka, India

ISBN-13 (pbk): 979-8-8688-1879-0
https://doi.org/10.1007/979-8-8688-1880-6

ISBN-13 (electronic): 979-8-8688-1880-6

Copyright © 2025 by Jaydeep Chakrabarty, Harinee Muralinath

This work is subject to copyright. All rights are reserved by the Publisher, whether the whole or part of the material is concerned, specifically the rights of translation, reprinting, reuse of illustrations, recitation, broadcasting, reproduction on microfilms or in any other physical way, and transmission or information storage and retrieval, electronic adaptation, computer software, or by similar or dissimilar methodology now known or hereafter developed.

Trademarked names, logos, and images may appear in this book. Rather than use a trademark symbol with every occurrence of a trademarked name, logo, or image we use the names, logos, and images only in an editorial fashion and to the benefit of the trademark owner, with no intention of infringement of the trademark.

The use in this publication of trade names, trademarks, service marks, and similar terms, even if they are not identified as such, is not to be taken as an expression of opinion as to whether or not they are subject to proprietary rights.

While the advice and information in this book are believed to be true and accurate at the date of publication, neither the authors nor the editors nor the publisher can accept any legal responsibility for any errors or omissions that may be made. The publisher makes no warranty, express or implied, with respect to the material contained herein.

    Managing Director, Apress Media LLC: Welmoed Spahr
    Acquisitions Editor: Anandadeep Roy
    Development Editor: James Markham
    Editorial Assistant: Jessica Vakili

Cover designed by eStudioCalamar

Distributed to the book trade worldwide by Springer Science+Business Media New York, 1 New York Plaza, New York, NY 10004. Phone 1-800-SPRINGER, fax (201) 348-4505, e-mail orders-ny@springer-sbm.com, or visit www.springeronline.com. Apress Media, LLC is a Delaware LLC and the sole member (owner) is Springer Science + Business Media Finance Inc (SSBM Finance Inc). SSBM Finance Inc is a **Delaware** corporation.

For information on translations, please e-mail booktranslations@springernature.com; for reprint, paperback, or audio rights, please e-mail bookpermissions@springernature.com.

Apress titles may be purchased in bulk for academic, corporate, or promotional use. eBook versions and licenses are also available for most titles. For more information, reference our Print and eBook Bulk Sales web page at http://www.apress.com/bulk-sales.

Any source code or other supplementary material referenced by the author in this book is available to readers on GitHub. For more detailed information, please visit https://www.apress.com/gp/services/source-code.

If disposing of this product, please recycle the paper

For humanity.

The kindness that code cannot write, and the understanding that data cannot contain.

Table of Contents

About the Authors xi

About the Technical Reviewer xiii

Prologue xv

Chapter 1: The Value Compass – Navigating the AI Hype 1

    Why Business Value Matters 4

    Escaping the "Death by POC" trap 16

    From Idea to Real-World Use: A Generative AI Implementation Workflow 19

        Step 1: Senior Leadership Education 19

        Step 2: Use Case Ideation 19

        Step 3: Stakeholder Workshop 19

        Step 4: Prioritization 19

        Step 5: Rapid POC Development 20

        Step 6: MVP Creation 20

        Step 7: Deployment and Measurement 20

    Anya's Notes 24

        Concepts in Practice 24

    The AI Value Compass: A Strategic Framework for AI Implementation 24

        Vector 1: Business Challenge Identification 25

        Vector 2: AI Capability Mapping 26

        Vector 3: Value and Impact Assessment 27

        Vector 4: Ethical Implementation Feasibility 28

        Implementing the AI Value Compass 29

    Navigating the Initiatives 30

        Framework for Evaluating AI Initiatives: The Degree of Unknowns 30

        Avoiding the "Death by POC" Trap 34

TABLE OF CONTENTS

The Generative AI Implementation Workflow: Charting Your Course to AI Success 37
    Key learnings from this chapter 41

Chapter 2: The GenAI Idea Maze – Finding Gold Among the Glitter 43

Inbox Overflow: The GenAI Proposal Deluge 43
Mind the Gap: Educating the Organization 45
Mapping the AI Landscape 47
The Use Case Detective's Toolkit 50
Anya's Notes 55
    Concepts in Practice 55
First Steps into the AI World 55
    Three Waves of Innovation 56
    The Data Dilemma 57
Mind the Gap: Cultivating AI Understanding 58
    The Need for AI Literacy 58
    Making AI Education Engaging and Practical 60
    Understanding AI's Core Capabilities 61
The Use Case Detective's Toolkit 66
    The Strategic Foundation: "Should We Build?" 67
    The Tactical Roadmap: "How Do We Build?" 70
The Framework in Action: Transforming Fashion Retail 72
    Starting with "Should We Build?" 72
    Moving to "How Do We Build?" 73
    Framework Insights 75
    Real Impact 75
When Theory Meets Reality 76
Key Learnings from This chapter 78

Chapter 3: Proof or Dare – Reimagining POCs in the GenAI Playground 81

POCs: Then and Now 81
Blueprint for GenAI POCs 84
From Architecture to Action: Implementing and Demonstrating GenAI POCs 90

TABLE OF CONTENTS

Anya's Notes 99
    Concepts in Practice 99
Understanding the Evolution of POCs in the AI Era 100
    Accelerated Technology Evolution 100
    Resource Sustainability Challenge 101
    The Value Realization Gap 102
The Bento Box Approach: Rethinking POC Architecture 103
    Building with Bento Box: From Concept to Code 104
From Blueprint to Reality: Orchestrating AI Implementation 106
Shifting Principles to Practice: Our Learnings from the Field 110
    Building the Foundation 111
    Innovation in Action 111
Leveraging Talent: Building Teams and Frameworks That Scale 112
Show, Don't Just Tell: The Demo That Covers "Wow" to "How" 114
    Making the Invisible Visible 115
    Key Learnings from This Chapter 118

Chapter 4: Code to Scale – Engineering GenAI for Production 121

Architecting for the Big Leagues 124
Taming the Data Beast 126
Guardrails and Security 129
Anya's Notes 132
    Concepts in Practice 132
From POC to Production – Scaling GenAI for Enterprise 132
    The Reality of Scale: When Success Creates New Challenges 133
    Architecting for the Big Leagues 135
    Building with Governance in Mind: From Day One to Enterprise Scale 146
    Key Learnings from This Chapter 151

TABLE OF CONTENTS

Chapter 5: The Goblet of Governance - Habits of Security and Ethics 155
A Timely Guide 155
Governance at Speed 156
AI Governance Framework – Establishing the Foundation 161
Data Governance: The Backbone of AI Governance 167
Risk Management Framework 170
Ethical AI Implementation 173
Operational Governance 175
The Security Investment Pyramid 177
Anya's Notes 184
    Concepts in Practice 184
Guardrails: Building Habits for Governance, Security, and Ethics 184
Reframing the AI Landscape 186
    Layered Security – The AI Security Onion 189
    Practical Guardrails in Action 195
Compliance Discovery Canvas 200
    Integrated Risk Management and Policy Frameworks 204
    The Economics of Security – Investment for Resilience 212
    Operationalizing Governance – From Concept to Everyday Practice 222
Key Learnings from This Chapter 233

Chapter 6: The Age of Agents - From Scripts to Sidekicks 237
Think Fast, Think Slow: The Art of AI Agency 240
The Reality of Real-World Data: FinCorp's Story 246
Finding Our Way: The Agent Assessment Framework 250
Anya's Notes 256
    Concepts in Practice 256
Genesis and Evolution of AI Agents 257
    The Timeline of LLMs and Their Engineering 258
    The Limits of "Vanilla" LLMs 259

TABLE OF CONTENTS

Enter Compound Systems: A Step Toward Agentic Thinking 260
What Is This Control Logic, by the Way 261
Core Components of Agentic Systems: ReAct Design principle... 266
Mixture of Experts: A Deeper Look into Efficient LLM Architecture 270
Strategic Implementation Framework for AI Agents.. 274
A New Horizon: Where AI Agents Go from Here 279
Key Learnings from This Chapter.. 283

Index.. **287**

About the Authors

Jaydeep Chakrabarty is a versatile technology leader with over two decades of experience across full-stack development, infrastructure, experience and visual design, project management, quality analysis, and security. He is passionate about open-source projects and has contributed to notable initiatives such as Talisman, OpenStack, Reportmine, Taiko, and EEG studies. He has served as the Head of AI and Generative AI for Thoughtworks in India and the Middle East, and he is currently the Director of AI in Tech at Piramal Finance. He regularly shares his insights through national newspapers, including *The Hindu*'s tech column, and other prestigious national and international publications. He has been recognized with multiple awards for his visionary leadership, including Asia's Leadership Award, Global Technology Influencer of the Year (Dubai), and the Most Impactful and Visionary Personality to Look For in 2025.

Harinee Muralinath is a senior technology and security leader, currently serving as the Business Information Security Officer (BISO) for India and the Middle East at Thoughtworks. Throughout her career, she has played diverse roles in software delivery, including quality analysis, development, and project management. She established the security practice at Thoughtworks India as the Security Practice Lead and went on to serve as Capability Lead, Head of Capability, and Head of Security for India as well as the Global Community Lead for Security. Harinee is deeply passionate about building quality in software delivery, believing it is more of a cultural shift than a technical one. She is driven by her fascination with cultivating an organic culture of security and ethical practices; innovation and open source contributions are her constant motivations.

ABOUT THE AUTHORS

Recognized with Women in Corporate Awards and as a Woman in Tech leader in India, Harinee believes in growing with the community. She regularly shares her knowledge through national and international conferences, published insights, and mentoring programs that encourage young innovators and women in technology.

About the Technical Reviewer

Saurabh Mittal is a distinguished technology leader and the **Chief Technology Officer (CTO)** of the Retail Finance business at Piramal Finance. With over two decades of experience in building and scaling cutting-edge technology platforms, he is at the forefront of driving digital transformation in the financial services industry.

As CTO, Saurabh is spearheading the ambitious agenda to reimagine Piramal Finance as a world-class, tech-first institution. His core mission is to build a robust, cloud-native technology stack and embed Artificial Intelligence (AI) and Machine Learning (ML) into the fabric of the lending business. This strategy aims to create a more agile, customer-centric, and data-driven organization, capable of delivering seamless financial solutions to millions across India. A key initiative under his leadership is the establishment of the Piramal Innovation Lab in Bengaluru, a hub dedicated to developing next-generation fintech products and platforms.

Saurabh's career is marked by a series of leadership roles where he has successfully blended deep technical expertise with sharp business acumen. Before joining Piramal Finance, Saurabh was at Amazon, where he led engineering teams for one of the company's core e-commerce fulfillment and supply chain platforms.

Earlier, he served as the CTO at Medlife, the pioneering online pharmacy, where he was instrumental in building the entire technology and product portfolio from the ground up. His leadership was a key driver in scaling the company into one of India's largest e-health platforms.

His early career was forged at Nokia, where he built innovative Value-Added Services (VAS) for leading telecom operators in the Indian and global markets.

In recognition of his significant contributions to the technology landscape of the financial sector, Saurabh was recently honored as one of the "**ET NOW TOP 100 BFSI TECH LEADERS 2025.**"

ABOUT THE TECHNICAL REVIEWER

He holds both a Master of Technology (M.Tech) and a Bachelor of Technology (B.Tech) in Electrical Engineering from the prestigious Indian Institute of Technology (IIT), Bombay. His work continues to influence the direction of fintech innovation, driven by his vision to leverage technology to create accessible and efficient financial services for all.

Prologue

It was early 2023, on a warm evening in Bengaluru, and we had just stepped out of a long, intense meeting. We had spent the afternoon with the senior leadership of a renowned global company – a sharp CXO and their forward-thinking Chief Data Officer – diving deep into the technical and strategic complexities of generative AI. As we stood on the curb, waiting for a cab that seemed destined never to arrive, we started to unpack the meeting.

It had gone remarkably well. The concepts had landed, and the intricate ideas we discussed had resonated not just with the tech leads, but with the business leaders. Why? What made the difference?

As another cab cancelled on us, we decided to find a nearby café. Over coffee, we pinpointed the reason for our success: we hadn't just presented facts; we told a story. We had used a "show and tell" approach, grounding abstract frameworks in relatable scenarios that made the potential of AI tangible and real.

It was in that moment that Harinee turned to Jaydeep and said, "We should write a book about this."

The idea was immediate and powerful. What if we could capture this method? What if we could write a book that didn't just *explain* AI concepts but allowed readers to *experience* them? A book with a fictional narrative, where a protagonist, Dr. Anya, navigates the very real challenges of convincing a board, guiding a team, and building responsible AI. This fictional journey, we realized, would be the most authentic way to teach the practical art of AI implementation.

That conversation sparked the very book you now hold, and its unique structure is a direct result of that realization.

How to Read This Book

This book is your organization's insider view of AI implementation. Through the eyes of our protagonist, Dr. Anya's experiences, you'll witness the realities of integrating AI into business operations, technical infrastructure, and application development. You will experience complex concepts distilled into practical insights, relevant for every level of your organization, from strategic decision-makers to hands-on developers.

PROLOGUE

Why Include a Story?

While understanding AI concepts is crucial, the real value lies in seeing how these concepts are applied in real-world scenarios. Dr. Anya's narrative allows readers to experience different challenges and solutions firsthand, demonstrating how AI can be translated into compelling business cases, efficient technical solutions, and innovative applications. This approach lets you live through these experiences, gaining deeper insights into the practical application of AI.

This isn't just theory – it's a roadmap drawn from the frontlines of AI adoption, designed to help you navigate the technical complexities, organizational challenges, and creative opportunities of AI integration. Here's how to extract maximum value from these pages.

Understanding the Structure

1. **Immersive Narrative:** Each chapter opens with a scene from Dr. Anya's professional life, immersing you in the day-to-day challenges of AI development and deployment. These stories, inspired by real-world events, make complex concepts more relatable and easier to grasp.

2. **Dr. Anya's Notes:** In the second part of each chapter, you'll find a summary of key learnings. These notes provide a structured technical overview, consolidating the concepts, frameworks, and methodologies discussed in the narrative.

How to Approach Each Chapter

- **Engage with the Story:** Let yourself be drawn into Dr. Anya's world. Pay attention to the scenarios, strategies, and interactions she encounters.

- **Reflect and Relate:** Connect the situations to your own experiences or potential scenarios in your professional environment.

- **Explore the Notes:** Delve into Dr. Anya's notes for in-depth discussions of key concepts and techniques, providing the technical foundation to apply these ideas in your own work.

The Unique Nature of AI

AI is not just a technology; it's an ecosystem, a shift in behavior, a habit. This book conveys this holistic view by showing how AI permeates every aspect of technology and business, from strategic planning to product development and organizational growth.

Who Should Read This Book

- **CXOs and Business Leaders:** Gain insights into how AI can drive strategic growth and innovation within your organization.

- **Technical Professionals:** Learn practical techniques for AI development and deployment through real-world scenarios and detailed technical explanations.

- **Enthusiasts and Learners:** Immerse yourself in the world of AI, from conceptualization to production, and understand how technology can be applied to solve real business problems.

Final Thoughts

This book offers more than just technical knowledge – it provides a window into the strategic thinking, ethical considerations, and practical problem-solving that drive AI innovation. Through Dr. Anya's narrative, you'll gain the insights needed to navigate the complexities of AI implementation in your own organization. Whether you're a business leader, a technical professional, or an AI enthusiast, this journey will equip you with the perspective and tools to thrive in our AI-driven future.

CHAPTER 1

The Value Compass – Navigating the AI Hype

The gentle chime of my smartwatch nudged me awake at 5:30 AM. As I laced up my running shoes, I smiled at the irony – here I was, about to lead a discussion on cutting-edge AI at one of India's most innovative tech consultancies, yet I still preferred my morning run to be a tech-free escape. No fitness trackers, no smartphones – just me, the pavement, and my thoughts. It was my way of clearing my head before diving into the digital world.

By 6:30 AM, freshly showered and sipping my morning chai, I was already deep in thought about the day ahead. The aroma reminded me of my childhood, spent in various corners of India – a fitting backdrop for TechNova's mission to blend global tech expertise with local insights.

At 52, I, Dr. Anya, had witnessed my fair share of technological revolutions. But this generative AI boom? It was something else entirely. As I reviewed my notes for the board meeting, my phone buzzed with a message from my daughter – a quick good luck wish that brought a smile to my face. Family always grounded me, especially before big meetings like this.

TechNova's office was a hub of activity when I arrived at 8:30 AM. The open-plan space buzzed with energy – developers huddling around whiteboards, UX designers gesticulating over prototypes, and the distinct hum of a dozen different languages being spoken. This was TechNova – where innovation met social responsibility, and cutting-edge technology was always in service of human needs.

As I made my way to the boardroom, I exchanged quick hellos with team members, my mind already mapping out the conversation ahead. TechNova wasn't just any tech company – we were consultants, thought leaders, and above all, champions of ethical technology. Our approach to AI would need to reflect all of these values.

CHAPTER 1   THE VALUE COMPASS – NAVIGATING THE AI HYPE

The boardroom was abuzz when I entered. Around the table sat the familiar faces of TechNova's leadership: Zara Iyer, our CEO and a fierce advocate for diversity in tech; Aryan Malhotra, CFO with a passion for sustainable business models; Dr. Kiara Reddy, CTO and open-source enthusiast; Kabir Kapoor, Head of Client Relations with a knack for translating tech-speak into business value; and several other board members, each bringing a unique perspective to our mission.

Zara stood, her presence commanding the room's attention. "Good morning, everyone. We're here to discuss our generative AI strategy. The tech world is buzzing, and we need to ensure TechNova isn't just keeping up, but leading the charge – ethically and innovatively." She paused, her gaze sweeping the room before landing on me. "Dr. Anya, we brought you on board six months ago for moments like this. The floor is yours."

As I rose, I felt a familiar calm settle over me. This wasn't just another meeting – it was a chance to shape the future of TechNova, to ensure that our approach to AI was not just innovative, but progressive, socially responsible, and business-aligned.

"Thank you, Zara," I began, my voice steady and warm. "Before we dive into strategies and technologies, I'd like us to take a step back and consider a crucial question: What do we really want from generative AI? And more importantly, how can we ensure it aligns with our mission to drive positive change through technology?"

Kabir, our ever-enthusiastic Head of Client Relations, couldn't contain himself. "I've seen what ChatGPT can do! It's incredible. We could use it to enhance our clients' customer service, create more inclusive content, maybe even democratize coding. The possibilities for social impact are endless!"

I nodded, acknowledging his enthusiasm with a smile. "You're right, Kabir. The possibilities do seem endless. But that's precisely why we need to be strategic. We can't chase every shiny new application, even if it promises social good. We need to focus on where AI can drive real business value for our clients while staying true to our ethical standards."

Dr. Kiara Reddy, our CTO, leaned forward, her brow furrowed. "But Anya, if we don't move fast, we'll be left behind. Our competitors are already announcing AI initiatives left and right. How do we balance our thoughtful approach with the need for speed?"

"I understand the pressure, Kiara," I replied, remembering similar concerns from my days as a computer engineer and later as a consultant. "But let me ask you this: how many of those initiatives do you think will still be relevant in a year? In five years? More importantly, how many will have made a genuine positive impact?"

A thoughtful hush descended upon the room as my question hung in the air.

CHAPTER 1 THE VALUE COMPASS – NAVIGATING THE AI HYPE

I walked to the whiteboard, marker in hand, feeling a familiar surge of energy. This was where my years of experience across various roles – from data scientist to product owner to CXO advisor – came into play.

"Look," I said, drawing a simple compass on the board, "generative AI is incredible. It's revolutionizing industries. But it's not a magic wand. We can't just sprinkle some AI dust and expect miracles or ethical outcomes. We need to start with our business goals, our clients' needs, and our commitment to positive social impact. Then we find the path to value."

Aryan, our CFO, raised an eyebrow. "A compass, Anya? We need concrete plans, not metaphors."

I smiled, reminded of the many times I'd bridged the gap between technical concepts and business realities. "Bear with me, Aryan. This compass has four key points: Business Challenge Identification, AI Capability Mapping, Value and Impact Assessment, and Ethical Implementation Feasibility. By navigating these four points, we can ensure that our AI initiatives are not just technologically advanced, but also strategically sound, ethically grounded, and truly impactful (Figure 1-1).

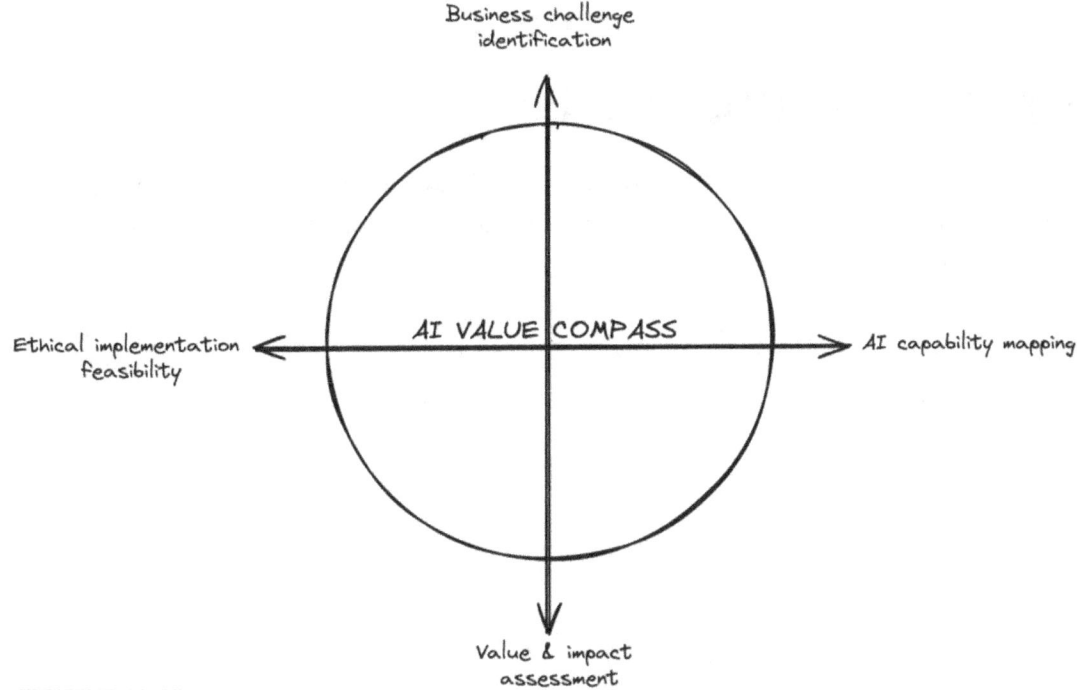

Figure 1-1. AI Value Compass

As I explained each point, I could see the wheels turning in the minds of the board members. We were about to embark on a journey – not just to implement AI but to transform our business and, potentially, the world around us. And with my decades of experience guiding me, I was ready to lead the way.

"Now," I said, capping the marker, "let's start with the first point of our compass. What are the key business and social challenges TechNova and our clients are facing right now?"

The room fell silent for a moment, then Kabir spoke up, his earlier excitement tempered with thoughtfulness.

"Well, one challenge we're facing is helping our clients navigate the AI landscape without getting caught up in the hype," Kabir offered. "Many of them are eager to implement AI, but they're not always sure how it aligns with their business goals."

"Excellent point, Kabir," I nodded. "It highlights another important aspect we need to consider. As a services organization, we're used to thinking about advancing our services. But to truly help our clients, we need to step into a product business mindset. Also, this brings us to a crucial topic: Why business value matters in AI implementation, particularly with generative AI."

Why Business Value Matters

I drew two interlinked circles on the whiteboard (Figure 1-2). "On one side, we have innovation. On the other side, business impact. Our challenge is to find the optimal balance between these two."

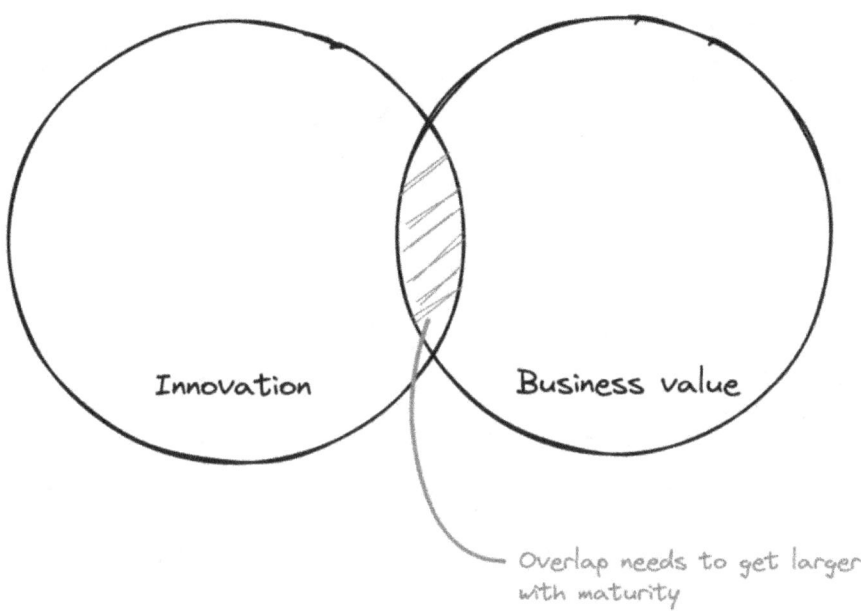

Figure 1-2. *The overlap of Innovation and Business value*

Zara leaned forward, her interest piqued. "But Anya, isn't there inherent value in experimentation, especially with how rapidly generative AI is evolving?"

"Absolutely, Zara," I replied. "Innovation is crucial, and the wow factor of generative AI is undeniable. But here's where many companies, including some of our clients, fall into a trap."

I added a series of small circles branching off from the 'innovation' circle. "They get caught up in the excitement of what AI can do. They run POC after POC, each one more impressive than the last. The responses are quick, the results are flashy, and it's easy to get carried away."

CHAPTER 1   THE VALUE COMPASS – NAVIGATING THE AI HYPE

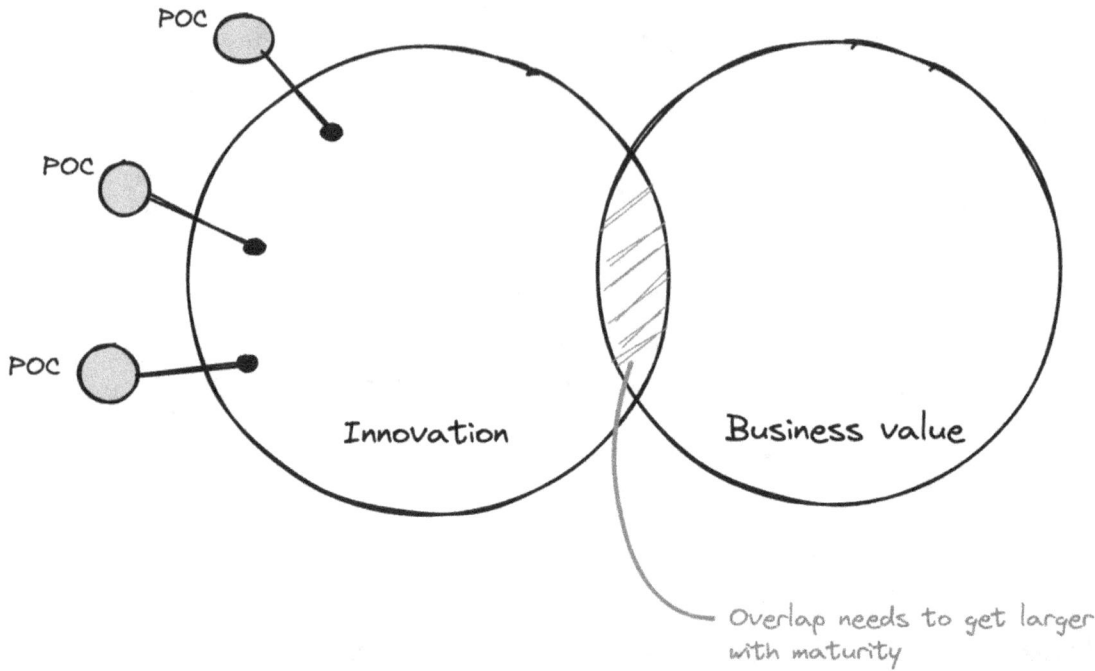

Figure 1-3. Proofs of concepts pushing innovations

Aryan, our CFO, raised an eyebrow. "I've seen this happen. Suddenly, we're six months in with a dozen POCs and no clear path to ROI."

"Exactly," I said, drawing a line connecting the small circles back to the 'business impact' circle. "That's when reality sets in. Someone asks, 'What value are we actually getting from all this?' And that's when the pendulum swings hard in the other direction, frantically searching for any use case that can demonstrate business value."

BALANCING INNOVATION AND BUSINESS VALUE IN AI PROJECTS

- Align AI initiatives with specific business goalsand resources for both research and applied AI.
- Develop a framework to assess potential business impact of new AI capabilities.
- Balance business-focused POCs with forward-looking innovation projects.
- Ensure most POCs tie to specific business challenges, while allowing room for exploratory innovation.

- Educate clients on the importance of this balance.
- Position as a strategic partner driving both innovation and business value.

Remember: Invest in today's needs while innovating for tomorrow's opportunities. This dual approach keeps the organization competitive and future-ready.

I paused, letting the scenario sink in. "But here's the thing: we can't afford to swing between these extremes. At TechNova, we need to chart a course that embraces both innovation and business value from the start."

Dr. Kiara nodded thoughtfully. "So how do we strike that balance, especially when we're working with clients who might be caught up in the AI hype?"

"Great question, Kiara," I responded. "It starts with our approach. For every AI initiative, whether it's for TechNova or our clients, we need to ask two key questions:

1. How does this push the boundaries of what's possible? This addresses the innovation aspect.
2. How can this drive tangible business outcomes? This ensures we're focused on value creation."

I drew a bridge between the two circles (Figure 1-4). "Our job is to be this bridge. We need to foster innovation that's grounded in business reality. This means:

- Allocating resources for pure research and experimentation, but with clear timelines and evaluation criteria.
- Tying every client POC to specific business challenges or opportunities from the outset.
- Developing a framework to quickly assess the potential business impact of new AI capabilities.
- Educating our clients on the importance of this balanced approach."

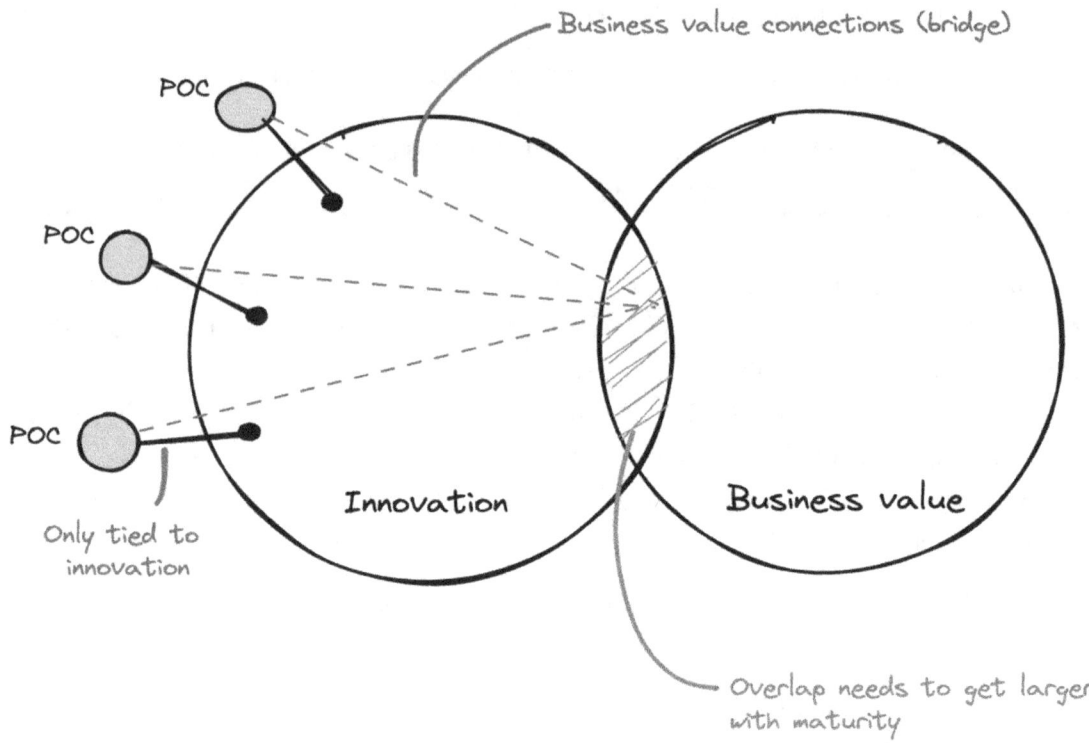

Figure 1-4. Finding the bridge with business value

Kabir chimed in, "This could be a key differentiator for us. Many of our competitors are either too cautious or too caught up in the hype."

"Exactly," I agreed. "By mastering this balance, we position TechNova not just as a technology implementer, but as a strategic partner that drives both innovation and business value."

I capped the marker and looked around the room. "Remember, our goal isn't just to create impressive demos or to squeeze out short-term profits. It's to harness the power of AI – especially generative AI – to create sustainable, long-term value for our clients and for TechNova itself. This balanced approach is how we'll do it."

The room buzzed with energy as the team began to discuss how we could implement this balanced approach in our current projects.

As the initial excitement settled, I noticed Dr. Kiara leaning forward, her brow furrowed in concentration. "Anya," she began, "I see how identifying business challenges is crucial, but how do we ensure we're choosing the right AI technologies to address these challenges?"

I smiled, appreciating Kiara's astute question. "That brings us to the second point of our Value Compass: **AI Capability Mapping**."

Turning back to the whiteboard, I drew a large rectangle across the top. "Let's start with our Business Challenges layer," I said, labeling it accordingly. "Within this, we have various use cases identified across different functions of an organization."

I began listing under the rectangle: "HR, IT, Legal, Contact Center..." I paused at 'Contact Center', circling it. "Let's focus on this one for our example."

Underneath, I drew a smaller box labeled 'Customer Query Resolution'. "This is one of the key use cases within our Contact Center function," I explained.

"Now, how do we map AI capabilities to this specific challenge?" I asked rhetorically. Below our diagram, I drew the 'AI Technology/Capability Layer'. "This is where we identify which AI technologies can address our use case."

I started connecting the 'Customer Query Resolution' box to different points on the AI Technology Layer. "For this use case, we might need a combination of technologies. Generative AI could help in crafting personalized responses," I said, highlighting the connection. "Machine Learning could be used for classifying and routing queries; And Natural Language Processing would be crucial for understanding the nuances of customer inquiries," I continued highlighting.

Aryan raised his pen slightly, and asked "So we're not limited to just one type of AI for a single use case?"

"Exactly, Aryan," I nodded, pleased with his observation. "It's not about choosing one AI technology, but rather combining them effectively. Each technology plays a specific role in addressing different aspects of our use case."

I paused, allowing this to sink in before moving on. "Now, an often overlooked but crucial aspect is ensuring we have the right skills to implement these technologies."

I drew a small icon representing a person below our diagram. "This is where you start Skill Gap Analysis. As we map out the required technologies, we might realize we don't have enough NLP or Machine Learning engineers in our organization."

I connected this icon to the AI Technology Layer with a dotted line. "This analysis helps us identify where we need to upskill our team or potentially hire new talent."

Dr. Kiara nodded thoughtfully. "This approach seems much more comprehensive than just jumping on the latest AI trend."

"Precisely, Kiara," I agreed. Stepping back from the board to take in the full picture we'd created (Figure 1-5), I concluded, "By mapping AI capabilities to specific business challenges in this way, we ensure our AI initiatives are not just technologically advanced, but also practically applicable and valuable to our clients."

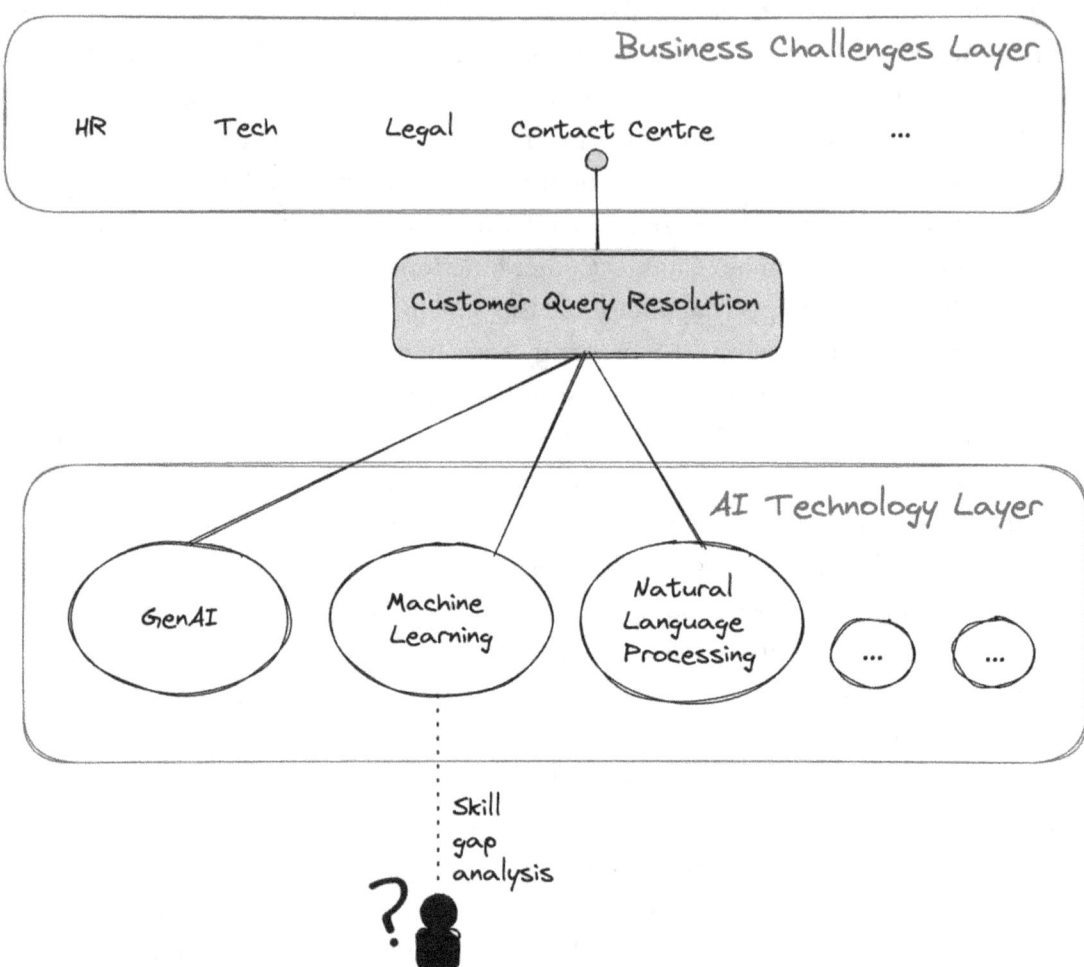

Figure 1-5. Mapping AI capabilities to business challenges

The room hummed with energy as everyone absorbed the diagram.

As I finished explaining AI Capability Mapping, I paused, allowing the information to sink in. The room was quiet, each member of the team processing what they'd just learned. I took a sip of water, gathering my thoughts for the next crucial part of our discussion.

"Now that we've covered AI Capability Mapping," I began, my voice breaking the contemplative silence, "it's time we address a critical aspect of AI implementation that often gets overlooked: **Value and Impact Assessment.**"

I gestured to the "Value and Impact Assessment" quadrant on our Value Compass diagram. "When organizations invest in AI – and make no mistake, these investments can be substantial – it's crucial to establish clear measures of success and impact."

I could see nods of agreement around the room. Aryan, our CFO, seemed particularly focused, his eyes fixed on the whiteboard.

"Think of it this way," I continued, "AI isn't just about implementing cutting-edge technology. It's about driving real, measurable value for our business and our clients. Without a robust framework for assessing this value, we risk pouring resources into initiatives that look impressive but don't actually move the needle on our key performance indicators."

"Let's consider a more detailed example," I said, turning back to the whiteboard. "Imagine we're proposing an AI-powered customer service assistant. At first glance, it might seem straightforward, but the value assessment is quite complex."

I drew a vertical line down the middle of the board, dividing it into two sections (Figure 1-6). On the left, I wrote "POTENTIAL BENEFITS" in large letters, and on the right, "COST."

"On the benefits side," I explained, writing '15%' in the board, "we're aiming for a 15% increase in customer satisfaction scores. This isn't just a feel-good metric; it directly impacts our bottom line."

I drew two branches from the customer satisfaction score: "Customer retention" and "Potential upsells."

"These are the tangible outcomes of improved customer satisfaction," I elaborated.

Aryan nodded, his financial acumen kicking in. "And I assume we'd need to quantify that impact in terms of revenue?"

"Right," I replied. "But that's just one part of the equation. On the cost side, things get interesting."

I turned to the right side of the board, drawing branches under the "COST" heading.

"First, we have the Large Language Model," I said, writing it down. "Whether it's open-source or from a private cloud provider, there's a significant cost involved in training, fine-tuning, and running the model."

Dr. Kiara leaned forward. "And if we want it to be voice-enabled, that's another layer of complexity and cost, right?"

"Spot on," I agreed, adding "Text to speech Model" as another branch. "For a voice-enabled chatbot, we'd need to factor in costs for text-to-speech capabilities."

I added a third branch: "Application development cost."

"This covers the expenses for integrating these components and building the actual application," I explained.

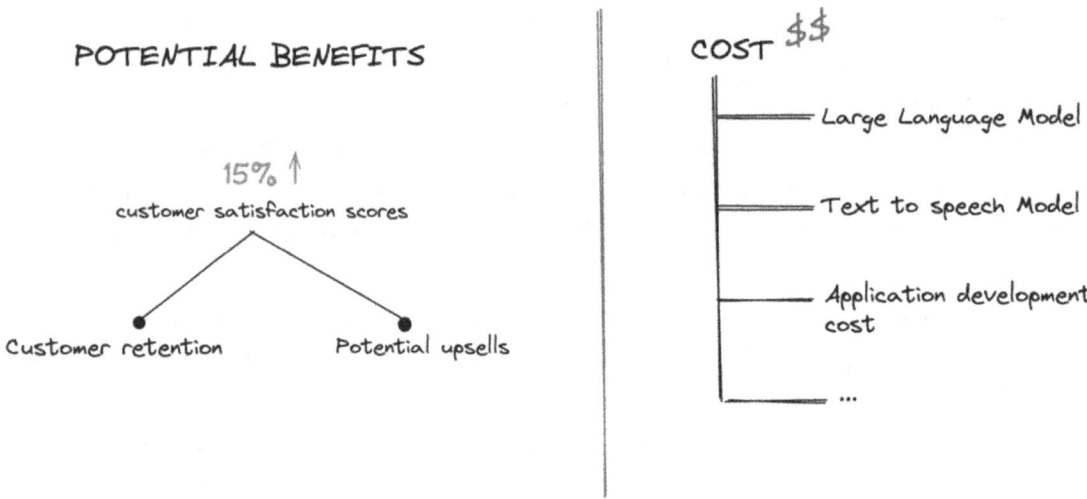

Figure 1-6. Listing potential benefits and costs

"The key here," I continued, "is to balance these potential benefits against the costs. Some benefits are easily quantifiable, like increased customer retention. Others might be less tangible but equally important: being seen as an industry innovator or gathering unprecedented insights into customer needs."

I underlined the '15%' on the benefits side. "The crucial point is this: we need clear, predefined metrics for our benefits before we even start the initiative. Whether it's a 15% increase in customer satisfaction or a specific revenue target from upsells – we need to know what success looks like from the outset."

Kabir nodded, then raised his hand. "Anya, couldn't we use proof of concepts as a way to assess value? That seems like a straightforward approach."

I appreciated Kabir's suggestion. "That's an excellent point, Kabir. Proof of concepts, or POCs, can indeed be valuable tools. However," I paused, making sure I had everyone's attention, "they also come with their own set of risks and limitations when it comes to value assessment. If you don't mind, I'd like to circle back to that important topic after we've covered the core elements of Value and Impact Assessment. It ties into a larger discussion about common pitfalls in AI implementation that I think will be crucial for us to understand."

Kabir nodded, looking intrigued.

"Coming back to our value assessment," I continued, "it's about finding the right balance. On one side, we have quantifiable benefits like reduced call handling times and increased first-call resolution rates. On the other hand, we have our costs and potential risks. The art is in making sure the benefits outweigh the costs and risks in a meaningful way."

Zara nodded thoughtfully. "So the value isn't always directly monetary."

"Correct, sometimes the value is in positioning ourselves at the forefront of customer service technology. But here's the crucial point – we need clear, predefined metrics for all of these factors before we even start the initiative."

The room fell silent as the team absorbed the complexity of the value assessment process. Then Aryan spoke up, his voice filled with newfound appreciation. "I see now why this is so critical. Without this kind of thorough analysis, we could easily pour resources into a 'shiny' AI project without truly understanding its impact."

I nodded, feeling a sense of progress. "That's exactly right. By conducting this kind of comprehensive value and impact assessment, we ensure that our AI initiatives aren't just technologically impressive, but truly valuable to our business, our clients, and potentially, the entire industry."

I gestured back to our Value Compass on the board, specifically to the 'Value and Impact Assessment' quadrant. "This thorough analysis we've just discussed is what brings this part of our compass to life. It ensures that every AI initiative we undertake is grounded in real, measurable value."

Zara nodded, her eyes moving between the different sections of our compass. "I can see how all these pieces fit together now. It's not just about the technology or the potential; it's about a holistic approach to AI implementation."

"Exactly," I agreed, stepping away from the whiteboard. "By considering all these factors, we position ourselves to make informed decisions about which AI initiatives to pursue and how to implement them effectively."

The room buzzed with a new energy. What had started as a theoretical discussion had evolved into a practical framework that everyone could visualize using in their day-to-day work.

As we delved deeper into the Value and Impact Assessment, a notification sound from Kabir's smartwatch broke our concentration. He glanced at it, then looked up with an apologetic smile. "Sorry about that. It's just my AI health assistant reminding me to take a walk."

CHAPTER 1   THE VALUE COMPASS – NAVIGATING THE AI HYPE

The interruption sparked an idea. "Actually, Kabir, your AI assistant provides a perfect segue into our next topic," I said, seizing the moment. "While we've been discussing the technical and financial aspects of AI implementation, there's a crucial element we haven't touched on yet – one that's exemplified by the very AI that just interrupted us."

I pointed to the last quadrant of Value Compass on the white board. "**Ethical Implementation Feasibility**. It's not just about what AI can do, but what it should do, and how it should do it."

The team's attention sharpened, sensing the shift in our discussion.

"Think about it," I continued. "Kabir's AI health assistant has access to his personal health data, activity patterns, and possibly even his location. It's making decisions about when to interrupt him, potentially influencing his behavior and health outcomes. The ethical implications are significant."

I could see the realization dawning on their faces as they considered the broader implications of AI in their own lives.

"As we push the boundaries of AI," I said, my voice taking on a more serious tone, "we must never lose sight of our ethical responsibilities. This isn't just about compliance or ticking boxes. It's about ensuring that our AI solutions align with our values and consider their broader societal implications."

I paused, feeling the weight of what I was about to share. "If I may speak candidly," I continued, my voice softening, "there are two things that keep me up at night when I think about AI implementation."

The team leaned in, curious about this personal revelation.

"First," I explained, "as AI increasingly enters our workflows and daily lives, it's making decisions that profoundly impact people. Whether it's determining when to remind someone to take a walk, or more critically, deciding on loan eligibility or insurance premiums, these AI-driven decisions have real-world consequences for individuals. The pressure to ensure these systems are not just efficient, but fair and accurate, is immense."

I could see nods of understanding around the room.

"Second," I continued, "there's a dangerous misconception that because machines make these judgments, they can't be biased. This couldn't be further from the truth. AI systems can absolutely perpetuate and even amplify existing biases if we're not vigilant."

Zara spoke up, her voice filled with concern. "How do we address these issues, Anya?"

I turned back to our Value Compass, pointing to the Ethical Implementation Feasibility quadrant. "It starts with a comprehensive approach. We need to ensure our AI solutions align with our ethical framework, analyze bias and fairness, prioritize transparency and explainability, protect data privacy and security, evaluate societal impact, and establish clear governance structures."

I began listing these elements on the board, explaining each in turn. As we discussed bias analysis, transparency measures, and data protection strategies, I could see the team grappling with the complexity and importance of these considerations.

"In regions like India," I added, "we must also adhere to specific regional guidelines and governance rules. But our ethical framework should go beyond mere compliance. We need to establish organizational guidelines that ensure ethical practices at every step."

Kabir looked thoughtful. "Can you give us a concrete example of how this might apply to our customer service AI?"

I nodded, appreciating his request for practical application. "Certainly. For our customer service AI, ethical considerations might include ensuring the system doesn't discriminate against customers based on demographic factors. For example, a tone analysis model might treat a native English speaker differently from someone with an accent, or it could misinterpret certain cultural communication styles as negative or rude. We might implement a 'right to human review' for AI-made decisions. And we'd need to establish clear data usage policies to protect customer privacy."

As our discussion deepened, I could see a new level of understanding dawning on the team's faces. We weren't just talking about building powerful AI systems anymore; we were discussing how to build responsible, ethical AI that could positively impact lives while minimizing potential harm.

The room buzzed with questions and ideas as we explored the ethical dimensions of AI implementation. It was clear that this topic had struck a chord with everyone, highlighting the profound responsibility that comes with advancing AI technology.

As our meeting drew to a close, I felt a sense of accomplishment tinged with the weight of the challenge ahead. We had completed our journey around the Value Compass, equipping ourselves with a powerful framework for navigating the complex landscape of AI implementation.

"Remember," I said, looking around at each team member, "as we move forward with our AI initiatives, this ethical consideration isn't a final checkpoint. It's a guiding principle that should inform every decision we make, from conception to implementation and beyond."

The team nodded solemnly, the importance of our discussion evident in their expressions. We were no longer just tech innovators; we were becoming responsible stewards of a technology that had the power to reshape our world. And with our Value Compass to guide us, I was confident we were on the right path.

Escaping the "Death by POC" trap

As we wrapped up our discussion on the four components of the Value Compass, I could see the team processing the wealth of information we'd covered. The room buzzed with a mix of excitement and contemplation.

Suddenly, Kabir snapped his fingers, a look of realization crossing his face. "Anya, earlier you mentioned something about proof of concepts. How does that fit into all of this?"

I smiled, appreciating Kabir's sharp memory and the perfect segue he'd provided. "Thank you for bringing that up, Kabir. It ties directly into a critical challenge we face when implementing AI initiatives – one that I like to call the 'Death by POC' trap."

The dramatic term caught everyone's attention. Aryan leaned forward, a thoughtful frown on his face. "That sounds ominous. What exactly do you mean by 'Death by POC'?"

I nodded, acknowledging the gravity of the term. "It's a phrase coined by one of my former colleagues. It refers to a common pitfall in AI adoption that we need to be acutely aware of as we move forward with our strategies."

I turned to the whiteboard, writing "85%" in large numbers. "Did you know that 85% of companies fail to move beyond the Proof of Concept (POC) phase in their AI initiatives? This is what we mean by 'Death by POC', and it's a real threat to AI adoption and value realization."

The weight of the statistic seemed to settle over the room like a heavy blanket.

"But how is this possible?" Zara asked, her brow furrowed. "Especially when we're emphasizing the importance of business value from the start?"

"It's a common pitfall," I explained. "Companies get excited about AI's potential, run multiple POCs, but struggle to translate that into real-world applications. To avoid this trap, we need a clear roadmap for moving from POC to production."

I began outlining my thoughts on the board, explaining each point:

1. Set clear success criteria before starting the POC.

2. Time-box POC development (typically 4–8 weeks).

3. Involve stakeholders from both technical and business sides.

4. Focus on solving real business problems, not just showcasing technology.

5. Plan for scalability from the start.

6. Establish a clear path to production before beginning the POC.

As I finished writing, Kabir raised his hand. "Anya, these steps make sense for product-focused POCs, but what about other areas of AI integration – like improving internal processes or supporting strategic decisions?"

I smiled, appreciating Kabir's insightful question. "Excellent point, Kabir. There's another important aspect we need to consider," I said, turning to a fresh section of the board. "POCs aren't always about products. They can also be about processes and practices, especially when we're talking about AI integration."

Kabir looked intrigued. "Can you give us an example?"

I nodded, "Certainly. Let's consider an organization aiming to become 'AI-first'. This transformation requires two key elements: continuous integration of AI and positive disruption."

I drew two columns on the board:

Continuous AI Integration	Positive Disruption
Enhancing existing processes and workflows	Exploring novel, transformative ideas

"For continuous integration," I explained, "we might run a POC on using AI coding assistants like GitHub Copilot in the development lifecycle. But here's the key – we're not just testing if it can write code from scratch."

Dr. Kiara leaned in, "Because that's not realistic for most established organizations, right?"

"Exactly," I affirmed. "Instead, we'd focus on how these tools can enhance existing workflows. For instance, can we use AI to help developers add new features to existing codebases more efficiently?"

Zara nodded thoughtfully. "This approach could help address concerns from our development teams. They might worry AI will replace their jobs."

"Precisely," I agreed. "By showing how AI can handle routine tasks, we demonstrate that it frees developers to focus on more complex problem-solving and solution architecting – tasks that still very much require human expertise."

Aryan, ever focused on the bottom line, chimed in. "And for the 'positive disruption' side?"

"That's where our research lab comes in," I explained. "We dedicate resources to exploring truly novel applications of AI. These POCs might not have immediate practical applications, but they keep us at the forefront of innovation."

I turned back to the group. "The key is balance. We run practical POCs to enhance our current processes and workflows, while also investing in more speculative research. This dual approach ensures we're improving our current operations while also preparing for future opportunities."

BALANCING POCS FOR PROCESS AND INNOVATION

- Consider POCs for processes and practices, not just products.
- Focus on realistic scenarios that enhance existing workflows.
- Balance 'continuous integration' POCs with 'positive disruption' POCs.
- Use POCs to address employee concerns and demonstrate practical benefits.
- Highlight how AI can free up time for higher-value tasks (e.g., solution architecting).
- Include both development and non-development teams in process-focused POCs.
- Establish a dedicated 'research lab' for exploring cutting-edge, disruptive ideas.

Remember: Effective AI integration often means enhancing existing processes rather than replacing them entirely. POCs should demonstrate this value clearly.

"Now," I continued, returning to our original discussion, "let's talk about how we can apply these principles to escape the POC trap and move toward real-world implementation." I turned to a fresh section of the whiteboard.

From Idea to Real-World Use: A Generative AI Implementation Workflow

I began sketching out a workflow diagram, explaining each step as I went along.

Step 1: Senior Leadership Education

"The first crucial step," I emphasized, "is educating senior leadership about generative AI's capabilities and limitations."

Zara nodded in agreement. "I've encountered misconceptions myself. Just last week, a client asked if generative AI could predict their December sales based on data up to July."

"Exactly," I replied. "That's a common misunderstanding, but it's important to clarify the distinctions. While generative AI does involve prediction in its process of generating content, it's not typically used for forecasting numerical trends like sales predictions. For that specific task, we'd want to use predictive analytics or time series forecasting models."

Step 2: Use Case Ideation

"Once leadership understands generative AI's capabilities, we can move to use case ideation," I continued. "This is where we brainstorm potential applications across various domains – text, audio, image, and video generation."

Kabir chimed in, "Should we involve business leaders in this process?"

"Absolutely," I affirmed. "Their proximity to business challenges makes them invaluable in identifying high-impact use cases."

Step 3: Stakeholder Workshop

"Next, we conduct a workshop with stakeholders to refine these ideas and create a clear mental model for evaluation," I explained.

Step 4: Prioritization

"After the workshop, we need to prioritize," I said, drawing a funnel on the board. "We'll likely have many ideas, but we need to focus on those with the highest potential impact."

Aryan leaned forward, "How do we determine that impact?"

"Great question," I responded. "We tie each use case to specific, measurable business goals. For instance, instead of just saying 'improve customer engagement', we might aim to 'increase customer engagement by 15% within six months.'"

Step 5: Rapid POC Development

"Once we've prioritized, we move to rapid POC development," I continued. "For generative AI, this should be quick – no more than 2-3 weeks."

Dr. Kiara looked concerned. "Is that enough time to develop something meaningful?"

"In the world of generative AI, it can be," I assured her. "The goal is to create a working application that demonstrates the core idea, even if it's using dummy data. This gives stakeholders something tangible to evaluate."

Step 6: MVP Creation

"If the POC shows promise, we move quickly to creating a Minimum Viable Product," I explained. "This is where we integrate with actual systems and data, implement necessary guardrails, and create a path to production."

Step 7: Deployment and Measurement

"Finally, we deploy the MVP to actual users and start measuring its impact," I concluded. "This is where we validate those initial goals we set – like the 15% increase in customer engagement."

Zara nodded enthusiastically. "And we can use this data to refine the solution and inform future projects."

"Exactly," I agreed. "It's an iterative process of continuous improvement."

FROM IDEA TO REAL-WORLD USE: IMPLEMENTING GENERATIVE AI

- Start with senior leadership education on generative AI capabilities and limitations.

- Conduct use case ideation sessions across various domains (text, audio, image, video).
- Hold stakeholder workshops to refine ideas and create evaluation frameworks.
- Prioritize use cases based on specific, measurable business goals and potential impact.
- Develop rapid POCs (2–3 weeks) to demonstrate core functionality.
- Create MVPs that integrate with actual systems and implement necessary guardrails.
- Deploy to users and measure impact against initial goals.

Remember: The journey from idea to implementation is iterative. Stay focused on creating tangible business value, but remain open to pivoting based on insights gained during the process. Continuous stakeholder engagement and rapid feedback loops are key to successful generative AI implementation.

As I finished explaining the 'Death by POC' trap and our strategies to avoid it, a palpable shift in the room's atmosphere caught my attention. The initial skepticism had transformed into a collective sense of purpose and excitement.

Kabir was the first to break the contemplative silence. "You know, when I walked in here this morning, I thought AI was just about flashy demos and futuristic concepts. But now..." He paused, shaking his head in amazement. "Now I see it's about reshaping our entire approach to problem-solving."

Zara nodded vigorously, her eyes alight with possibilities. "Exactly! We're not just talking about implementing new technologies; we're discussing a fundamental shift in how we create value for our clients."

"And for society at large," Dr. Kiara added, her typically reserved demeanor giving way to enthusiasm. "The ethical considerations we've discussed... they're not just checkboxes. They're our responsibility as leaders in this field."

Aryan, who had been quietly processing everything, finally spoke up. "I came in here worried about ROI and bottom lines. But now I see that if we approach this right, the value creation potential is... well, it's beyond anything we've tackled before."

Their words filled me with a sense of accomplishment and excitement for what lay ahead. This wasn't just a successful presentation; it was the beginning of a journey that could redefine TechNova's future.

CHAPTER 1   THE VALUE COMPASS – NAVIGATING THE AI HYPE

"I'm thrilled by your insights," I said, unable to keep the smile from my face. "What we've outlined today – our Value Compass, our strategies for avoiding common pitfalls – these are the foundations upon which we'll build our AI initiatives."

Zara stood up, her posture radiating determination. "We need to strike while the iron is hot. Anya, can you lead a workshop next week? We should start applying this framework to our current projects immediately."

"Absolutely," I agreed. "Let's set that up. And I want all of you to come prepared with at least one potential use case from your departments. We'll run them through our Value Compass together."

As the team filed out, their animated discussions about potential AI applications echoing down the hallway, I felt a mix of excitement and responsibility settle over me. We had taken the first step toward harnessing the true potential of AI, not just for TechNova but for all those our work would impact.

I gathered my notes, my mind already racing with ideas for our upcoming workshop. The challenges ahead were significant, but the energized faces of my colleagues told me we were ready to face them head-on.

The buzz of my phone pulled me from my thoughts. A message from my daughter lit up the screen: "Hope your meeting went well, Mom! Will you be home for dinner?"

I glanced at my watch. Just past 5 PM. "On my way. Save me some of dad's famous butter chicken," I texted back.

The familiar streets of Bengaluru passed by as I drove home, the day's meetings gradually fading from my mind. A catchy tune on the radio had me humming along, my thoughts drifting to the evening ahead.

As I stepped into our home, I was greeted by the aroma of Ray's cooking and the sound of Anvi's animated voice from the kitchen.

"...and then our neural network started classifying cats as toasters. Can you believe it?" Anvi was saying as I walked in.

Ray, stirring in a pot on the stove, laughed. "Sounds like your machine learning models have a sense of humor."

"Hey, Mom's home!" Anvi exclaimed.

"Welcome home," Ray said, turning to me with a smile. "Dinner's almost ready. How about a quick change while I set the table?"

Over dinner, our conversation meandered through various topics. Anvi talked about her upcoming ML project presentation, discussing the challenges of fine-tuning her models. Ray shared his excitement about a new photography exhibit he was planning, and I found myself fully present, savoring both the food and the company.

After we cleared the table, I settled into my favorite armchair with my journal and a cup of chai. It was my nightly ritual – a few moments to reflect on the day and jot down my thoughts.

As I wrote, I could hear Anvi and Ray in the living room, debating which board game to play. Their playful argument brought a smile to my face.

Just as I was finishing up, Anvi poked her head into the room. "Mom, we're setting up Sequence. Want to join? I promise we won't gang up on you this time."

I glanced at my half-filled journal page. The day's reflections could wait. "Count me in," I said, closing the book. "But I'm picking the snacks."

As we gathered around the coffee table, I felt a sense of contentment. The challenges at TechNova were exciting, but these moments at home were what gave those challenges meaning. Both were essential parts of my life, each enriching the other in ways I was still discovering.

Later that night, as the house quieted down, I returned to my journal to add a final thought: "Another day of balancing AI strategies and family life. Sometimes I wonder which requires more strategic thinking!"

Anya's Notes
Concepts in Practice

The AI Value Compass: A Strategic Framework for AI Implementation

Artificial Intelligence stands at the forefront of technological innovation, promising transformative impacts across industries. Yet, for many organizations, the path to successful AI implementation remains unclear. How can businesses harness AI's potential while ensuring strategic alignment and ethical responsibility? Here is a structured approach to decipher this: **the AI Value Compass** (Figure 1-7).

This strategic framework comprises four essential components that will collectively generate a comprehensive list of AI initiatives for further prioritization:

1. Business Challenge Identification
2. AI Capability Mapping

3. Value and Impact Assessment

4. Ethical Implementation Feasibility

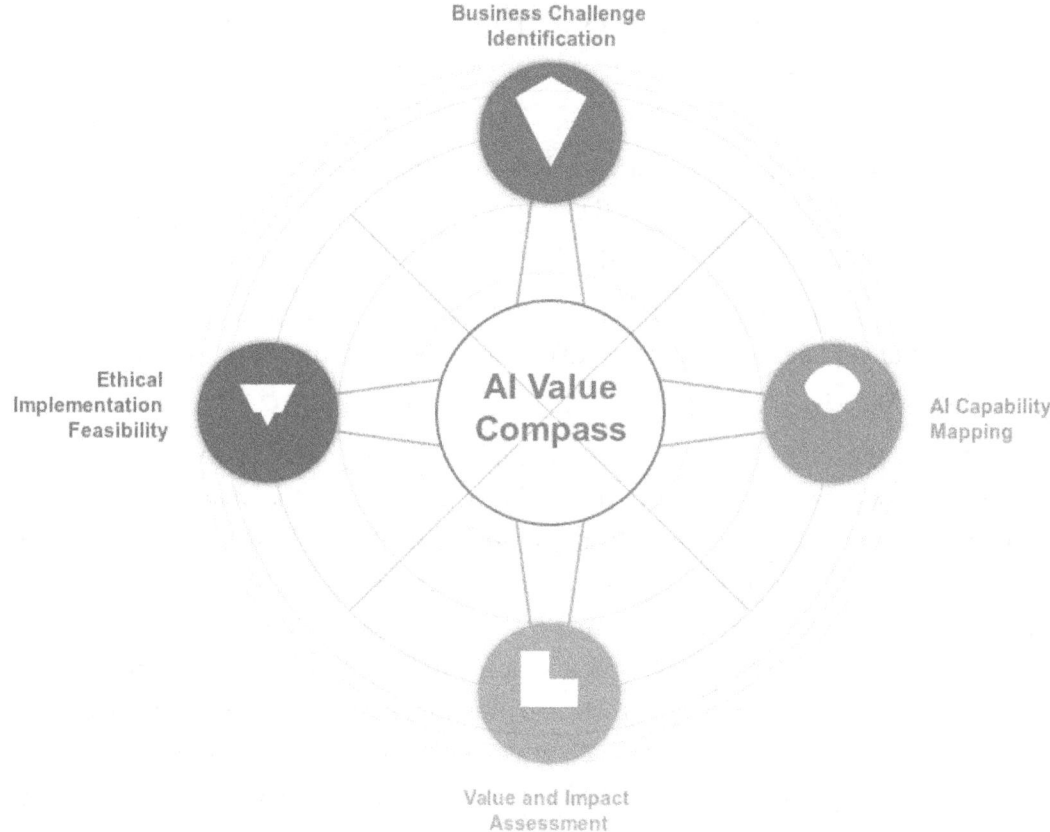

Figure 1-7. AI Value Compass

Vector 1: Business Challenge Identification

The foundation of any successful AI initiative is a clear understanding of the business problem it aims to solve. This component involves:

- **Problem Definition:** Clearly articulate the specific issue or opportunity the AI initiative will address. This should be precise, measurable, and tied to business outcomes.

- **Scope Delineation**: Define the boundaries of the challenge. What areas of the business will be affected? What are the limitations of the current approach?

- **Stakeholder Analysis**: Identify all parties affected by or involved in addressing this challenge. This might include employees, customers, partners, and regulators.

- **Current State Assessment**: Analyze existing processes, technologies, and strategies currently used to address the challenge. This provides a baseline for measuring improvement.

- **Goal Setting**: Establish clear, measurable objectives for the AI initiative. These should be SMART: Specific, Measurable, Achievable, Relevant, and Time-bound.

A critical aspect of this phase is recognizing that while generative AI can be incredibly impressive, not every use case will provide the necessary value. It's easy to get wowed by AI's capabilities, but organizations, especially mid-sized ones with limited resources, must prioritize use cases that bring the most value. For instance, a customer service use case might have a higher impact compared to an internal developer tool, depending on the business context. It is also important to have a clear communication with business leaders and collectively define the objective. For example, instead of a vague goal like "improve customer service," a well-defined challenge might be "Reduce average customer query resolution time by 30% within 6 months while maintaining or improving customer satisfaction scores."

Vector 2: AI Capability Mapping

Once the challenge is defined, the next step is to identify which AI technologies are best suited to address it. This involves:

- **Technology Landscape Analysis**: Survey the current state of AI technologies relevant to the identified challenge. This might include machine learning, natural language processing, computer vision, or other AI subfields.

- **Capability Assessment**: Evaluate the specific capabilities of relevant AI technologies. What can they do? What are their limitations?

- **Maturity Evaluation**: Assess the readiness of these technologies for real-world implementation. Consider factors like reliability, scalability, and track record in similar applications.

- **Integration Requirements**: Determine how the AI solution would integrate with existing systems and processes. What additional infrastructure or resources might be needed?

- **Skill Gap Analysis**: Identify any gaps in your organization's current capabilities to implement and maintain the AI solution. This might inform training or hiring needs

It's essential to acknowledge that not all solutions will require generative AI. Some might benefit more from traditional AI or even non-AI solutions. The goal is to find the right technology fit for the problem at hand. For instance, a challenge involving customer query resolution, AI capability mapping might identify natural language processing for understanding customer queries, machine learning for classifying and routing issues, and potentially a knowledge graph for providing relevant information to customer service representatives.

Vector 3: Value and Impact Assessment

This component focuses on quantifying the potential benefits of the AI solution and weighing them against the costs and risks involved. Identifying KPIs correctly is crucial. Organizations need to understand their measures of success upfront to balance the risks and expected ROI effectively. This assessment helps determine if the potential ROI justifies the risks involved. It includes:

- **ROI Projection**: Estimate the financial returns of the AI implementation. This should consider both direct cost savings and potential revenue increases.

- **KPI Impact Analysis**: Predict how the AI solution will affect key performance indicators relevant to the identified challenge.

- **Cost Analysis**: Evaluate all costs associated with the AI implementation, including technology costs, human resources, training, and ongoing maintenance.

- **Risk Assessment**: Identify potential risks and challenges in implementing the AI solution. This might include technical risks, operational risks, and strategic risks.

- **Opportunity Cost Evaluation**: Consider what other initiatives might be foregone by pursuing this AI project and weigh the relative benefits.

- **Sensitivity Analysis**: Assess how changes in key variables might affect the projected value and impact of the AI solution.

Example: For the customer service AI solution, a value assessment might project a 25% reduction in query resolution time, translating to $2 million in annual cost savings, a 15% increase in customer satisfaction scores, and a potential risk of initial disruption to existing workflows, mitigated by a phased implementation approach.

Vector 4: Ethical Implementation Feasibility

The final component ensures that the AI solution aligns with organizational values and considers broader societal implications. This involves

- **Ethical Framework Alignment**: Ensure the AI solution adheres to your organization's ethical guidelines and values.

- **Bias and Fairness Analysis**: Evaluate the potential for bias in the AI system and implement measures to ensure fair outcomes across different user groups.

- **Transparency and Explainability**: Determine how decisions made by the AI system can be explained and understood by stakeholders, including end-users.

- **Data Privacy and Security**: Assess how the AI solution will handle sensitive data and ensure compliance with relevant data protection regulations.

- **Societal Impact Evaluation**: Consider the broader implications of the AI solution on society, including potential job displacement or changes in user behavior.

- **Governance Structure**: Establish clear lines of responsibility and accountability for the AI system's decisions and outcomes.

In regions like India and elsewhere, it's vital to adhere to regional guidelines or governance rules. Ethical frameworks should not only meet these requirements but also include organizational guidelines that ensure ethical practices beyond mere compliance.

Example: For the customer service AI, ethical considerations might include ensuring the system doesn't discriminate against customers based on demographic factors, implementing a 'right to human review' for AI-made decisions, and establishing clear data usage policies to protect customer privacy.

Implementing the AI Value Compass

The AI Value Compass is not a linear process but an iterative one. Each component informs and influences the others, creating a comprehensive framework for AI decision-making. Organizations should revisit each component regularly throughout the AI implementation journey, adjusting their approach as new information becomes available or circumstances change.

By systematically addressing each point of the compass, organizations can

- Align AI initiatives with core business objectives
- Select the most appropriate and effective AI technologies
- Quantify and justify AI investments
- Ensure ethical and responsible AI implementation

Implementing the AI Value Compass requires a mindset shift within the organization. It's about balancing excitement with value, ensuring that AI initiatives are not only innovative but also impactful and responsible. This framework helps create a balanced approach, fostering innovation while maintaining a focus on tangible business value and ethical responsibility.

The culmination of applying the AI Value Compass will be a comprehensive list of AI initiatives that can be prioritized based on their potential impact and feasibility. Let's learn to navigate this comprehensive list to guide the strategic allocation of resources and ensure that the most valuable AI projects are pursued first, leading to effective and efficient AI implementation.

Navigating the Initiatives

In the pursuit of AI-driven transformation, organizations often find themselves at a crossroads: Should they chase cutting-edge innovations or focus on proven solutions that deliver immediate business value? The answer, as is often the case in complex business environments, lies in striking a delicate balance.

The Importance of Balance

It's crucial to recognize that many bright talents within an organization are motivated by innovation. Simply focusing on immediate business value risks stifling creativity and missing out on groundbreaking opportunities. Conversely, pursuing innovation without regard for business outcomes can lead to resource drain and lack of tangible results. The key is to strike a balance that satisfies both the innovative spirit and the need for concrete business value.

Framework for Evaluating AI Initiatives: The Degree of Unknowns

To effectively balance innovation and business value in AI initiatives, we've developed a framework that categorizes projects based on their "degree of unknowns" (Figure 1-8). This approach helps organizations maintain a diverse portfolio of AI projects, ensuring both short-term wins and long-term breakthroughs.

Understanding the Degree of Unknowns:

The "degree of unknowns" refers to the level of uncertainty surrounding the solution to a given AI use case. It encompasses factors such as technical feasibility, potential impact, and alignment with existing processes. Projects with a higher degree of unknowns tend to be more innovative and potentially disruptive, but also carry greater risk.

We categorize initiatives into three levels:

1. Low
2. Medium
3. High

Example: AI in Hiring Processes

Let's consider two AI initiatives in the hiring process to illustrate this concept:

1. **Low to Medium Degree of Unknowns:** Use Case: Using generative AI or large language models to create interview questionnaires based on job descriptions and candidate resumes. Why it's Low to Medium: We have a good understanding of language models' capabilities in processing and generating text. The inputs (job descriptions and resumes) and outputs (questionnaires) are well-defined. While there might be some unknowns in terms of accuracy and relevance, the overall approach is relatively straightforward.

2. **High Degree of Unknowns:** Use Case: Developing an AI system that analyzes a candidate's spoken responses, facial expressions, and body language during a video interview to provide deeper insights into their thought processes and suitability for the role. Why it's High: This involves multiple complex technologies working together:

    - Natural Language Processing to understand spoken responses
    - Computer Vision to analyze facial expressions and body language
    - Advanced AI algorithms to interpret these inputs and derive meaningful insights
    - Ensuring fairness and eliminating bias in this complex system

3. **The unknowns here are significant:** Can we accurately interpret non-verbal cues across diverse candidates? How do we ensure this doesn't introduce new biases? Can we make this system fairer and more effective than traditional methods?

Balancing Your AI Portfolio:

1. Prioritize low-degree-of-unknown initiatives for quick wins and to build trust in AI investments.

2. Allocate medium strategic investment to projects with a medium degree of unknowns. These typically last 3–5 months and drive sustainable value.

CHAPTER 1 THE VALUE COMPASS – NAVIGATING THE AI HYPE

3. Select one or two high-degree-of-unknown projects for focused, long-term innovation efforts.

Benefits of High-Degree-of-Unknown Projects:

1. Potential for groundbreaking solutions not yet explored in the industry
2. Opportunity to establish thought leadership
3. Positioning the organization as an innovator and trendsetter

By maintaining a balanced portfolio across these categories, organizations can ensure they're driving immediate value while also investing in potential game-changing innovations. The high-degree-of-unknown projects, while riskier, offer the chance to significantly differentiate the organization and potentially reshape entire industries.

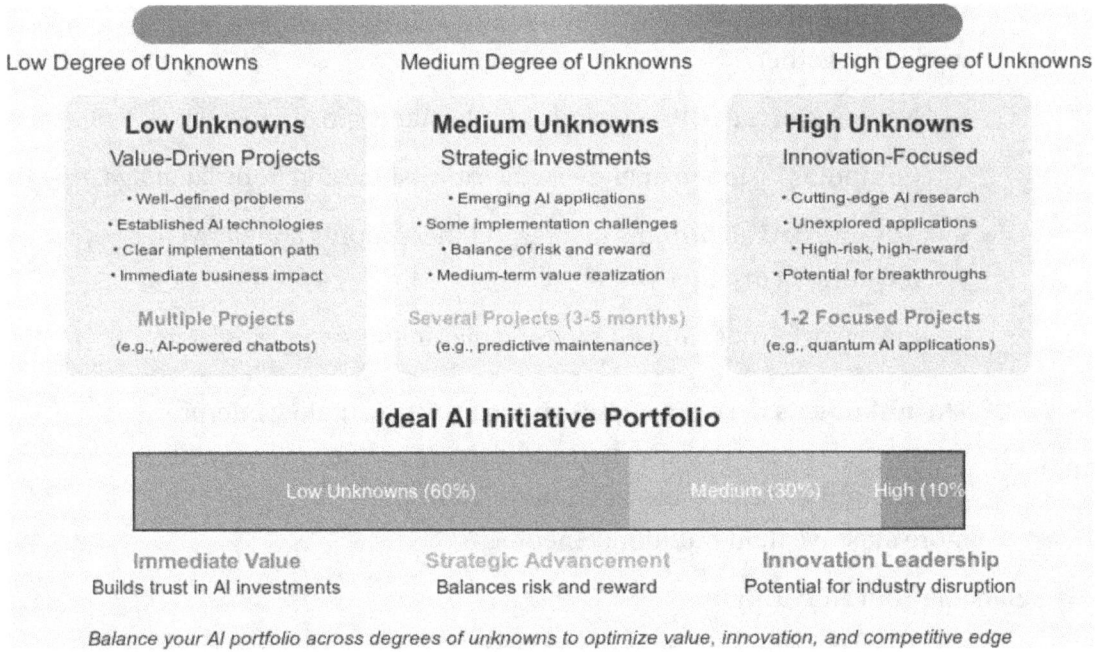

Figure 1-8. *Framework for evaluating AI initiatives*

Balancing Continuous Improvement and Positive Disruption while prioritizing your initiatives

The degree of unknowns in AI initiatives provides a framework for organizations to balance enhancing existing processes with pursuing transformative innovations. This equilibrium is crucial for maintaining current operations while positioning for future breakthroughs.

Continuous Improvement: Low to Medium Degree of Unknowns. These initiatives focus on enhancing existing processes and workflows, typically spanning one to three months. They aim for quick wins and tangible business value. Examples include automating routine customer service tasks, implementing AI-driven quality control in manufacturing, or enhancing data analysis for more informed decision-making.

Positive Disruption: Medium to High Degree of Unknowns. These transformative projects push boundaries and seek groundbreaking solutions, often spanning three to 12 months or longer. They might involve developing AI-driven product innovations, creating new AI-enabled business models, or pioneering AI applications in unexplored areas of the industry.

After all, it is the Human–Machine Handshake!

When implementing AI, particularly in continuous improvement initiatives, creating synergy between human expertise and AI capabilities is crucial. This process involves

1. Analyzing existing workflows
2. Identifying areas where humans face challenges or spend significant time
3. Deploying targeted AI solutions in these areas
4. Ensuring smooth handoffs between AI-driven and human-driven parts of the process

This approach maximizes the strengths of both humans and AI, leading to more effective and sustainable implementations.

Fostering Innovation Culture

To fully leverage the potential of high-degree-of-unknown projects, organizations must foster a culture of innovation. This involves creating safe spaces for exploring speculative AI applications, encouraging bold thinking, and rewarding innovative ideas. Cross-functional collaboration brings diverse perspectives to spark creative AI applications, while treating unsuccessful high-unknown projects as valuable learning experiences further enhances the innovation process.

By adopting this balanced approach within the degree of unknown framework, organizations can drive immediate value through AI while positioning themselves for future breakthroughs. This strategy ensures that AI implementation enhances current operations while also opening doors to new possibilities, keeping the organization competitive and forward-thinking in the rapidly evolving AI landscape.

Avoiding the "Death by POC" Trap

Proofs of Concept (POCs) are essential in AI implementation, serving as a crucial step to validate ideas and demonstrate potential value. However, organizations must be wary of falling into the "Death by POC" trap – an endless cycle of exciting demonstrations that never translate into real-world implementation. This trap is often fueled by the adrenaline rush that comes with seeing AI's impressive capabilities, leading both creators and business stakeholders to continuously pursue new ideas without bringing any to fruition.

The key to avoiding this trap lies in maintaining a controlled approach to innovation while still pushing boundaries. Here's how to strike this delicate balance:

1. **Set Clear Success Criteria:**

    - Define specific, measurable outcomes for each POC before starting.

    - Ensure these criteria are directly linked to business value.

    - Example: For a customer service chatbot POC, success criteria might include "Accurately respond to 80% of frequently asked questions" and "Reduce average response time by 30%."

    Why it matters: Clear criteria help control the "adrenaline rush" by providing objective benchmarks for success. They prevent the temptation to continually expand the POC's scope based on initial excitement.

2. **Time-box Development**

    - Set strict time limits for POCs, typically 4–8 weeks.

    - If a POC can't demonstrate value within this time frame, reevaluate its potential.

Why it matters: Time-boxing creates a sense of urgency and prevents POCs from dragging on indefinitely. It forces teams to focus on demonstrating core value quickly, rather than getting lost in perfecting every feature.

3. **Plan for Scalability from the Start:**
   - Design POCs with real-world implementation in mind.
   - Whenever possible, use actual organizational data rather than dummy data to get a clearer picture of potential outcomes.
   - Consider how the solution would integrate with existing systems and processes.

   Why it matters: This approach bridges the gap between POC and production, making it easier to transition successful POCs into full-scale implementations. It also helps stakeholders envision the real-world application, tempering excitement with practical considerations.

4. **Involve Business Stakeholders**
   - Engage business leaders throughout the POC process.
   - Regularly check in to ensure the POC is aligning with business expectations and needs.
   - Use these check-ins to decide whether to continue investing time and resources in the POC.

   Why it matters: Regular engagement helps maintain alignment between technical possibilities and business needs. It allows for course correction and helps manage expectations, preventing the unchecked growth of enthusiasm that can lead to unrealistic demands.

5. **Establish a Clear Path to Production**
   - Before starting a POC, outline the steps required to move from POC to full-scale deployment.
   - Include considerations for data requirements, infrastructure needs, and change management.
   - Create a timeline for moving from POC to pilot to full implementation.

Why it matters: Having a clear path to production helps stakeholders understand that the POC is not an end in itself, but a step toward real-world implementation. It keeps the focus on practical outcomes rather than just technological demonstrations.

6. **Learn from Failures**
   - Treat unsuccessful POCs as learning opportunities.
   - Document insights gained and apply them to future initiatives.
   - Conduct postmortem analyses to understand why a POC didn't meet expectations.

Why it matters: This approach helps teams maintain perspective, recognizing that not every exciting idea will translate into business value. It promotes a culture of continuous learning rather than chasing one "wow factor" after another.

7. **Celebrate and Communicate Successes**
   - When a POC demonstrates value, quickly move to pilot or full implementation.
   - Share successes across the organization to build momentum for AI adoption.
   - Highlight the journey from POC to implementation, emphasizing the disciplined approach that led to success.

Why it matters: Celebrating successes provides positive reinforcement for the disciplined approach to POCs. It shows that controlled innovation leads to real-world impact, encouraging a balanced approach to future initiatives.

Controlled Adrenaline Rush: The Key to Successful AI Implementation

While the excitement generated by AI's capabilities can be a powerful motivator, it's crucial to channel this energy productively. The "controlled adrenaline rush" approach involves

1. Embracing the excitement of new possibilities while maintaining a clear focus on business objectives
2. Allowing teams to explore innovative ideas within defined parameters

3. Regularly pausing to assess progress and realign with strategic goals

4. Balancing quick wins (low degree of unknowns) with more speculative projects (high degree of unknowns)

5. Creating a culture that values both innovation and practical implementation

By adopting this balanced approach, organizations can harness the motivational power of AI's potential while avoiding the pitfall of endless, unproductive POCs. This strategy allows for continuous innovation while ensuring that efforts ultimately translate into tangible business value and real-world AI implementations.

Remember, the goal is not to stifle creativity or limit exploration, but to ensure that innovation is directed toward achievable, value-driven outcomes. By maintaining this balance, organizations can successfully navigate the exciting but complex landscape of AI implementation, turning promising concepts into powerful, business-transforming realities.

The Generative AI Implementation Workflow: Charting Your Course to AI Success

Implementing generative AI requires a structured approach that balances innovation with practical execution. This seven-stage workflow guides organizations from initial concept to real-world deployment, ensuring AI initiatives deliver measurable value (Figure 1-9).

1. **Leadership AI Compass: Orienting Decision-Makers**

   Equip your decision-makers with a clear understanding of generative AI's potential and limitations:

   - Conduct focused workshops on AI technologies and their business implications.

   - Present case studies demonstrating successful AI implementations and potential pitfalls.

   - Address common misconceptions about AI capabilities.

By the end of this stage, your leadership team should be able to make informed decisions about AI initiatives, setting realistic expectations for the journey ahead.

2. **Idea Incubator: Cultivating AI Applications**

    Generate a diverse range of potential AI applications across various domains:

    - Organize cross-functional brainstorming sessions.
    - Encourage ideas spanning text, audio, image, and video applications.
    - Document and categorize proposed use cases based on business impact and technical feasibility.

    This creative phase should result in a comprehensive list of potential AI use cases, providing a rich pool of ideas for your organization to explore.

3. **Stakeholder Synergy: Aligning Vision and Expertise**

    Refine ideas and create a comprehensive evaluation framework:

    - Facilitate discussions between technical experts and business stakeholders.
    - Develop criteria for assessing use cases, including alignment with business goals and technical feasibility.
    - Create a shared mental model for evaluating AI initiatives.

    The outcome is a refined list of use cases and a clear, collective understanding of how to assess AI initiatives moving forward.

4. **Strategic Sieve: Filtering for High-Impact Initiatives**

    Select high-impact use cases for development using the degree of unknowns framework:

    - Apply the degree of unknowns scale (Low to High) to each use case.
    - Evaluate potential business impact and resource requirements.

- Select a balanced portfolio of initiatives, including both low-risk improvements and innovative projects.

This critical stage results in a prioritized list of AI initiatives, balanced across the spectrum of innovation and practicality.

5. **Rapid Realization: Proving Concepts at Speed**

    Quickly validate the feasibility and potential impact of selected use cases:

    - Develop time-boxed proofs of concept (typically 2–3 weeks).
    - Use dummy data to demonstrate core functionality.
    - Evaluate POCs against predefined success criteria.

    This stage produces validated concepts ready for further development or refinement, providing tangible evidence of AI's potential in your organization.

6. **MVP Forge: Crafting Real-World Solutions**

    Develop a minimum viable product integrated with actual systems and data:

    - Implement necessary security and ethical guardrails.
    - Integrate with existing infrastructure and data sources.
    - Conduct iterative testing and refinement.

    The result is a functional AI solution ready for controlled deployment, bridging the gap between concept and real-world application.

7. **Launch Pad: Deploying and Measuring Impact**

    Launch the AI solution and assess its real-world performance:

    - Deploy the MVP to a controlled user group.
    - Monitor key performance indicators (KPIs) closely.
    - Gather user feedback and iterate on the solution.

    This final stage yields a deployed AI solution with measurable impact and a clear path for ongoing improvement and scaling.

CHAPTER 1   THE VALUE COMPASS – NAVIGATING THE AI HYPE

Generative AI Implementation Workflow

1. Leadership AI Compass: Orienting Decision-Makers
- Conduct focused workshops on AI technologies
- Present case studies of AI implementations
- Address common AI misconceptions
- Pitfall: Overpromising capabilities
- Pitfall: Lack of engagement

2. Idea Incubator: Cultivating AI Applications
- Organize cross-functional brainstorming
- Encourage diverse AI applications
- Document and categorize use cases
- Pitfall: Misalignment with strategy
- Pitfall: Narrow focus

3. Stakeholder Synergy: Aligning Vision and Expertise
- Facilitate expert-stakeholder discussions
- Develop use case assessment criteria
- Create shared evaluation framework
- Pitfall: Dominant voices
- Pitfall: Lack of focus

4. Strategic Sieve: Filtering for High-Impact Initiatives
- Apply degree of unknowns framework
- Evaluate business impact and resources
- Select balanced initiative portfolio
- Pitfall: Resource dilution
- Pitfall: Subjective decisions

5. Rapid Realisation: Proving Concepts at Speed
- Develop time-boxed POCs (2-3 weeks)
- Use dummy data for core functionality
- Evaluate against success criteria
- Pitfall: Over-engineering
- Pitfall: Scope creep

6. MVP Forge: Crafting Real-World Solutions
- Implement security and ethical guardrails
- Integrate with existing systems
- Conduct iterative testing and refinement
- Pitfall: Scalability issues
- Pitfall: Integration challenges

7. Launch Pad: Deploying and Measuring Impact
- Deploy MVP to controlled user group
- Monitor KPIs closely
- Gather feedback and iterate
- Pitfall: Focusing only on technical performance
- Pitfall: Lack of user support

A structured approach to navigate complexities and ensure successful outcomes in AI implementation

Figure 1-9. *Generative AI implementation workflow*

Throughout this journey, remember to

- Balance continuous improvement (low to medium unknowns) with positive disruption (medium to high unknowns).
- Identify optimal collaboration points between AI and human expertise.
- Foster an innovation culture that encourages calculated risk-taking while maintaining focus on business value.

By following this systematic workflow, organizations can effectively navigate the complexities of generative AI implementation, turning promising concepts into value-driving realities. Each stage builds upon the last, creating a cohesive process that maximizes the chances of successful AI adoption and impact.

Key learnings from this chapter

In a world buzzing with AI hype, how do you separate genuine opportunities from expensive distractions? This chapter provides the strategic foundation for your entire AI journey. It argues that successful AI implementation isn't about chasing the latest trend; it's about a disciplined, value-driven approach that starts with your most critical business challenges.

Here are the key frameworks you've discovered to navigate the AI landscape with purpose and precision:

1. **The Guiding Principle: The AI Value Compass** How do you ensure your AI initiatives are strategically sound from the very beginning? The **AI Value Compass** is your essential tool. It forces you to evaluate every idea against four crucial vectors, ensuring a holistic approach:

    - **Business Challenge Identification:** What specific, measurable problem are you solving?
    - **AI Capability Mapping:** Is this the right technology for the job?

- **Value and Impact Assessment:** What is the quantifiable ROI?
- **Ethical Implementation Feasibility:** Is this solution responsible, fair, and safe?

2. **The Portfolio Strategy: Balancing Innovation with Impact** How do you build a balanced AI portfolio that delivers both immediate wins and long-term breakthroughs? This chapter introduces a framework for diversifying initiatives based on their **"degree of unknowns."** You've learned to categorize projects to manage risk and drive innovation simultaneously:

   - **Low Unknowns:** Quick, value-driven projects that build trust and momentum.
   - **Medium Unknowns:** Strategic investments that balance risk and reward.
   - **High Unknowns:** Focused, high-risk projects that push boundaries and establish thought leadership.

3. **The Implementation Roadmap: Avoiding "Death by POC"** How do you move from an exciting proof of concept to a real-world, value-generating solution? We outlined a **seven-stage implementation workflow** designed to escape the "Death by POC" trap — where promising ideas never make it to production. This structured process guides you from initial leadership education and use case ideation to rapid POC development, MVP creation, and finally, deployment and measurement.

Your Path Forward

This chapter has equipped you with the mental models to think like a strategist, ensuring that every dollar and every hour invested in AI pushes your organization forward. But how do you translate these strategies into concrete plans for specific use cases? To master the art of identifying and validating the perfect AI opportunities for your team, dive back into the detailed pages of this chapter and put these frameworks into action.

CHAPTER 2

The GenAI Idea Maze – Finding Gold Among the Glitter

Inbox Overflow: The GenAI Proposal Deluge

"Anya! You've got to hear this!"

Kabir's voice rose above the morning bustle of TechNova's open office, his excitement cutting through the usual hum of keyboards and muted conversations. I glanced up from my tablet just in time to see him weave around a cluster of desks, narrowly sidestepping Anita from Accounting's precarious stack of papers.

"Good morning, Kabir," I said with a smile. "What's got you so energized? Did someone finally fix the coffee machine?"

He chuckled as he reached my desk, his eyes bright with enthusiasm. "Better than that. I've been thinking about an idea that could really benefit our financial clients."

I leaned back, intrigued. Kabir always had a keen eye for opportunities. "I'm all ears."

He took a seat, leaning forward slightly. "I've been considering how we could use Generative AI to analyze a vast array of data – news articles, social media trends, economic indicators – to provide deeper insights into market movements."

I raised an eyebrow, impressed. "That sounds promising. Integrating diverse data sources could give our clients a significant edge."

"Exactly," he nodded. "With our expertise, I believe we can develop a tool that helps them navigate market complexities more effectively."

I thought for a moment. "How do you envision integrating this with our current services?"

CHAPTER 2   THE GENAI IDEA MAZE – FINDING GOLD AMONG THE GLITTER

"Well," he admitted, "I was hoping to collaborate with you on that. I think the potential is there, but aligning it with our offerings is key."

"I appreciate you bringing this to me," I said warmly. "Let's set up a meeting with the analytics team. We can explore how to develop this further."

Kabir's face lit up. "That would be great. I'll start preparing some notes."

"Perfect. I'm looking forward to seeing what we can create together."

As Kabir headed back to his desk, I felt a surge of optimism. His idea had real merit, and his collaborative approach was exactly what we needed.

Turning back to my computer, I noticed my overflowing inbox. Email after email featured subject lines brimming with AI enthusiasm:

- "AI-Powered Coffee Scheduler: Never Miss a Break!"
- "GenAI Fashion Advisor: Your Personal Stylist Awaits!"
- "AI Wellness Coach: Mindfulness in Minutes!"

I chuckled softly, amused by the creativity but aware of the mounting challenge. The excitement around AI was palpable, yet the sheer volume of ideas was becoming overwhelming.

Opening a new document, I began organizing my thoughts.

Observations

- **Enthusiasm Abounds:** The team is eager to innovate using AI.
- **Perception of AI as a Cure-All:** There's a tendency to see AI as a magical solution to any problem.
- **Need for Direction:** We require a way to channel this creativity effectively.

Action Plan

1. **Develop an AI Literacy Program**
   - **Objective:** Educate the team on the realistic capabilities and limitations of AI.
   - **Approach:** Host workshops, share case studies, facilitate discussions.

2. **Establish a Proposal Review Framework**
      - **Criteria:** Feasibility, alignment with business goals, resource requirements.
      - **Process:** Create a cross-functional committee to evaluate and prioritize ideas.
   3. **Foster Collaborative Innovation**
      - **Initiatives:** Encourage teams to collaborate on refining proposals.
      - **Support:** Provide resources and mentorship to develop viable projects.

Leaning back, I gazed out the window at the bustling city below. The blend of towering skyscrapers and cranes constructing new buildings mirrored our situation – a fusion of established success and emerging possibilities.

A smile tugged at the corner of my lips. We had the talent and the drive; now it was a matter of steering this enthusiasm in the right direction. With a clear plan, we could transform these imaginative ideas into real innovations that would propel TechNova forward.

Feeling energized, I began drafting an outline for the AI literacy program. It was time to harness this wave of creativity and turn it into tangible progress.

Mind the Gap: Educating the Organization

By mid-afternoon, my office resembled a collage of creativity. Sticky notes in every conceivable color plastered the walls, each bearing an AI idea from enthusiastic team members: "Predictive maintenance for equipment," "Personalized learning platforms," "AI-driven customer support." The clock read 2:15 PM, but the weight of the proposals made it feel much later.

I leaned back in my chair, stretching to relieve the tension in my shoulders. The afternoon sun filtered through the blinds, casting striped patterns across my desk cluttered with reports and scribbled notes. The initial excitement of the morning was waning, replaced by the realization that we needed a structured way to harness all this energy.

CHAPTER 2   THE GENAI IDEA MAZE – FINDING GOLD AMONG THE GLITTER

A soft knock drew my attention to the doorway. Zara stood there, holding two steaming mugs.

"Thought you might need a caffeine boost," she said with a sympathetic smile.

"You're a mind reader," I replied, grateful for the interruption. "I was just debating whether to tackle another proposal or surrender to the chaos."

She laughed, settling into the chair across from me. "Looks like it's been quite the day."

"That's an understatement," I sighed, accepting the mug. "The team's enthusiasm for AI is off the charts, but we're swimming in ideas without a clear direction."

Zara glanced around at the colorful notes covering the walls. "I've heard some of the suggestions floating around. There's definitely no shortage of creativity."

"True," I acknowledged. "But without a way to focus it, we're at risk of spreading ourselves too thin."

She took a sip of her coffee. "Have you thought about how we might channel this effectively?"

"I have," I said, pausing to collect my thoughts. "I'm considering an AI literacy campaign to give everyone a solid understanding of what Generative AI can actually do. But I don't want it to be just another mandatory training that people dismiss."

She nodded thoughtfully. "Maybe we could make it more interactive. Workshops where teams bring real challenges they're facing and we explore how AI might help."

"That's a great idea," I agreed. "It would make the sessions relevant and engaging."

"And if we involve department heads," she added, "we can tailor the content to each team's needs."

"Exactly," I said, feeling a spark of optimism. "We could help cultivate an 'AI intuition' throughout the company."

Zara smiled. "I like that term. But we'll need to figure out how to measure the impact."

"Good point," I replied. "Perhaps we can track the quality of proposals over time by measuring outcomes like cost savings, time efficiency, or improved business processes from AI-integrated projects."

"That would provide tangible results to share with the board," she said.

For a moment, we sat quietly, letting the office sounds drift around us, as we gathered our thoughts.

"It's a big undertaking," I mused.

"But a necessary one," Zara said firmly. "The team's eager to contribute; they just need the right guidance."

I glanced at the cluttered whiteboard in the corner. "What do you say we move this to the conference room? We could use more space to map out our plan."

"Great idea," she agreed, standing up. "I'll grab my notebook."

As we walked down the hallway, the air felt cooler, and the distant sounds of meetings and phone calls faded into the background. My mind buzzed with possibilities, but also with the challenges that lay ahead.

"Do you think people will be receptive?" I asked.

She considered for a moment. "If we present it as an opportunity rather than an obligation, I think so. People want to be part of something meaningful."

"Let's make sure that's the message," I said.

We entered the conference room, its large windows offering a panoramic view of the city bathed in the late afternoon light. The spacious table and expansive whiteboard provided the perfect setting to flesh out our ideas.

"Alright," Zara said, uncapping a marker. "Let's get to work."

I felt a renewed sense of purpose as we began outlining the campaign. The road ahead wouldn't be easy, but with a clear plan and a collaborative effort, we could turn the team's enthusiasm into tangible progress for TechNova.

Mapping the AI Landscape

The conference room door closed behind us with a soft click, sealing out the muffled sounds of the bustling office. Zara and I settled into the expansive space, placing our notebooks and pens on the polished wooden table. The mid-afternoon sun streamed through the floor-to-ceiling windows, casting warm hues across the room and illuminating the blank whiteboard that awaited our ideas.

"Feels good to have some space to think," Zara remarked, glancing around. "It's been quite a day."

"Tell me about it," I agreed, uncapping a marker. "But I think we're onto something with this AI literacy campaign."

She nodded, flipping open her notebook. "So, where should we start?"

I moved toward the whiteboard, tapping the marker thoughtfully against my palm. "I was thinking we could structure the workshop around the core capabilities of Generative AI. Break it down into fundamental functions that everyone can understand and relate to."

"That's a solid idea," Zara said, joining me at the board. "It would help demystify the technology."

I began writing:

- **Generation**: Creating new content
- **Summarization**: Condensing information
- **Translation**: Converting between languages
- **Correction**: Refining existing content
- **Classification**: Organizing data
- **Question Answering**: Providing insights and information

As I wrote, Zara leaned in to read. "These cover the main functionalities," she observed. "But we should also consider the types of data our teams work with."

"Good point," I replied, adding another list beside the first:

- **Text**
- **Images**
- **Audio**
- **Video**
- **Code**

She picked up a different colored marker. "If we connect these capabilities with the data types, we can create relevant examples for each department," she suggested.

"Exactly," I said, drawing lines between the lists. "For instance, 'Summarization' and 'Video' could help us condense lengthy training videos or event recordings, making valuable insights easily accessible for the team."

"Or 'Generation' and 'Text' could enable our marketing team to create immersive content, tailored precisely to our audience's interests and experiences – a fully personalized approach," Zara added. "That would be game-changing."

We continued mapping out connections, the whiteboard gradually filling with lines and annotations. The room buzzed with a quiet energy as ideas flowed freely. Occasionally, one of us would pause to think, then add another connection or note.

After a while, I stepped back to survey our work. The whiteboard was now a tapestry of arrows, boxes, and annotations – a visual map of potential applications.

"This is starting to look promising," I observed. "But I wonder if it's still a bit abstract for some people."

Zara crossed her arms, contemplating. "You might be right," she admitted. "Not everyone thinks in terms of charts and diagrams."

"Maybe we need to ground it with real-world examples," I suggested. "Case studies or success stories that illustrate these concepts in action."

"That could help," she agreed. "People relate better to stories than to theoretical models."

I made a note in my tablet. "We should also consider adding interactive elements," I added. "Hands-on activities where teams can experiment with AI tools relevant to their work."

"Engagement is key," Zara affirmed. "But we should be mindful not to overwhelm them. We need to strike the right balance."

"Absolutely," I said. "And we can't ignore the potential concerns. Some might be apprehensive about AI replacing jobs or making their roles obsolete."

"True," she said thoughtfully. "We need to address those fears head-on – maybe include a section on how AI can augment their work rather than replace it."

"Great idea," I replied. "And perhaps discuss ethical considerations, like data privacy and the importance of human oversight."

The sunlight outside was still bright but had begun to soften, casting gentle shadows across the room. I glanced at the clock on the wall – it was approaching 3:30 PM.

"Time flies when you're mapping out the future," Zara remarked, following my gaze.

I smiled. "Indeed. Maybe we should take a short break?"

"Good idea," she agreed. "I could use a snack to recharge."

We capped our markers and stepped back from the whiteboard, our minds buzzing with ideas yet acknowledging the need to pause. As we left the conference room, the hallway felt quieter than earlier. The office was still humming with activity, but there was a subtle shift as some teams wrapped up meetings or took their own breaks. At the snack station, we each grabbed a granola bar and some fruit. I poured myself a cup of herbal tea, and quickly dialed Anvi. "Hey, Mom!" she answered, her voice bright. "Guess what? We finally got our ML model to stop mixing up cats with toasters!"

"That's progress!" I laughed. "Can't wait to hear all about it tonight.""

CHAPTER 2   THE GENAI IDEA MAZE – FINDING GOLD AMONG THE GLITTER

The Use Case Detective's Toolkit

The setting sun painted the conference room in hues of orange and gold, casting long shadows across our whiteboard filled with AI capabilities and data types. The day's brainstorming had been intense, and Zara and I both felt the weight of the challenge ahead. The city skyline beyond the windows was beginning to glow with the lights of evening, a reminder of the hours we had spent immersed in our work.

I absently twirled a marker between my fingers, the faint scent of ink a subtle accompaniment to our thoughts. "We've mapped out the possibilities," I mused, breaking the contemplative silence. "But it feels like we've given everyone a map without any directions. They might see where they want to go with AI but have no idea how to get there."

Zara leaned against the table, her gaze fixed on the intricate web of ideas we'd drawn. "So, you're thinking we need to provide a compass of sorts? A guide to help them navigate from idea to implementation?""

I nodded slowly. "Exactly. We've identified the core capabilities of Generative AI and how they intersect with different data types. But without a structured approach, the team might feel overwhelmed or, worse, pursue impractical projects."

She sighed softly, crossing her arms. "I see your point. Maybe we need to develop some kind of framework or toolkit that walks them through the process of evaluating and developing AI use cases."

"Yes," I agreed, feeling a spark of excitement. "A 'Generative AI Canvas' or something similar. It would help them think critically about their ideas and assess feasibility before diving in."

Zara tilted her head, considering. "But what should this toolkit include? We don't want it to be so complex that it becomes a barrier."

"Good question." I moved back to the whiteboard, erasing a section to make space. "Let's think about the key components that are essential for evaluating an AI use case."

She joined me at the board, marker in hand. "First, there needs to be a clear **Problem Statement**," she suggested. "What is the specific challenge or opportunity they're addressing?"

"Agreed." I wrote it down, underlining it for emphasis. "And they should outline the **Current Workflow** – how things are done now. That way, they can identify inefficiencies or pain points."

"Right," she said. "Then, they can propose how AI could improve or transform that workflow – the **Proposed AI Solution**."

"Exactly." I added that to the list. "But we also need them to consider the **Business Impact**. How will this solution contribute to our goals? Will it save costs, increase revenue, improve customer satisfaction?"

"That's crucial," Zara affirmed. "And what about **Technical Feasibility**? Do we have the data, the technology, and the expertise to implement this solution?"

"Good point." I wrote it down. "We can't ignore the **Ethical and Responsible AI Considerations** either. They need to think about data privacy, potential biases, and the ethical implications of their solution."

She nodded thoughtfully. "And perhaps include **Risk Assessment**. What are the potential risks if the AI doesn't perform as expected? What are the consequences of failure?"

"Yes, and let's not forget to consider **Alternatives to AI**," I added. "Sometimes, a non-AI solution might be more appropriate or cost-effective."

We stepped back to look at the list:

1. Problem Statement
2. Current Workflow
3. Proposed AI Solution
4. Business Impact
5. Technical Feasibility
6. Ethical and Responsible AI Considerations
7. Risk Assessment
8. Alternatives to AI

Zara tapped the marker against her chin. "This seems comprehensive, but do you think it's approachable for everyone? Some might find this process daunting."

I leaned against the table, contemplating. "Perhaps we can provide guiding questions under each section to help them think through the points. Make it more of a facilitated exercise than just a form to fill out."

"That's a good idea," she agreed. "For example, under Problem Statement, we could ask: 'What is the issue you're trying to solve? Who does it affect? Why is it important?'"

"Yes," I said, scribbling down her suggestions. "And under Current Workflow: 'How is the process currently handled? What are the limitations or challenges?'"

CHAPTER 2   THE GENAI IDEA MAZE – FINDING GOLD AMONG THE GLITTER

"Under Proposed AI Solution, we might ask: 'How do you envision AI addressing this problem? What capabilities would it need?'" Zara added.

"Exactly. For Business Impact, questions like: 'What benefits do you expect? How will success be measured?'" I continued.

She looked thoughtful. "For Technical Feasibility: 'What data is required? Do we have access to it? What technology or infrastructure is needed?'"

"And under Ethical Considerations: 'Could this solution introduce bias? How will you ensure data privacy? Are there legal or regulatory concerns?'" I added.

"Risk Assessment could include: 'What are the potential failure points? What is the impact if things go wrong?'" she said.

"And for Alternatives to AI: 'Are there simpler solutions? Have other methods been tried?'" I finished.

We both paused, taking in the expanded framework. The whiteboard was now a detailed roadmap (Figure 2-1) guiding teams through a thorough evaluation of their AI ideas.

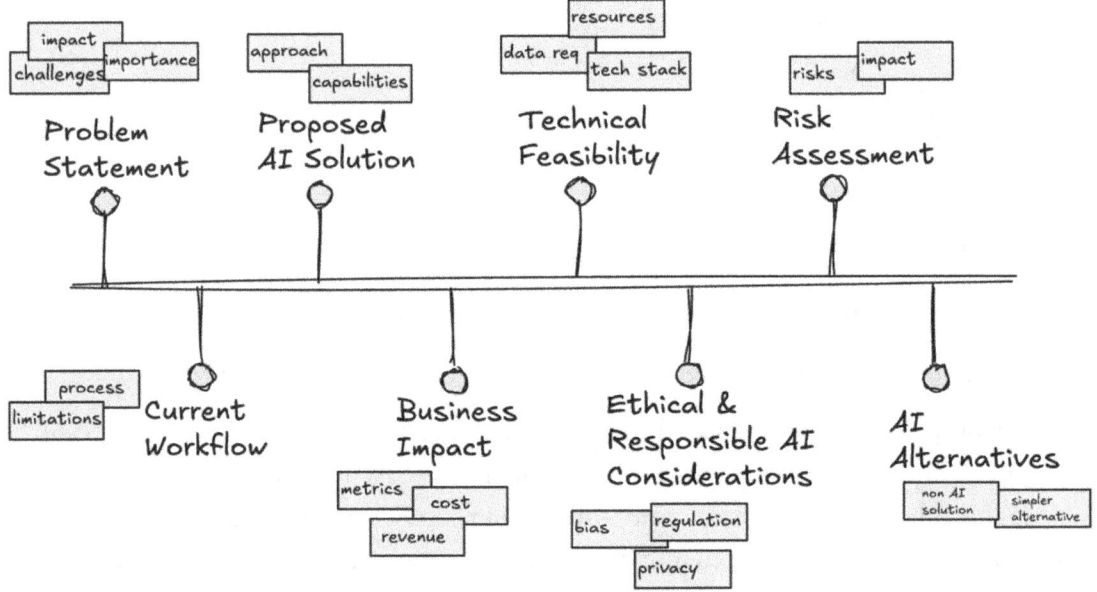

Figure 2-1. *Roadmap to validate AI ideas*

"This feels more actionable," Zara remarked. "But we need to ensure that teams have support in using this toolkit."

52

"Agreed," I said. "Maybe we can organize workshops or training sessions to walk them through the process. Encourage cross-functional collaboration so that different perspectives are included."

She raised an eyebrow. "Cross-functional teams might help, but coordinating them could be challenging."

I sighed, acknowledging the potential hurdles. "True. But if we start with a pilot program involving a few teams, we can work out the kinks before scaling up."

"That's sensible," she agreed. "We can select teams that are eager to participate and have clear use cases in mind."

I glanced at the clock – it was nearing 6:00 PM. The office noise had dwindled, and the sky outside had deepened to a rich amber.

"Maybe we should wrap up for today," I suggested. "We can refine the toolkit tomorrow and start planning the pilot."

Zara stretched her arms, a hint of fatigue showing. "I think that's a good idea. My brain is starting to protest."

I smiled. "Mine too. But I feel like we've made significant progress."

As we began tidying up, I felt a mix of satisfaction and apprehension. Satisfaction at having crafted a practical framework, and apprehension about the challenges of implementing it.

"Do you think the teams will embrace this?" Zara asked, stacking her notes.

"It's hard to say," I admitted. "Some might see it as extra work or be skeptical of its value."

She nodded. "We'll need to communicate the benefits clearly. Maybe share success stories or examples where such a framework led to successful AI implementations."

"Good idea," I said, shutting down my laptop. "We can also gather feedback from the pilot teams to make improvements."

We turned off the lights, leaving the whiteboard illuminated by the soft glow of the city lights outside. Walking down the corridor, the quietness of the office felt almost surreal after the day's busyness.

"Any plans for tonight?" Zara asked as we waited for the elevator.

I chuckled softly. "Honestly, I think a quiet dinner and maybe a good book. You?"

"Sounds about the same," she replied. "Though I might skip straight to sleep."

The elevator doors opened with a gentle ding, and we stepped inside. As we descended, I reflected on the day's events.

"Despite the challenges, I'm optimistic," I said, breaking the silence. "We're tackling important issues, and I believe it will make a difference."

Zara smiled faintly. "I admire your optimism. It's contagious."

"Well, we need at least one optimist on the team," I joked.

As we exited the building, the cool evening air was refreshing. The city was alive with the sounds of traffic and distant chatter, a stark contrast to the stillness inside the office.

"Thanks for your partnership today," I told Zara as we parted ways. "Couldn't have done it without you."

"Likewise, Anya," she replied warmly. "See you bright and early tomorrow."

"Looking forward to it," I said.

Walking toward my car, I allowed myself a moment to breathe deeply, appreciating the night's calm. The path ahead with the AI framework was uncertain, but I felt a renewed sense of purpose. There would be obstacles – resistance, misunderstandings, unforeseen complexities – but we had taken a meaningful step.

As I drove home, the rhythmic hum of the engine provided a backdrop to my thoughts. The framework we'd developed was more than a tool; it was a catalyst for change, encouraging thoughtful engagement with AI rather than hasty adoption.

Tomorrow would bring new challenges and, hopefully, new insights. For now, I was content to embrace the quiet satisfaction of progress made, however incremental.

Anya's Notes
Concepts in Practice

First Steps into the AI World

Every organization's journey with AI begins with a moment of collective awakening. We see it time and again – the day after a company announces its AI initiative, ideas start flowing from every corner of the organization. It's like watching a garden bloom overnight, with ideas sprouting from the most unexpected places.

At a global manufacturing firm, within days of their AI announcement, proposals emerged from every department – from shop floor supervisors suggesting AI-powered quality control to HR teams envisioning AI-driven talent development. This sudden burst of creativity, while exhilarating, reveals something profound about how organizations begin to grapple with AI's potential.

CHAPTER 2   THE GENAI IDEA MAZE – FINDING GOLD AMONG THE GLITTER

Three Waves of Innovation

What you'll encounter are three distinct waves of innovation, each bringing unique opportunities and challenges to manage (Figure 2-2). The first wave comes from the problem solvers – those individuals who've been wrestling with complex business challenges for years. They see AI as a potential answer to their long-standing problems. Like the finance director who proposed an AI system to predict market trends, their enthusiasm often outpaces their understanding of AI's actual capabilities, but their intimate knowledge of business problems proves invaluable.

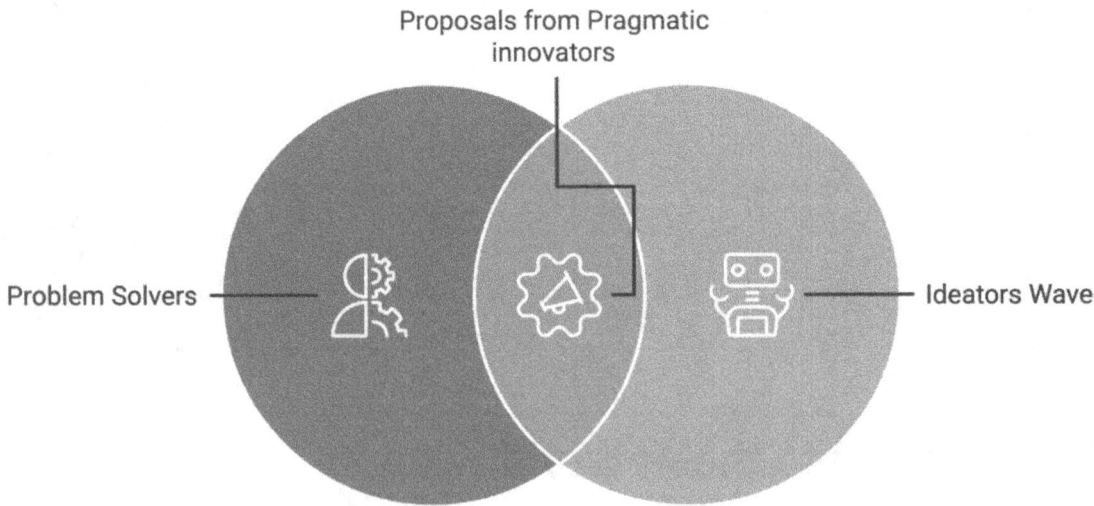

Figure 2-2. Three waves of innovation

Then comes what we call the wave of ideators. Suddenly, every process becomes a candidate for AI enhancement. We have seen proposals for AI-powered coffee machines that learn your preferences, AI fashion designers that predict next season's trends, and AI therapists promising instant solutions to complex emotional challenges. While these ideas might seem fantastical, they often contain valuable insights about process improvements and user experience enhancements.

The third wave is perhaps the most interesting – the pragmatic innovators. These individuals take time to understand both AI's capabilities and their organization's needs. Their proposals, while still ambitious, show a more nuanced understanding of how

AI might realistically transform their work. At a recent client, a procurement manager proposed using AI not to completely automate purchasing decisions but to augment the team's ability to identify patterns in supplier performance and pricing trends – a perfect example of balanced thinking about AI's capabilities.

Let's look at some examples

Consider the market prediction system proposed by an executive at a recent workshop. At first glance, it seemed like yet another over-ambitious AI project – using generative AI to predict market trends by analyzing everything from news articles to weather patterns. But examining this proposal reveals several crucial insights about early AI adoption.

First, it reflects our natural desire to automate complex decision-making processes. Who wouldn't want a system that could reliably predict market trends? Second, it shows an intuitive understanding of AI's data-processing capabilities – the idea that AI could integrate diverse data sources isn't wrong, even if the specific application might be misguided.

Most tellingly, it highlights a common misconception about generative AI's capabilities. While these systems excel at creating content and finding patterns, pure prediction tasks are better suited to traditional machine learning approaches. This distinction often becomes the first step in developing a more sophisticated understanding of AI's capabilities.

This proposal also revealed what we call the "integration paradox" – the assumption that more data sources automatically lead to better insights. The executive wanted to analyze everything from social media sentiment to weather patterns, not realizing that each additional data source introduces new complexities, biases, and potential points of failure.

The Data Dilemma

In the rush to keep pace with the development of AI, organizations often fall into what we call the "data hoarding trap." Like collectors who amass objects believing quantity equals value, companies stockpile data assuming it will fuel their AI ambitions. But perhaps nothing reveals more about an organization's AI maturity than how it thinks about data.

CHAPTER 2   THE GENAI IDEA MAZE – FINDING GOLD AMONG THE GLITTER

A business might hold a vast data lake – decades of transaction records, customer profiles, and market analyses – and yet struggle to generate meaningful insights. The problem isn't a lack of data; it is a lack of focus.

Data must be approached with the question of relevance. Do not ask "How much data do we have?" but ask "What does our data tell us?"

The lesson is clear and crisp: data quality trumps quantity every time. Well-structured, relevant data – even in smaller amounts – provides a stronger foundation for AI success than vast repositories of unstructured information. It's like the difference between a carefully curated art collection and a warehouse full of random paintings. AI models don't need to know everything; they need to know the right things. The value lies not in the volume, but in the curation.

But this realization leads us to a broader challenge. As organizations begin to understand the importance of data quality over quantity, they face a more fundamental question: How do we build the knowledge and skills needed to make these distinctions? How do we help teams understand not just the potential of AI, but its practical requirements and limitations? This is where the real work of AI adoption begins – in cultivating a deeper understanding of what AI truly needs to succeed.

Mind the Gap: Cultivating AI Understanding

The Need for AI Literacy

Imagine an organization that has just provided its employees with access to powerful generative AI tools. It's like giving everyone a high-end digital camera without any photography training. While some might naturally capture stunning photos, many will struggle with basic composition, lighting, and focus. The tools are powerful, but their effective use requires understanding.

This scenario is playing out in organizations worldwide. The democratization of AI through tools like ChatGPT has created an interesting paradox. While anyone can prompt an AI system to generate content, few understand how to harness its true potential or recognize its limitations. It's akin to having access to a sophisticated kitchen without knowing the principles of cooking – you might be able to follow basic recipes, but creating a fine dining experience requires deeper understanding.

The consequences of this knowledge gap manifest in various ways. Consider these real-world scenarios:

A marketing team excitedly proposes using generative AI to predict next year's consumer trends. While this sounds innovative, it reveals a fundamental misunderstanding – confusing generative AI's ability to create content with predictive analytics' ability to forecast trends. It's like using a food processor to wash dishes – wrong tool, wrong job.

A product team suggests using AI to make complex business decisions autonomously, not realizing that AI excels at processing information and identifying patterns but lacks the nuanced judgment and contextual understanding that human decision-makers bring. This is similar to expecting a calculator to develop a business strategy – it can crunch the numbers, but it can't understand the human and market dynamics that influence strategic choices.

An HR department proposes using generative AI to conduct entire job interviews, missing the crucial distinction between AI's ability to analyze responses and the human skill needed to assess cultural fit and interpersonal dynamics. It's comparable to trying to evaluate a chef by having them only fill out a questionnaire about cooking.

These misalignments between expectations and reality underscore why AI literacy isn't just desirable – it's essential. Organizations need a structured approach to help their teams understand

- What generative AI can and cannot do
- How to identify appropriate use cases
- When to use AI and when to rely on human expertise
- How to combine AI capabilities with human skills

This understanding needs to go beyond superficial knowledge. It must enable people to think critically about AI applications in their specific domains. Just as financial literacy helps employees make better business decisions, AI literacy enables them to make better technology choices.

The goal isn't to turn everyone into AI experts, but rather to develop what we might call "AI intuition" – the ability to recognize meaningful opportunities for AI application while avoiding common pitfalls. This intuition becomes the foundation for sustainable AI adoption and innovation.

CHAPTER 2   THE GENAI IDEA MAZE – FINDING GOLD AMONG THE GLITTER

Making AI Education Engaging and Practical

Traditional technology training often resembles a lecture hall – an expert speaks, everyone listens, and then they're expected to apply what they've learned. With AI, this approach falls remarkably short. It's like teaching someone to ride a bicycle by having them watch a PowerPoint presentation.

The Challenge of Engagement

Consider what typically happens in most organizations. A series of mandatory training sessions are scheduled. Employees attend, perhaps even take notes about neural networks and machine learning algorithms. They pass the quiz at the end. Yet, when they return to their desks, they struggle to connect these concepts to their daily work.

This disconnect isn't surprising. AI isn't just another tool to learn – it represents a fundamentally new way of thinking about problem-solving and work itself. Teaching it requires an approach that bridges theory and practice, abstract concepts and concrete applications.

Learning Through Discovery

Imagine instead a workshop where a sales team brings their actual customer interaction data. Rather than just learning about AI's capabilities in theory, they discover how AI could help them personalize customer communications more effectively. As they experiment with different approaches, they naturally encounter both the possibilities and limitations of the technology.

Or picture a product development team working with a simple AI prototype. Instead of being told what AI can do, they experience firsthand how it might accelerate their design process – and where human creativity remains irreplaceable. These hands-on experiences create what psychologists call "authentic learning" – knowledge that sticks because it's directly relevant to the learner's world.

The Power of Contextual Learning

Effective AI education must be contextualized for different roles and departments:
For executives, it might focus on strategic decision-making and resource allocation. A CFO doesn't need to understand the intricacies of large language models, but they do need to know how AI investments could impact their bottom line and what questions to ask when evaluating AI initiatives.

For middle managers, the emphasis might be on identifying opportunities and managing AI-enhanced teams. A customer service manager needs to understand how AI could augment their team's capabilities without replacing human empathy and judgment.

For frontline staff, the focus should be on practical application within their specific domains. A content writer needs to understand how to effectively collaborate with AI tools while maintaining their unique creative voice.

Creating Learning Momentum
The key to successful AI education lies in creating what we might call "learning momentum." Start with simple, relatable examples that demonstrate immediate value. For instance:

- Show a marketing team how AI can help brainstorm campaign ideas, not by replacing their creativity but by expanding their creative possibilities.

- Demonstrate to technical writers how AI can help document code more efficiently, while still requiring their expertise to ensure accuracy.

- Help product managers see how AI can analyze customer feedback at scale, while they focus on deriving strategic insights.

As teams experience these initial successes, their curiosity naturally leads them to explore more sophisticated applications. This organic growth in understanding is far more effective than trying to force-feed complex concepts from the start.

Understanding AI's Core Capabilities

When most people think about generative AI, they imagine a magical black box that can do almost anything. It's like having a mystical assistant who claims to be able to cook any dish, paint any picture, or solve any puzzle. The reality, while still remarkable, is more nuanced and specific.

Breaking Down the Magic
Generative AI's capabilities span six core functions, each a distinct skill that enables it to create, interpret, and refine content by recognizing patterns in data (Figure 2-3).

Generation – Creating Something New

Imagine a chef creating a new recipe. They don't conjure it from nowhere – they draw upon their knowledge of ingredients, cooking techniques, and flavor combinations. Similarly, generative AI creates new content by drawing patterns from its training data. When it generates text, code, or images, it's combining and adapting what it has learned, not truly creating from scratch.

Question Answering – Understanding and Responding

This is like having a knowledgeable librarian who has read every book in the library. They can quickly find and synthesize information to answer your questions. However, just like a librarian, AI can only work with the information it has been trained on – it can't provide insights about events or developments beyond its training data.

Summarization – Distilling the Essential:

Think of this as similar to a skilled journalist who can take a complex story and capture its essence in a compelling headline and brief article. The AI identifies key points and patterns, condensing lengthy content while preserving the most important information.

Translation – Bridging Communication Gaps

This goes beyond just converting between languages. Like a cultural interpreter, AI can translate between different forms of expression – turning a technical document into simple explanations, or converting written descriptions into visual concepts.

Correction – Refining and Improving

Similar to an editor who catches errors and suggests improvements, this capability allows AI to identify mistakes, enhance clarity, and improve quality. However, like any editor, it works best when refining rather than completely rewriting.

Classification – Making Sense of Information

This is akin to a skilled organizer who can look at a cluttered room and create a logical system for arranging everything. AI can analyze information and sort it into meaningful categories based on patterns it recognizes.

Core Capabilities of Generative AI

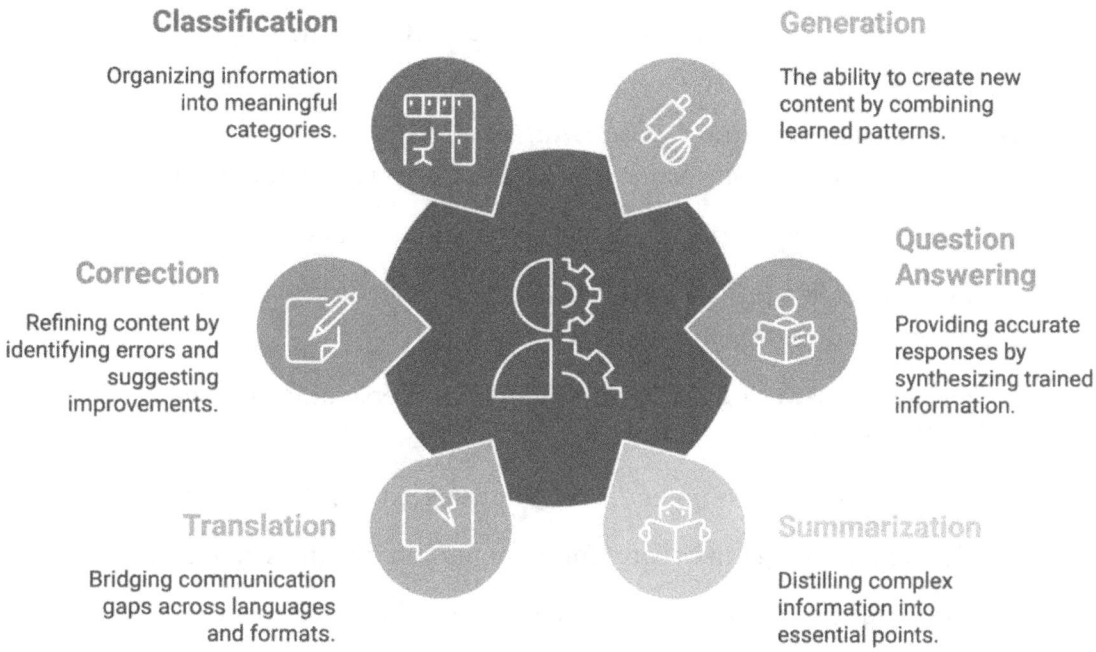

Figure 2-3. AI's core capabilities

From Capabilities to Business Solutions

The real power of understanding these core capabilities lies in recognizing how they can address specific business challenges. Consider how different departments might leverage these capabilities in unique ways:

Marketing and Customer Engagement:

Imagine a marketing team planning a global product launch. Instead of viewing AI as just a content generation tool, they might orchestrate its capabilities like a conductor:

- Generation creates initial campaign concepts and copy variations.

- Translation adapts content for different markets while maintaining brand voice.

- Summarization crafts bite-sized social media posts from longer content.

- Classification analyzes customer responses to refine messaging.
- Correction ensures brand consistency across all materials.
- Question Answering helps create detailed FAQs for customer support.

Software Development and Documentation:
For a development team, the same capabilities take on a different meaning:

- Generation helps write initial code structures and documentation.
- Summarization provides overviews of large codebases, creates concise code comments and release notes.
- Question Answering assists developers in understanding complex code sections.
- Correction identifies potential bugs and suggests optimizations.
- Classification organizes code components and identifies patterns.
- Translation converts technical specifications into user-friendly documentation.

Financial Services and Analysis:
In financial operations, these capabilities transform data into insights:

- Summarization distills lengthy financial reports into key points, or even produces condensed highlight reels from long earnings calls or investor meetings.
- Classification categorizes transactions and identifies patterns.
- Generation creates initial draft reports and analysis.
- Question Answering helps investigate financial anomalies.
- Correction validates data entries and calculations.
- Translation makes financial information accessible to non-experts.

When we combine these capabilities
The true art lies in combining these capabilities to solve complex business problems. Think of it like cooking – while individual ingredients are important, the magic happens in how you combine them. Here's a real-world example:

A customer service improvement initiative might combine (Figure 2-4)

- Generation to create personalized responses
- Question Answering to find relevant solutions
- Summarization to capture the essence of each issue
- Translation to communicate in the customer's preferred language
- Correction to ensure accuracy and appropriate tone
- Classification to categorize incoming customer queries

This orchestrated use of capabilities creates a solution far more powerful than any single capability alone.

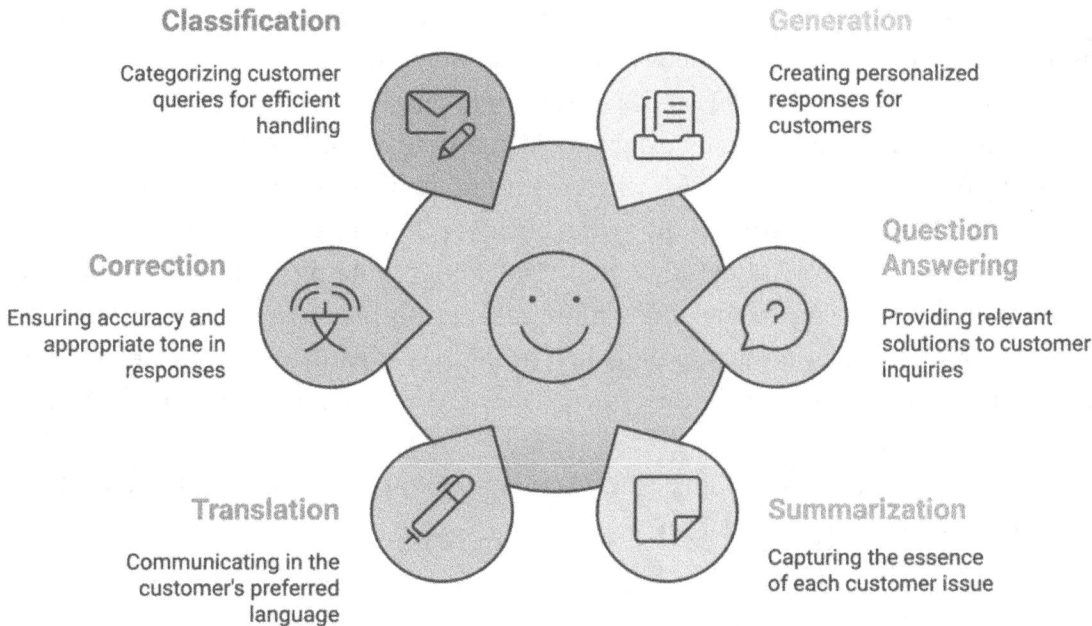

Figure 2-4. *AI capabilities for customer service improvements*

Avoiding Common Missteps: Lessons from the Field

As organizations begin to experiment with these capabilities, certain patterns emerge – patterns that can either limit or expand the potential of AI solutions. Think of it like learning to paint. A novice might stick to using just one color, missing the richness that comes from combining different hues. Similarly, organizations often limit themselves by focusing too narrowly.

Consider a content team that sees AI only as a text generator. They use it to create blog posts and social media content, which is valuable, but they're missing the bigger picture. By understanding the full palette of capabilities, they might discover how AI could also analyze content performance, adapt messaging for different audiences, and identify emerging topics their readers care about.

Another common tendency is what we might call the "magic solution" approach. It's like expecting a Swiss Army knife to build an entire house. While the tool is versatile, effective construction requires understanding how to use each tool in concert with others. One organization wanted to use AI to "completely automate customer service" – a goal that sounds ambitious but overlooks the intricate dance between AI capabilities and human skills needed for effective customer interaction.

Perhaps the most subtle misstep is starting with technology rather than understanding. It's like buying an expensive kitchen gadget and then trying to figure out what to cook with it. We see this when teams excitedly propose "We need to use generative AI!" before clearly defining what business challenge they're trying to solve.

The path to effective AI implementation isn't about avoiding these natural learning steps – it's about moving through them more consciously. Just as a chef learns to combine ingredients by understanding their properties, organizations can create more powerful solutions by understanding how different AI capabilities can work together to address real business needs.

Yet a crucial question remains: How do we systematically identify and validate the right use cases for our organization?

The Use Case Detective's Toolkit

Organizations face a critical challenge that extends far beyond the technical complexities of implementation. The fundamental question isn't how to implement generative AI – it's determining what to implement in the first place. This challenge calls for a structured approach that bridges the gap between possibility and practicality, between enthusiasm and execution.

The Generative AI Canvas framework (Figure 2-5) emerges as this bridge. It's a comprehensive evaluation system that transforms the abstract potential of generative AI into concrete, actionable plans. The framework operates through two distinct but interconnected canvases, each serving a crucial role in the journey from concept to implementation.

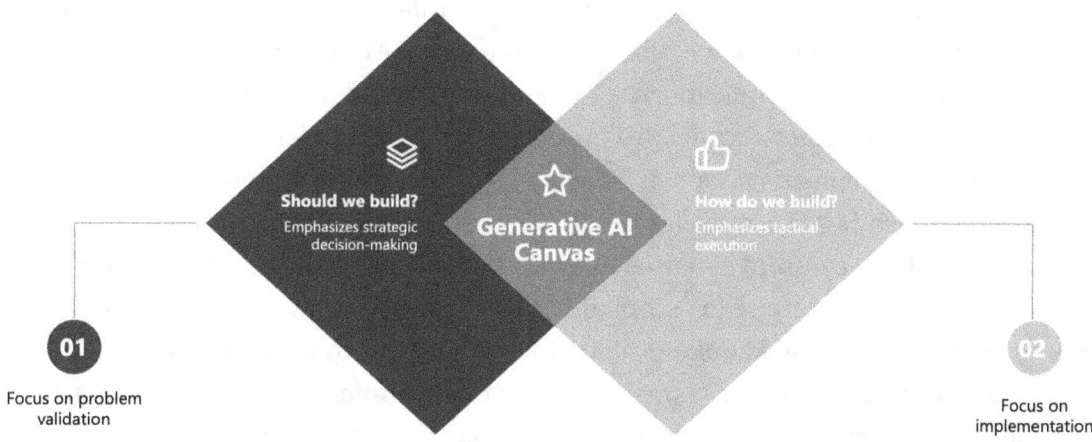

Figure 2-5. Generative AI Canvas bridging problem validation with implementation

The Strategic Foundation: "Should We Build?"

The first part of the canvas addresses the foundational question that every organization must answer before committing resources to an AI initiative. This isn't merely about technical feasibility – it's about strategic alignment, ethical considerations, and organizational readiness (Figure 2-6).

At the heart of this canvas lies the **Problem Statement**. This isn't simply a space to declare AI aspirations; it's where organizations articulate the genuine business challenges they face. The key lies in precision and clarity. Rather than stating "We need AI for customer service," a proper problem statement might read: "Our customer support team struggles to maintain consistent response quality across time zones while handling a 40% increase in inquiry volume." This level of specificity transforms vague aspirations into addressable challenges.

The **As-Is Workflow** section serves as a mirror, reflecting current operational realities. Here, organizations map out existing processes not just as procedures, but as living systems with their own rhythms, bottlenecks, and inefficiencies. This reflection often reveals surprising insights – sometimes what appears to be a candidate for AI automation is actually a process begging for basic streamlining.

When organizations reach the **Solution** section, they're asked to bridge the gap between problem and possibility. This isn't about listing AI capabilities; it's about articulating how specific applications of generative AI would transform current workflows into more efficient, effective processes. This section demands both imagination and pragmatism – a balance between what's possible and what's practical.

The **Responsible AI** section elevates the discussion beyond pure functionality. Here, organizations confront essential questions about ethics, bias, and transparency. This isn't a checkbox exercise in compliance; it's a crucial examination of how AI implementation affects stakeholders, data privacy, and organizational trust.

Organizational Fit pushes teams to look beyond technical capabilities to cultural readiness and structural alignment. This section often reveals the hidden barriers to AI adoption – not in technology but in organizational dynamics and team preparedness.

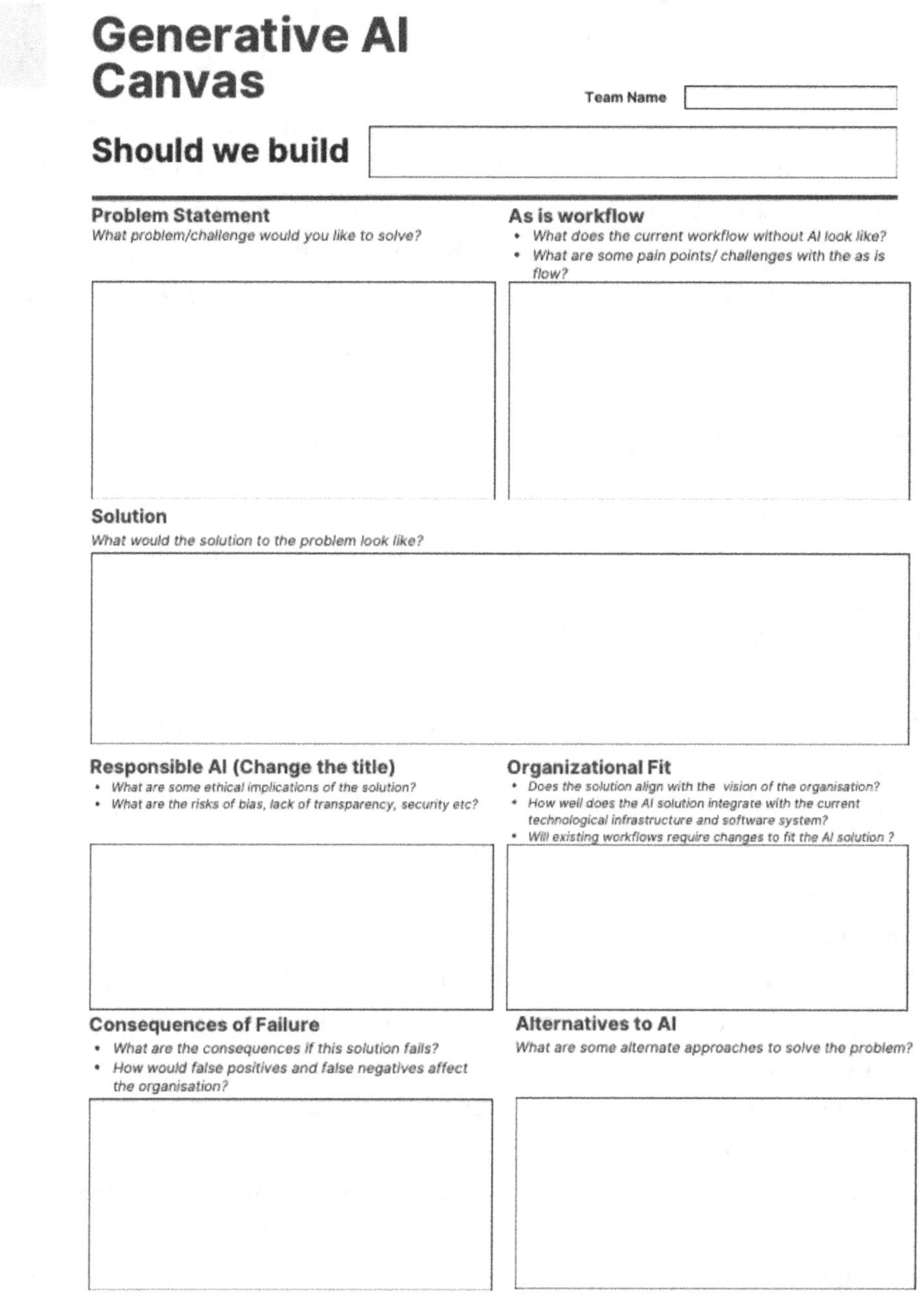

CHAPTER 2   THE GENAI IDEA MAZE – FINDING GOLD AMONG THE GLITTER

Generative AI Canvas

Team Name [ ]

Should we build [ ]

Problem Statement
What problem/challenge would you like to solve?

As is workflow
- What does the current workflow without AI look like?
- What are some pain points/ challenges with the as is flow?

Solution
What would the solution to the problem look like?

Responsible AI (Change the title)
- What are some ethical implications of the solution?
- What are the risks of bias, lack of transparency, security etc?

Organizational Fit
- Does the solution align with the vision of the organisation?
- How well does the AI solution integrate with the current technological infrastructure and software system?
- Will existing workflows require changes to fit the AI solution?

Consequences of Failure
- What are the consequences if this solution fails?
- How would false positives and false negatives affect the organisation?

Alternatives to AI
What are some alternate approaches to solve the problem?

Figure 2-6. *Generative AI Canvas template: Should we build?*

The **Consequences of Failure** section might seem pessimistic, but it serves a crucial role. By examining potential failure modes, organizations build resilience into their solutions from the start. This isn't about fear; it's about foresight.

The **Alternatives to AI** section broadens the organizational lens, prompting teams to consider solutions that don't rely on artificial intelligence. Here, the focus shifts from the allure of new technology to the practicalities of existing resources and strategies. This isn't about dismissing AI's potential, rather, it's about ensuring that the most straightforward and effective solutions aren't overlooked. Sometimes, challenges can be addressed through process optimizations, policy revisions, or adopting new practices.

The Tactical Roadmap: "How Do We Build?"

The second part of the canvas transforms strategic intent into tactical execution. This is where abstract possibilities become concrete plans, where "what if" transforms into "how to" (Figure 2-7).

The Outcomes section demands specificity in success definition. Rather than vague goals of "improved efficiency," organizations must articulate precise, measurable objectives. This precision guides everything that follows, from technical requirements to success metrics.

Success Criteria takes these outcomes and transforms them into measurable benchmarks. This section forces organizations to answer the crucial question: "How will we know we've succeeded?" The criteria established here become the compass that guides development and implementation.

The **Data Requirements** section might appear straightforward, but it often reveals the most surprising insights. Organizations must think beyond simple data availability to data quality, accessibility, and sustainability. This section breaks down data needs into three crucial categories: case data for operation, training data for development, and feedback data for improvement.

Dependencies mapping reveals the interconnected nature of AI implementations. This isn't just about technical dependencies; it's about understanding how changes in one area ripple through the entire organization. This section often uncovers hidden connections that could impact implementation success.

The **Adoption Strategy** section acknowledges a crucial truth: the most technically perfect solution will fail without proper user adoption. This section guides organizations in planning the human side of AI implementation, ensuring that technical excellence translates into practical success.

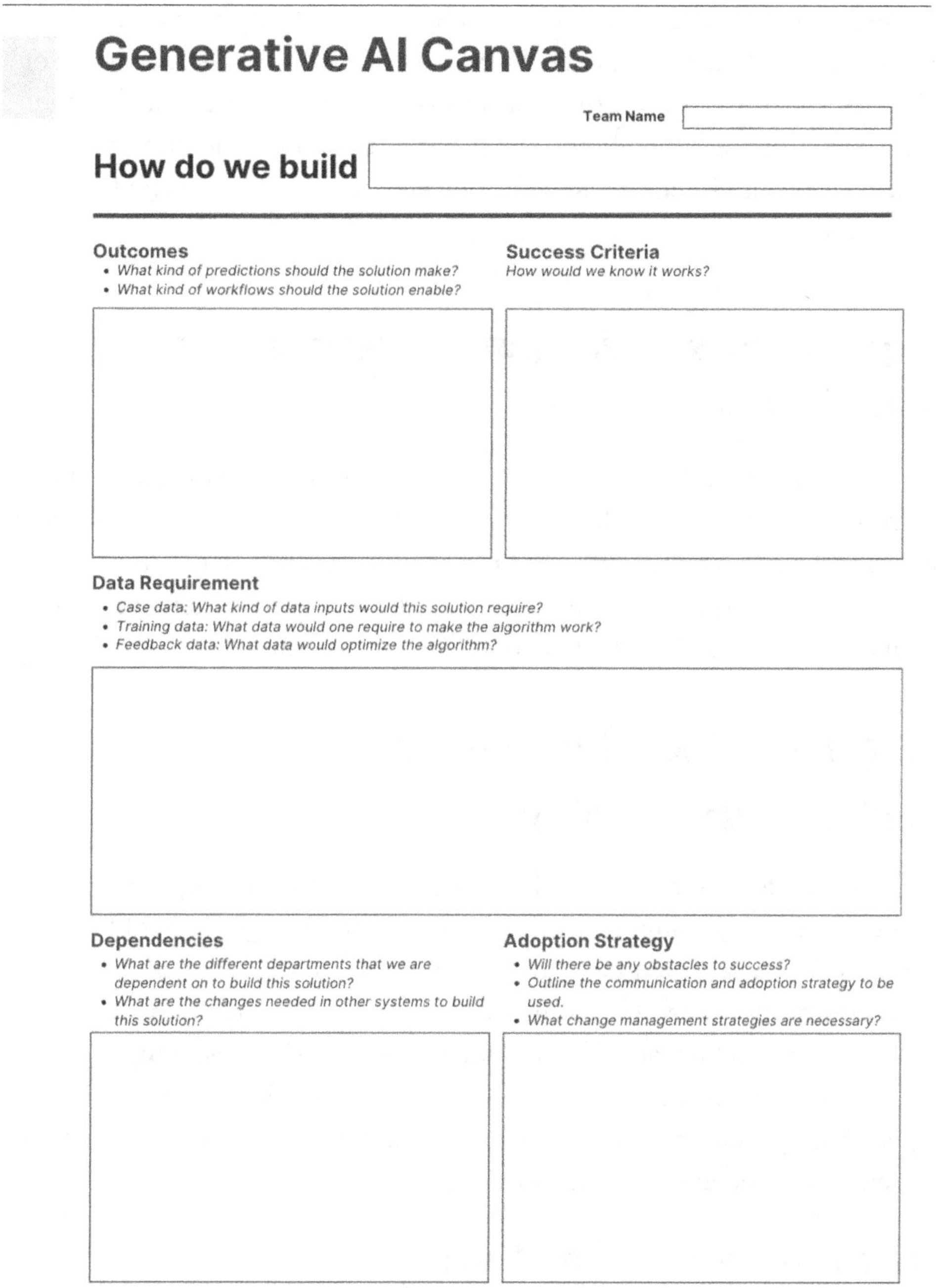

Generative AI Canvas

Team Name

How do we build

Outcomes
- What kind of predictions should the solution make?
- What kind of workflows should the solution enable?

Success Criteria
How would we know it works?

Data Requirement
- Case data: What kind of data inputs would this solution require?
- Training data: What data would one require to make the algorithm work?
- Feedback data: What data would optimize the algorithm?

Dependencies
- What are the different departments that we are dependent on to build this solution?
- What are the changes needed in other systems to build this solution?

Adoption Strategy
- Will there be any obstacles to success?
- Outline the communication and adoption strategy to be used.
- What change management strategies are necessary?

Figure 2-7. Generative AI Canvas template: How do we build?

Together, these canvases create a comprehensive framework for evaluating and planning generative AI initiatives. They transform the complex challenge of AI implementation into a structured journey of discovery and execution. In the following sections, we'll explore how this framework comes to life through a real-world implementation example, complete with code and practical insights that demonstrate its power in action.

The Framework in Action: Transforming Fashion Retail

Working with fashion retailers has taught us that the most impactful AI solutions often emerge from deeply understanding everyday business challenges. Let us share the story of a global fashion retailer who used this framework to revolutionize their product description process – a perfect example that illustrates how the Generative AI Canvas transforms abstract possibilities into concrete business value.

Starting with "Should We Build?"
Uncovering the Real Problem

"We need AI to write product descriptions" – this was the initial request from the retailer's merchandising team. However, as we worked through the Problem Statement section of our canvas, a more nuanced challenge emerged: "Our team spends 15 hours per day writing product descriptions for 500+ new items weekly across 12 markets, leading to delayed product launches and inconsistent brand messaging."

This refined problem statement revealed the true complexity of their challenge. It wasn't just about generating text; it was about maintaining brand consistency, ensuring cultural relevance, and accelerating time-to-market.

Understanding Current Workflows

Mapping the As-Is Workflow revealed a labyrinth of manual processes. Product descriptions began with merchandisers capturing technical details, then moved to copywriters who crafted engaging content, before finally reaching market teams for localization. Each piece required multiple reviews, leading to bottlenecks and delays.

I remember a particularly telling moment when a senior merchandiser pointed to a stack of product launch documents and said, "These have been waiting for descriptions for three weeks. That's three weeks these products could have been generating revenue."

Envisioning the Solution

The Solution section helped the team articulate a comprehensive vision for their AI assistant. They needed a system that could

- Generate initial product descriptions from technical specifications
- Adapt tone and style to match different product categories
- Provide market-specific variations while maintaining brand voice
- Suggest SEO-optimized content variations

Responsible AI Considerations

The fashion industry's nuanced relationship with cultural and gender sensitivity made the Responsible AI section particularly crucial. The team identified potential risks around cultural appropriation in product descriptions, gender-specific language concerns, and the need for market-specific sensitivity.

Organizational Readiness

The Organizational Fit assessment revealed both strengths and challenges. While the company had strong technical infrastructure, they needed to consider how AI would integrate with their existing product information management system and how it would affect their global content team's workflows.

Moving to "How Do We Build?"

Defining Success

The Outcomes section helped the team establish clear objectives:

- Reduce description creation time from 30 minutes to 5 minutes per product.
- Enable simultaneous multi-market launches.

- Maintain consistent brand voice across all markets.
- Improve product findability through optimized descriptions.

Data Foundation

The Data Requirements section revealed the rich data assets they could leverage:

- Historical product descriptions across markets
- Performance metrics for different description styles
- Customer search and engagement data
- Market-specific language preferences

What made this particularly interesting was discovering they had years of high-performing product descriptions that could train their AI system to understand what resonated with customers in different markets.

Building for Scale

The Dependencies section highlighted crucial integration points:

- Product information management system
- Translation management platform
- E-commerce content management system
- Analytics and performance tracking tools

Adoption Strategy

The team developed a thoughtful approach to rolling out their solution:

1. Begin with a single product category in one market.
2. Expand to all categories in that market.
3. Gradually roll out to other markets, incorporating learnings.
4. Enable full multimarket capabilities.

Framework Insights

What made this implementation particularly successful was how the framework helped the team maintain focus on business value while addressing technical complexity. It wasn't just about implementing AI – it was about solving a real business challenge that affected revenue, brand consistency, and market agility.

The framework revealed several crucial insights:

- The need for human oversight in culturally sensitive descriptions
- The importance of market-specific training data
- The value of maintaining brand voice across automated content
- The critical role of feedback loops in improving output quality

Real Impact

Six months after implementation, the results spoke for themselves:

- Product description creation time reduced by 80%.
- Market-specific launches accelerated by 65%.
- Consistent brand messaging across all markets.
- Improved search rankings due to optimized content.

But perhaps more importantly, the framework helped the team avoid common pitfalls. Instead of rushing to implement a generic solution, they built a system that truly understood their brand voice, respected cultural nuances, and integrated seamlessly with their existing workflows.

This fashion retail case demonstrates the power of our framework in bridging the gap between AI's potential and practical business value. It shows how systematic evaluation and planning can transform a seemingly straightforward need ("we need AI to write descriptions") into a comprehensive solution that delivers real business impact.

Remember, the framework isn't just a planning tool – it's a lens through which we can see the full complexity and potential of AI implementation in our specific business context. When used thoughtfully, it helps us move beyond the hype of AI to create solutions that deliver lasting value.

When Theory Meets Reality

While the framework helps organizations answer these critical questions – ensuring they're both **building the Right Thing and building Things Right** – the journey from framework to reality brings its own valuable lessons. We've spent years advising organizations about AI, and one truth consistently emerges: you can't truly understand AI's potential until you've experienced it firsthand. It reminds us of a workshop where a senior executive, after decades of making data-driven decisions, watched in amazement as AI analyzed years of customer feedback in minutes, revealing patterns his team had missed for months. "I get it now," he said, his eyes lighting up. "This isn't just faster analysis – it's a completely different way of seeing our business."

This moment of revelation, this shift from intellectual understanding to practical insight, is what transforms AI from a buzzword into a tangible tool. It's in these moments that people stop thinking about AI as magical technology and start seeing it as a practical instrument for solving real problems.

Discovering Through Doing
The journey to AI proficiency requires more than passive learning. True understanding emerges when people actively engage with AI tools to solve their own challenges. A marketing director might start skeptically, wondering how AI could possibly understand their brand voice. But when they experiment with AI to generate campaign variations, then use classification tools to analyze audience responses, their skepticism transforms into strategic thinking about how to integrate AI into their creative process.

Similarly, when developers first encounter AI-assisted coding, they often expect it to either write perfect code or produce unusable gibberish. The reality they discover through hands-on experimentation is more nuanced and ultimately more valuable – AI becomes a collaborative partner, suggesting approaches, helping with documentation, and catching potential issues early in the development cycle.

From Skeptics to Innovators
What makes these hands-on experiences so powerful isn't just the technical learning – it's the discovery of possibilities. When a finance team realizes they can use AI to not just summarize quarterly reports but to identify subtle trends and generate insights, they begin to reimagine their entire analytical process. When customer service managers see AI helping their teams respond to inquiries more effectively while maintaining the human touch, they start envisioning new ways to enhance customer experience.

But perhaps most importantly, hands-on experience teaches what AI can't do – a crucial understanding that no amount of theoretical knowledge can convey. It's in trying to push AI beyond its capabilities that teams develop a true appreciation for the balance between artificial and human intelligence.

Where Understanding Takes Root

This experiential learning creates what we call "practical wisdom" – the kind of deep understanding that comes from doing rather than just knowing. Teams learn to

- Recognize opportunities for AI application in their daily work
- Understand when AI can accelerate their efforts and when human judgment is crucial
- Develop an intuitive sense of how to combine different AI capabilities to solve complex problems
- Build realistic expectations about what AI can achieve

The result isn't just technical proficiency – it's a fundamental shift in how teams approach problem-solving. They stop seeing AI as either a threat or a silver bullet and start viewing it as what it truly is: a powerful tool that, when understood deeply, can enhance human capabilities in remarkable ways.

In an example, a team of financial analysts spent weeks learning about AI's analytical capabilities through presentations and documentation. Yet it wasn't until they used AI to analyze their own market reports that the potential became clear. Within hours, they uncovered market correlations they had missed in months of traditional analysis. More importantly, they began to see how AI could complement their expertise rather than replace it.

This transformation – from theoretical understanding to practical application – is what separates successful AI initiatives from those that remain stuck in the pilot phase. It's not enough to know what AI can do; teams need to experience it, experiment with it, and sometimes fail with it to truly understand how to harness its potential.

But how do we bridge this gap between understanding and implementation? How do we transform promising ideas into tangible solutions? This is where the art and science of proof-of-concepts comes into play. While traditional POCs focus on validating technical feasibility, the world of generative AI demands a different approach. We're no longer just proving that something can work – we're discovering how it should work within the complex fabric of organizational needs and human interactions.

CHAPTER 2   THE GENAI IDEA MAZE – FINDING GOLD AMONG THE GLITTER

As we step into this new frontier of POCs, we'll discover that the rules have changed. The rapid evolution of generative AI has transformed what was once a straightforward technical validation into an intricate dance of possibility and practicality. It's time to reimagine how we prove value in the generative AI playground.

Key Learnings from This chapter

Once your organization catches the AI bug, you'll face a new challenge: an overwhelming flood of ideas. How do you navigate this "idea maze" to find the projects that will deliver real value, not just excitement? This chapter provides the tools to move from a chaotic brainstorm to a structured, strategic pipeline of validated AI use cases.

Here are the key frameworks you've discovered to find the gold among the glitter:

1. **The Foundation: Building AI Literacy** You've learned that before you can evaluate ideas, your organization needs a shared language. This chapter outlines how to cultivate "AI intuition" by demystifying the technology. We broke down GenAI into its **six core capabilities** (like Generation, Summarization, and Classification), showing you how to map these fundamental skills to your specific business challenges and data types (text, image, audio, etc.).

2. **The Core Framework: The Generative AI Canvas** How do you systematically vet an idea and transform it from a "what if" into a "how to"? The **Generative AI Canvas** is your essential tool for this process. It provides a structured, two-part framework to ensure every project is both strategically sound and tactically viable:

    - **Part 1: "Should We Build?" – The Strategic Filter:** This first canvas forces you to validate the *why* behind an idea. It guides you to define the core business problem, map the current workflow, and critically assess the solution's organizational fit and ethical implications before you write a single line of code.

- **Part 2: "How Do We Build?" – The Tactical Roadmap:** Once an idea is validated, this second canvas helps you plan the *how*. It pushes you to define specific outcomes, measurable success criteria, data requirements, and a robust adoption strategy, turning a promising concept into a concrete project plan.

3. **The Proof: Learning Through Doing:** This chapter emphasizes that true understanding comes from experience. The frameworks provided are not just theoretical; they are designed to be used. By applying the Generative AI Canvas, your teams move beyond abstract discussions and gain practical wisdom, learning to distinguish a high-potential AI application from a solution in search of a problem.

Your Path Forward

This chapter has equipped you with a powerful toolkit to bring order to the creative chaos of AI ideation. You now have a method to ensure the best ideas rise to the top. But what happens when you've chosen a promising use case and need to prove its value without falling into the "POC trap"? To master the art of building proofs of concept that are designed to scale, dive back into the detailed pages of this chapter and put the canvas to work.

CHAPTER 3

Proof or Dare – Reimagining POCs in the GenAI Playground

POCs: Then and Now

The October morning carried a hint of winter as I prepared for another day at TechNova. Two weeks had passed since our framework discussions, and while teams were beginning to adopt structured approaches to AI implementation, something still nagged at me. My tablet displayed the latest statistics: 12 POCs initiated last quarter, four moved to production, and eight essentially abandoned – their code destined for the digital graveyard.

Standing by the kitchen window, waiting for my chai to steep, I watched leaves scatter across the backyard. Each leaf's journey reminded me of our POCs – some finding fertile ground, others simply drifting away. The pattern troubled me, especially given the resources invested in each proof-of-concept. If the tree was in a fertile ground, is it crazy to think that most of these fallen leaves may have become a new tree by itself? I know, maybe scientifically this analogy might stand out, but it resonated with me from the perspective of creation of reusable foundations.

My mind wandered to 2005, my first major POC at a financial services firm. We had three months to prove that automated trading algorithms could outperform human traders. The requirements were clear: demonstrate specific performance metrics using historical data. Clean, contained, predictable. Those early POCs followed a linear path – define requirements, build a prototype, validate, decide. Like a well-rehearsed play, each actor knew their role.

CHAPTER 3   PROOF OR DARE – REIMAGINING POCS IN THE GENAI PLAYGROUND

I smiled at the simplicity of those times. Today's POCs, particularly in AI, were different beasts entirely. Last week's insurance claim processing POC illustrated this perfectly. The team had created a compelling demonstration using public language models to analyze claims. Stakeholders were impressed by the demo's ability to extract key information from sample documents. Then reality struck – real claims contained sensitive health data, requiring strict privacy controls. The public models couldn't be used, and the POC's architecture wasn't designed to handle enterprise-grade AI models. Another prototype destined for the archive. And I totally empathize with teams to keep up the pace. The way new models, new frameworks, and new generative AI products are coming; they have to keep pace with them.

My phone buzzed with a message from the innovation team. Another POC using public APIs had impressed stakeholders but stumbled when faced with enterprise integration. Classic scenario: quick implementation with OpenAI's public endpoints, promising demos, then the inevitable complications when trying to adapt it for production.

The challenges had multiplied exponentially with generative AI. Traditional POCs assumed stable requirements and controlled environments. But how do you prove a concept when the underlying technology evolves weekly? When each new model release could dramatically change capabilities? When data privacy and security couldn't be afterthoughts but needed to be baked into the foundation?

I thought about our email enhancement POC from last month. The team had built directly against public APIs, creating an impressive demonstration that helped users craft better emails. But when the time came to scale, to switch to enterprise endpoints, to handle sensitive data – the prototype proved too rigid, too monolithic to adapt.

The past year has taught us hard lessons about AI POCs. The traditional approach of building quick, disposable prototypes was failing us in three critical ways (Figure 3-1):

CHAPTER 3   PROOF OR DARE – REIMAGINING POCS IN THE GENAI PLAYGROUND

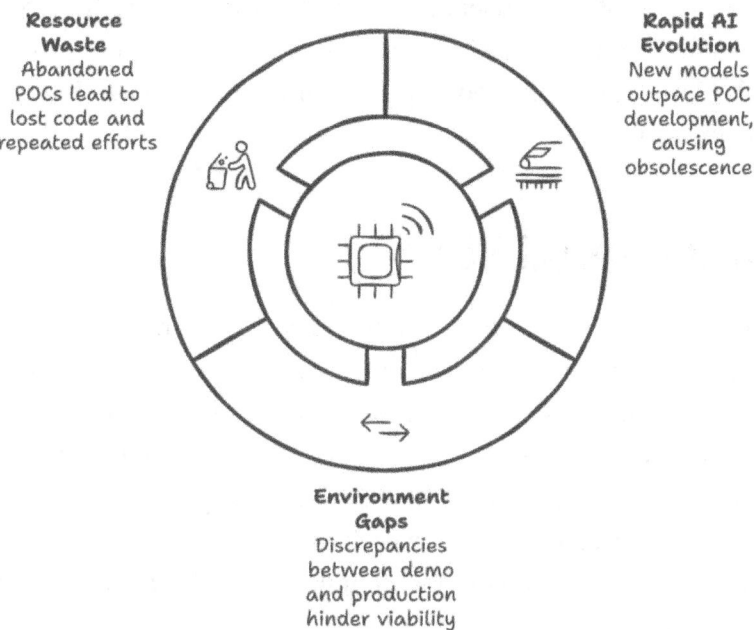

Figure 3-1. *Failures of traditional approach in building quick, disposable prototypes*

First, the speed of AI evolution meant that by the time a POC was complete, newer, more capable models were often available. POCs built as monolithic applications couldn't easily adapt to these changes.

Second, the gap between demonstration and production environments had widened dramatically. Running a POC with public AI models and synthetic data proved little about real-world viability. Enterprise data came with complexity that dummy datasets couldn't mirror – privacy requirements, security constraints, integration needs.

Third, the resource waste was becoming unsustainable. Each abandoned POC represented not just lost code but lost learning opportunities. Teams were solving the same problems repeatedly, reinventing components that could have been reused.

The realization that had been forming over weeks crystallized: we needed to stop thinking of POCs as disposable demonstrations and start viewing them as foundations for future growth. Why build a proof-of-concept that would be discarded when we could create reusable components? The concept of a GenAI stack began taking shape in my mind – modular services that could survive beyond any single proof-of-concept.

I grabbed my tablet, opening a fresh note. Imagine a text generation service, independent of any specific provider. Another service handling prompt management, separating system prompts from user inputs. Each component is discrete yet interconnected, like compartments in a bento box. This modular approach would allow teams to switch AI providers, scale components independently, and reuse services across multiple projects.

Blueprint for GenAI POCs

The drive to TechNova gave me time to refine the concept. This wasn't just about AI POCs – this philosophy could revolutionize how we approached all proof-of-concepts. Real data instead of synthetic datasets. Reusable microservices instead of monolithic prototypes. A foundation for growth rather than a temporary demonstration.

The morning traffic moved steadily along the highway, brake lights blinking in rhythm. My mind wandered to the microservices architecture we'd implemented last year – how it had transformed our deployment flexibility. If we applied similar principles to POCs...

By the time I reached the office, the morning bustle was in full swing. As I waited for the elevator, I spotted Sam from the architecture team heading for his morning coffee. In his three years at TechNova, he'd built some of our most robust microservices architectures. More importantly, he had an uncanny ability to see through complexity to elegant solutions.

"Sam!" I called out, catching up to him at the coffee station. He turned, the coffee cup paused midway to his mouth, eyebrows raised in friendly questions.

"Black, no sugar?" I asked, reaching for an extra cup at the coffee station.

"Thanks, Dr. Anya." Sam accepted the cup with a nod. The break room hummed with morning activity – developers grabbing their caffeine fix, analysts huddled over their phones.

"How's the new microservices architecture for the trading platform coming along?" I asked, remembering the robust design Sam had presented last month.

"Final testing phase. The separation of concerns really paid off – teams can deploy independently now." Sam's eyes lit up with quiet pride. Three years of architecting critical systems had earned him that confidence.

"That's actually why I wanted to catch you. Been thinking about our POC processes, especially for AI initiatives." I gestured toward the small meeting room nearby. "Got a minute?"

In the meeting room, I sketched our current POC pattern on the whiteboard. "We've had 12 POCs this quarter. Only four made it to production."

"That's actually better than industry average," Sam observed, setting his coffee down. "POCs are meant to validate ideas quickly. Not all should succeed."

"True. But look at why they're failing." I added notes beside the diagram. "The email assistant POC – technically solid, great demo, but couldn't handle enterprise data. The document analyzer – impressive with public models, fell apart when we needed private deployment."

Sam leaned forward, his expression thoughtful. "These are expected challenges when moving from proof-of-concept to production. That's why we keep POCs lightweight."

"What if that's the wrong approach for AI? We're treating these POCs like disposable prototypes, but..." A knock on the glass interrupted us. Through the wall, we could see the room's scheduled occupants waiting.

"Architecture room?" Sam suggested, already gathering his notes.

The architecture room, with its wall-to-wall whiteboards and dual displays, had seen countless system designs come to life. Sam claimed his usual spot near the main board while I pulled up the POC statistics on the display.

"You mentioned the trading platform earlier," I said, turning to Sam. "How many components from the initial POC survived to production?"

"None," Sam replied definitively. "Complete rebuild. That's normal for POCs."

"But what if it wasn't? What if we could build POCs with components designed to evolve?" I paused for a moment, considering the possibilities. "Think about how we handle microservices in production – isolated concerns, clear interfaces, independent scaling..."

Sam's expression shifted from skepticism to intrigue. "You want to apply production architecture principles to POCs? That's..." he paused, choosing his words carefully. "That's unconventional, Dr. Anya. The overhead alone would be significant."

"Specifically for generative AI, yes." I nodded, acknowledging the unconventional nature of the idea. "The traditional POC approach made sense when technology changed in predictable cycles. But look at what's happened just in the past two weeks – Anthropic enhanced their API and released a new Claude model, OpenAI announced updates and many more"

Sam nodded, his architectural mindset already processing the implications. "So every POC we build today might need updates tomorrow just to leverage these improvements."

"Right. Take Chen's email assistant. Brilliant implementation, but..."

"But when we tried to switch from public to enterprise endpoints, we hit a wall," Sam finished. "Had to rewrite the prompt handling, modify the response processing, restructure the data flow."

"Yet the core functionalities remain the same across most of our generative AI projects." I started listing on the whiteboard: "Text generation, prompt management, response handling, data preprocessing..."

Sam straightened, his expression shifting from polite interest to genuine engagement. "You're suggesting we modularize these common elements? Even for POCs?"

"Think about it – every generative AI POC needs these components. Instead of rebuilding them each time..." I paused, letting him follow the logic.

"We could create standardized, reusable services," Sam continued, professional reserve giving way to excitement. "But maintaining production-grade services for POCs... the overhead..."

"Would be justified by the flexibility we gain." I continued writing on the whiteboard, drawing some circles to explain. "Imagine each component like a well-designed module – independently deployable, easily maintainable, ready to scale."

Sam moved to the whiteboard, marker in hand. "Walk me through a concrete example. How would this work for something like the email assistant?"

He was already sketching the email assistant's current architecture – a typical monolithic POC structure. "Right now, it's all interconnected. The prompt handling, API calls, response processing..."

"Let's reimagine this," I said, moving to the adjacent whiteboard. "In traditional Japanese cuisine, there's this concept of a bento box. Each component of the meal sits in its own compartment, perfectly prepared and self-contained, yet part of a cohesive whole."

I drew a series of connected squares. "What if we approached our AI architecture the same way? Each core functions in its own container, independently maintainable but designed to work together."

"Take the email assistant. First compartment: text generation service." I labeled the box. "Its only job is handling interactions with AI models. Think of it as our universal translator for AI communications. Doesn't matter if it's OpenAI today, Claude tomorrow, or our own models next month."

Sam nodded, then pointed to the service boundary. "So this handles the raw interaction with AI endpoints?"

"Exactly. No business logic, no prompt engineering – just pure text generation capability. Like a well-trained chef who can cook anything but doesn't decide the menu."

"And the next compartment?"

"Prompt management service." I drew another box, connecting it to the first with a clear interface. "This is where the magic of context lives. When our email assistant needs to generate text, it doesn't just pass raw user input to the AI. Instead, it works with both services – prompt management provides the carefully crafted system prompts, defining the assistant's personality and guidelines, while text generation handles the AI interaction."

"So if we want to change how formal or casual the email tone is..." Sam started.

"We just modify the system prompt through the prompt service," I completed. "No need to touch the text generation service or any other parts of the application. Like adjusting a recipe without replacing the chef."

Sam grabbed a marker, adding a flow diagram. "The email assistant's front end would call these services in sequence then? Prompt service first to get the optimized prompt..."

"Then to text generation for the AI response," I nodded. "When we need to change how the assistant understands email context or adjust its writing style, we only update the prompt templates in one place. The text generation service continues its job, blissfully unaware anything changed."

"And if tomorrow we find a better AI model for email writing..."

"We only update the text generation service, while all our carefully tuned prompts remain intact in their own service." I drew the connection points between services. "It's about creating clear boundaries while ensuring smooth collaboration between components."

"Another example can be Document Processing Bentos," I continued "The micro services inside this can be used widely actually."

"Hmm, because documents are everywhere?" Sam asked, his focus on the practical implementation.

"That's where it gets interesting. Document preprocessing isn't just one service – and that's why, it's potentially its own bento box." I started a new diagram. "Think about document processing. We need classification services to identify document types, parsing services to extract structured data, matching services to find similar documents…"

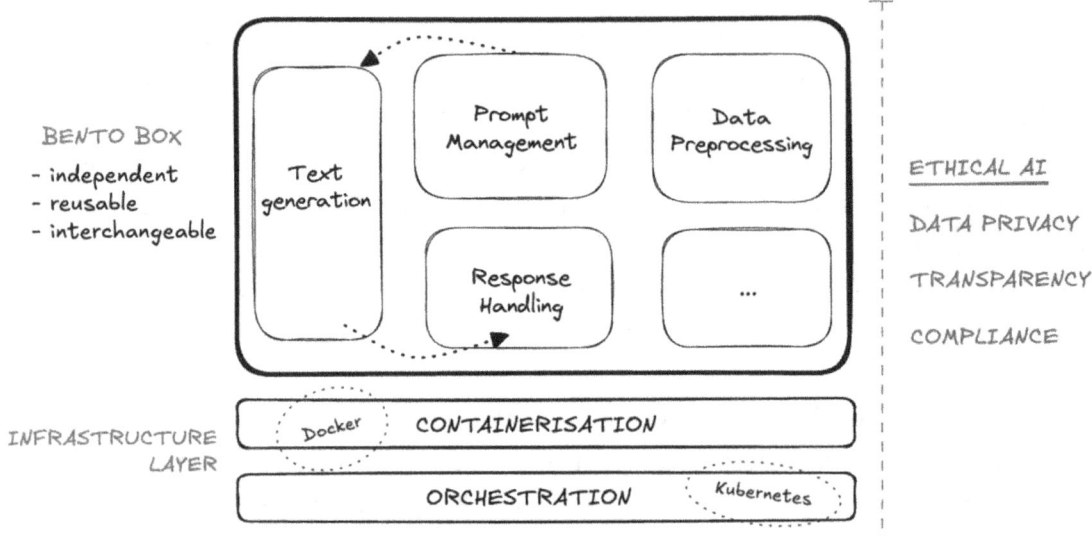

Figure 3-2. Introducing the Bento Box architectural approach

Sam straightened, his architectural instincts engaged. "Yeah, I am kind of getting it. If there is a use case now, where we have any of the above needs like classifying documents into multiple document types, we can use one or more services from this stack."

"Exactly. Just like a traditional bento box can stack, these service collections can be layered and combined." I drew connecting lines between the boxes. "For our current use case, the email assistant might use the text generation bento box for content creation, while pulling from the document services bento box for attachment processing."

Sam moved closer to the whiteboard, thoughtfully. "This could create a common language for discussing services across the organization. Instead of getting lost in technical details…"

"We can talk about which 'bento boxes' a solution needs. Business teams understand the metaphor, while technical teams grasp the architectural implications."

"And as we develop more specialized needs…" Sam sketched another container set.

"We create new compartments within the bento. Maybe one for analytics services, another for security and compliance." I pointed to the connections between boxes. "Each one self-contained but designed to work with others."

Sam stepped back, studying the expanding architecture. "This could fundamentally change how we structure our AI initiatives. Questions?"

"Many," I replied. "How do we handle service discovery between boxes? What about cross-box orchestration? Authentication between services?"

"Valid concerns," Sam said, jotting them down. "We'll need a solid containerization strategy. Kubernetes for orchestration, definitely. But first..." He drew a smaller diagram in the corner. "Let's prototype this with the email assistant. Start small, prove the concept. We can create some bento services for this use case and see while this POC is being developed, are there any further challenges from the back-end bento perspectives?"

Sam grabbed his laptop. "Let me create a mockup of a quick architecture diagram. Might help us spot potential issues."

While Sam worked on the architecture diagram, my mind shifted to our next challenge. Having a solid framework was one thing – successfully implementing and demonstrating it was another. We needed a practical approach that would align our technical architecture with business objectives while making the value clear to stakeholders.

"Sam," I said, looking up from my notes. "Before we dive deeper into the technical specs, we should consider how this plays out in reality. Mind if we grab Mei from the product team? Her experience with stakeholder demonstrations could be valuable here."

Sam nodded, saving his diagram. "Good call. This isn't just an engineering challenge – it's about providing business value."

We headed toward the product wing. In my mind, I was still thinking, how our Bento Box approach would need to demonstrate not just technical elegance, but practical impact. We need to think of some creative ways of showing stakeholders how this architecture could transform their AI initiatives from experiments into production-ready solutions.

CHAPTER 3   PROOF OR DARE – REIMAGINING POCS IN THE GENAI PLAYGROUND

From Architecture to Action: Implementing and Demonstrating GenAI POCs

The product wing occupied the east side of our floor, where the sun streamed through floor-to-ceiling windows. I spotted Mei in one of the conference rooms, deep in discussion with her team.

"Mind if we interrupt?" I asked from the doorway. Mei glanced at her team, then at her watch.

"We're just wrapping up. Give me five minutes?"

While her team filed out, Sam and I claimed the far end of the conference room. The walls still held remnants of their planning session – user stories, timeline charts, and iteration plans carefully mapped out.

"Mei's got a way of keeping products grounded in reality," Sam remarked quietly, studying their release timeline.

She joined us shortly, dropping into a chair with her ever-present notebook. "So, what brings the architecture team to my corner of the world?"

"We're revamping our AI POC approach," I began, "but we need to ensure we're not just solving technical problems. Your product launches always nail the balance between innovation and practical value."

Mei raised an eyebrow. "You've seen our AI pilot feedback. Half our stakeholders are excited about possibilities, the other half worried about practical implementation." She pulled out the latest metrics. "Time to market, security compliance, scalability against demand – these aren't just technical challenges."

"That's why we need your input," I said, as Sam began sketching our Bento Box concept. "We've developed a new architectural approach, but architecture alone won't drive adoption."

For the next 15-20 mins, we walked Mei through the entire concept of Bentos, whatever me and Sam discussed. I was glad to notice how Sam remembered everything and drew the beautiful sketch of the blueprint. Kind of assured me that my idea is actually feasible!

Mei studied Sam's diagram thoughtfully. As Head of Product Strategy, her focus had always been on sustainable delivery roadmaps.

"In just two weeks, we've seen significant interest in generative AI across departments," I said. "Legal's asking about contract analysis possibilities. Sales is exploring email automation. Marketing sees potential in content generation."

"That's where we need to think ahead," I continued. "While teams are still in the exploration phase, we have an opportunity to build the right foundation. Instead of rushing into individual solutions, we could invest in creating a robust GenAI stack."

Sam adjusted his diagram. "The architecture would support immediate needs while building reusable components for future projects."

Mei turned to her laptop, pulling up next year's strategic initiatives. "We're looking at significant AI exploration in the coming quarters. Having standardized components could change how we approach these projects."

"It's about building for scale from the start," I explained. "When teams move beyond initial testing to actual implementation, they'll need an infrastructure that can grow with their needs. The Bento Box approach gives us that flexibility while maintaining enterprise standards for security and compliance."

"The challenge," Sam noted, "will be balancing immediate needs with long-term architecture."

"I think we need to consider both timelines here," I said, moving to the whiteboard. "Teams need to demonstrate AI capabilities quickly, but we also need to build sustainably."

Sam nodded. "We could start with one component of the Bento Box – maybe the text generation service. It's fundamental to most AI projects we're seeing."

"And security considerations?" Mei asked, her product leadership experience evident in the question. "Enterprise data isn't something we experiment with."

"Yes, you are right!" I uncapped the marker and continued talking while going toward the white board, "I suggest as we create the first service, we make sure we have thought it through. For example, our text generation service can use Azure Open AI packages, to start with instead of public open ai service."

I sketched a simple timeline on the board:

- **Week 1-2**: Core text generation and document preprocessing services
- **Week 3-5**: Add prompt management service, expand security features around these services, like adding input and output validations, create orchestrators to manage multiple services from bentos.

"Pretty aggressive timelines," Sam commented, studying the board. "But if we do this, we could have initial services ready for teams to start building against within weeks."

"The key is clear documentation and APIs," I added. "As teams begin using these services, we'll learn what works, what doesn't. The architecture will evolve based on real usage patterns."

Mei made a note on her laptop. "I'll need to adjust some product timelines, but having reusable components could actually accelerate our later phases," she continued while closing the laptop, "Let me just quickly grab a coffee."

The morning sun had shifted, casting new shadows across our diagrams. Our proposed timeline sat on the whiteboard – around one month of careful service building, starting with core text generation and data preprocessing. I wanted to sort out the strategy resource planning as well, so that we have some idea on how to structure the teams properly.

"We'd also need the right team structure," I said finally.

"Let me show you what I'm thinking," Sam said, turning his laptop so I could see his team roster. "Liam and Mateo have been working on our containerization initiatives. They understand enterprise-grade service architecture."

I studied the screen, thinking about the dual tracks we needed to establish. "They could form the core of our Bento Box team. Focus solely on building these foundational services."

""While Priya leads the POC implementations," Sam added. "She has the right mix of technical skills and business understanding to help teams leverage these services effectively."

The afternoon light had softened, casting long shadows across the whiteboard where our earlier diagrams still stood. I added two columns: 'Bento Box Team' and 'POC Team'.

"The Bento Box team needs to start with the text generation services," I said. "Build it, secure it, document it. Make it a template for how we approach all our Generative AI services."

"Meanwhile, the POC team can start working with teams on defining their needs. By the time they're ready to build, they'll have reliable services waiting."

"And for the POC implementations themselves..." Sam began.

I sketched out the seven-day framework we'd need once the core services were ready. This wasn't just about quick demonstrations anymore – it was about building scalable solutions on top of proven foundations.

"Here's how I see the seven days playing out," I said, drawing a timeline across the whiteboard. "The key is having those Bento Box services ready and stable."

Day 1: Assessment and Architecture – "Day one is about understanding what we have and what we need," I explained, marking the first section. "The POC team meets with business stakeholders, maps their requirements against our available services.

Sam pulled up our service inventory on his laptop. "And if they identify gaps?"

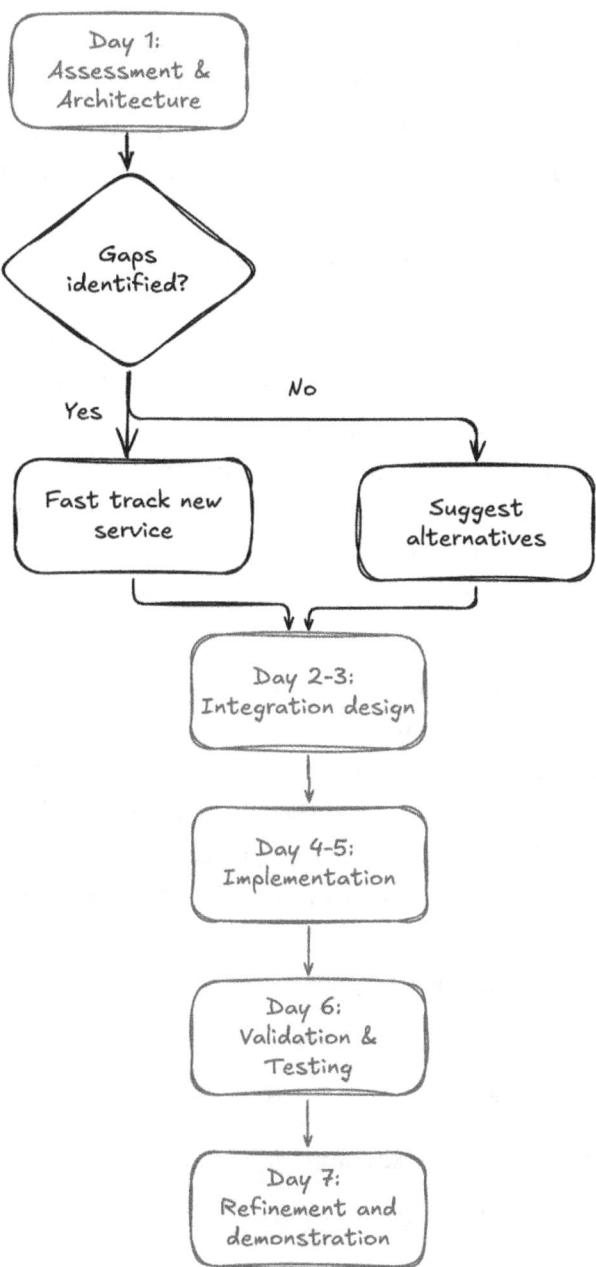

Figure 3-3. *Seven-day cycle for proof of concept*

"That feeds back to the Bento Box team. They either fast-track a needed service or suggest alternatives using existing components." I added a feedback loop to the diagram.

Days 2–3: Integration Design – "With known services, the POC team can move fast," I continued. "No time wasted building basic functionality. They focus on business logic, data flows, user experience."

"Removes a lot of technical debt up front," Sam noted, thinking about previous POCs that had struggled with basic infrastructure.

Days 4–5: Implementation – "This is where having solid services really shows its value," I said, filling in the middle section. "Instead of writing authentication, data preprocessing, or AI interaction code..."

"They just connect to existing services through standard interfaces," Sam finished, seeing the efficiency gain.

Day 6: Validation and Testing – "Real data, real security, real performance testing," I emphasized. "Because our services are production-grade from the start, we're not discovering fundamental issues at this stage."

Day 7: Refinement and Demonstration – "Final day is about polishing the implementation and preparing to show to stakeholders," I concluded. "No last-minute infrastructure fixes or security patches."

Sam studied the timeline. "This only works if those Bento Box services are truly production-ready."

"Exactly why we need dedicated teams and clear separation of concerns," I agreed. "One team builds the foundation, another innovates on top of it."

"Quality can't be an afterthought for either team," I said, moving to a clean section of the whiteboard. The afternoon had progressed, but this was crucial to get right.

Sam straightened in his chair, his architectural expertise coming to the fore. "For the Bento Box team, we need strict engineering standards." He moved to the whiteboard, taking the marker:

Core Engineering Requirements (Figure 3-4):

- Enterprise-grade security from day one
- Comprehensive service documentation
- Standardized APIs and integration patterns
- Performance benchmarks and monitoring
- Clear versioning strategy

CHAPTER 3   PROOF OR DARE – REIMAGINING POCS IN THE GENAI PLAYGROUND

"The teams can't work in isolation," Sam continued, adding another section. "We'll need structured interaction points."

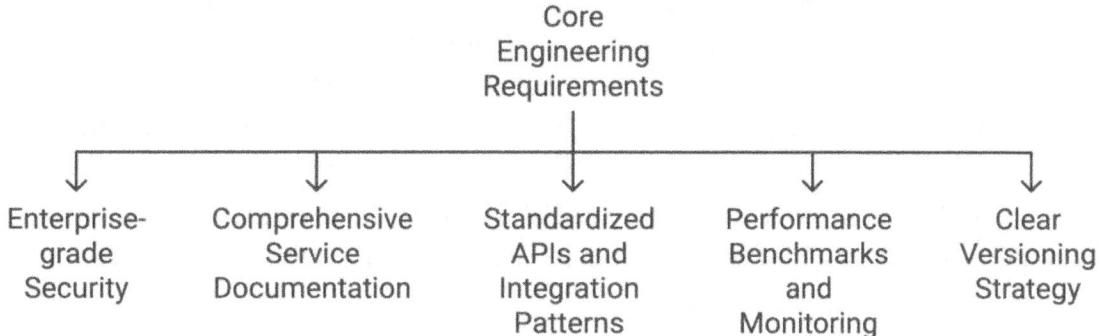

Figure 3-4. *Engineering standards*

He sketched out a communication cadence:

- Weekly architecture reviews where both teams align on patterns and challenges
- Service adoption workshops to ensure proper usage
- Regular integration pattern discussions
- Cross-team pairing sessions for knowledge transfer

I watched as he detailed the interaction points, appreciating how his experience with enterprise architecture brought clarity to our approach.

"This gives us quality control and knowledge sharing," Sam explained. "The POC team helps us validate service design, while the Bento Box team ensures we're building on solid foundations."

"Timeline for the first cycle?" I asked.

Sam pointed to the part where I previously wrote the timeline, "Nothing changes from what you wrote before. Two weeks to build our first production-ready text generation bento box. Then we can test the seven-day POC framework with a real project."

"Before we commit to timelines," we actually did not notice that Mei is back, "we should consider how we'll demonstrate these POCs and services. These services aren't just internal tools – they'll be the foundation for client solutions."

Her point landed with impact. While we had our technical approach mapped out, we needed to think beyond implementation to actual enterprise adoption.

"Agree" Sam said, "there's just to add to what you are saying, when clients see these POCs, their first question will be about production readiness."

Mei nodded. "That's been consistent feedback. They see the potential but want to know if they can actually start using it in their environment.""

"That's where our approach differs," I said. "Because we're building production-grade services from the start, the POC they see is already enterprise-ready. No major rewrites needed for production."

"It's not just about the technology though," Sam added. "Clients need to understand how they can integrate these services into their existing workflows, their security protocols, their data governance."

"And scale," Mei pointed out. "They might want to start with email processing in one department, then expand across the organization."

The conversation shifted to practical adoption scenarios. How a financial institution might start with document processing in their compliance department, then extend to customer service, then trading analysis – all using the same core services but with different configurations.

"This is about proving not just capability, but adaptability," I said. "Showing that what works in a POC can grow with their needs."

"Also, Enterprise readiness isn't something we just talk about," I said. "We need to show it in action."

Sam nodded thoughtfully. "A live demonstration that tells the complete story."

"Exactly," Mei moved to the whiteboard. "Take our HR chatbot POC. Instead of just showing how it answers policy questions, we demonstrate the entire spectrum of capabilities."

The Demonstration Journey:

1. **Start with the Expected**

    - Show the chatbot answering common HR queries.

    - Demonstrate accurate policy information retrieval.

    - Highlight natural conversation flow.

2. **Reveal the Safety Net**

    "Now this is where it gets interesting," she said. "We show what happens when someone tries to manipulate the system."

Sam caught on immediately. "Like attempting to extract sensitive employee data or bypass policy restrictions?"

"Precisely. We demonstrate our guardrails in action:

- Show an attempt to extract confidential information.
- Watch the system recognize and block the attempt.
- Demonstrate how it maintains security while staying helpful."

3. **Behind the Curtain** "Then we pull back the curtain," I added to Mei's list.

- The prompt management service enforcing security boundaries
- Data preprocessing ensuring sensitive information never reaches the model
- Real-time monitoring catching unusual patterns"

Mei leaned forward. "This kind of demonstration builds trust. It shows we're not just implementing AI – we're implementing it responsibly. This gives organizations confidence."

"And for client demonstrations," Sam added, "we can customize these scenarios to their specific security concerns."

I sketched a client demonstration flow (Figure 3-5):

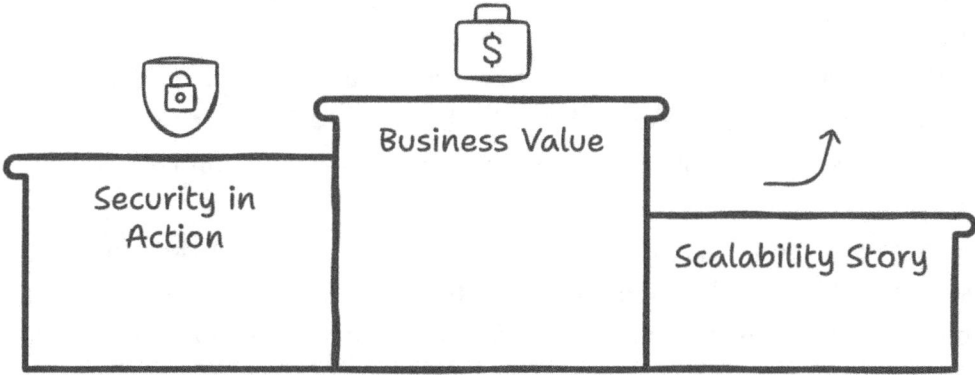

Figure 3-5. *Client demonstration flow*

1. **Business Value**
   - Solve their immediate challenge.
   - Show expected behavior.
2. **Security in Action**
   - Demonstrate protective measures.
   - Show how their specific compliance requirements are met.
   - Illustrate data handling safeguards.
3. **Scalability Story**
   - Start with one department.
   - Show expansion across teams.
   - Demonstrate consistent security and performance.

"This approach tells a complete story," I said. "From immediate value to long-term security and scalability."

We continued this discussion to create a structure to everything that we discussed. Then called it a day. We had moved beyond abstract discussions of architecture to a concrete demonstration of value and trust.

Over the next few weeks, this storytelling approach transformed our demonstrations. Teams didn't just showcase features – they revealed the intelligent guardrails protecting users, the scalable architecture enabling growth, and the thoughtful design ensuring security.

Sam's team embraced this narrative approach, creating demonstrations that showed both capability and responsibility. Each POC became a story of possibility and protection, showing stakeholders not just what AI could do, but how it could be trusted to do it safely.

The foundation was set. We had created not just an architecture for building AI solutions, but a framework for demonstrating their value, security, and scalability. Now it was time to see how this approach would transform the way organizations proved, built, and scaled their AI initiatives.

Just as I was finishing up my notes, my phone buzzed – Ray calling from home. I smiled, switching to speaker as I packed up my things.

"Hey," he greeted, his tone warm and familiar. "I'm guessing today was one of those big-picture days?"

I looked at the diagrams still scattered across the whiteboard. "Yeah, we dug deep. We're working on this 'Bento Box' concept – basically, modular building blocks for our AI projects. If it works, it could mean creating flexible foundations that don't need constant reworking."

"Like building something with pieces you can rearrange, without starting from scratch," he said, clearly thinking it over.

"Exactly," I replied, a little surprised at how well he got it. "It's ambitious, but if we pull it off, it could change how we handle all these evolving AI projects."

"Well, it sounds like you're building something lasting. I'll leave you to wrap up, but don't get so focused you miss dinner," he reminded, a lighthearted nudge to close the day.

"Noted," I replied with a smile. "See you soon."

Anya's Notes
Concepts in Practice

Understanding the Evolution of POCs in the AI Era

Over our decades of technology implementation experience, we've watched proof-of-concepts evolve from simple technical validations to complex enterprise initiatives. In the pre-AI era, we guided organizations through POCs that followed predictable patterns: define requirements, build a minimal viable solution, demonstrate functionality, and decide on implementation. The success criteria were clear, the technology stack was stable, and the path from POC to production was well understood.

But generative AI has fundamentally disrupted this established approach. In our recent work with enterprises adopting AI, we've observed several critical shifts that demand a new way of thinking about POCs.

Accelerated Technology Evolution

The pace of change in generative AI has no precedent in our experience. While traditional technology cycles gave organizations months or years to evaluate and implement solutions, we now see significant AI capabilities evolving weekly. Working with multiple enterprises, we've witnessed POCs become outdated before they even reach stakeholder review. A financial services client recently completed a document analysis POC using GPT-3.5, only to find GPT-4's capabilities would have fundamentally changed their approach.

The **Enterprise Reality Gap** (Figure 3-6) – Perhaps the most crucial challenge we've encountered is the widening gap between POC environments and enterprise requirements. We've seen countless impressive demonstrations using public AI models crumble when confronted with enterprise realities:

- **Data Privacy**: In healthcare implementations, we've had to completely rebuild POCs that initially used public APIs because they couldn't meet HIPAA requirements.

- **Compliance**: Our financial sector clients require detailed audit trails and controlled AI interactions that public models simply don't support.

- **Integration**: What works in isolation often fails when integrated with enterprise authentication, monitoring, and security systems.

- **Performance**: We've seen POCs that performed brilliantly with test data struggle under actual production workloads.

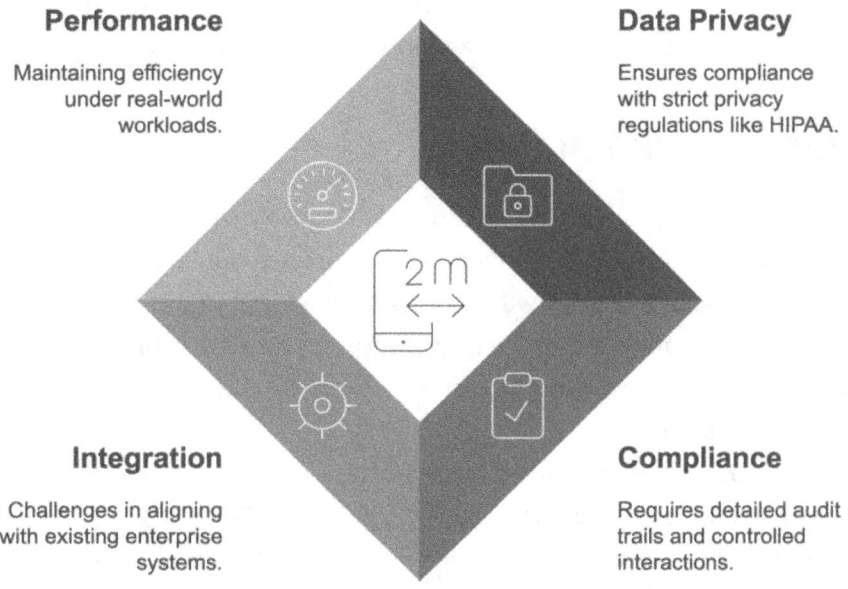

Figure 3-6. Enterprise Reality Gap

Resource Sustainability Challenge

Through our work with technology teams, we've identified a growing frustration with the traditional "throwaway POC" approach. Each discarded proof-of-concept represents more than just lost code – it represents

- **Lost Learning:** We've watched teams across different departments solve the same AI integration challenges repeatedly.

- **Redundant Development:** Basic capabilities like prompt management and response handling are rebuilt from scratch for each POC.

- **Missed Optimization:** Insights gained from one implementation rarely inform future projects, creating a cycle of repeated mistakes.

This pattern became particularly clear during a recent enterprise-wide AI initiative, where we found that different departments had independently built similar prompt management solutions five times. Each team had invested weeks solving the same problems, yet none of these solutions was robust enough for production use.

The Value Realization Gap

Perhaps most concerning is what we called in the previous notes section "Death by POC" – organizations continuously investing in proofs-of-concept without realizing actual business value. In our work with enterprise leaders, we frequently hear impressive metrics from POC demonstrations: "This will reduce processing time by 60%," or "We can automate 40% of these workflows." But these remain theoretical benefits until solutions reach production.

A manufacturing client recently showed us their AI initiative portfolio: 15 POCs completed over six months, each promising significant efficiency gains. Yet with only two making it to production, the actual return on their AI investment was minimal. This pattern repeats across industries – POCs generate excitement and promise, but without a clear path to production, they become expensive technical exercises rather than value-generating solutions.

The root cause isn't a lack of potential – our experience shows that generative AI can deliver remarkable business value. Rather, it's the disconnect between POC implementation and production requirements. Traditional POC approaches force organizations to essentially start over when moving to production, making the journey so resource-intensive that many promising solutions never make the transition.

This challenge is particularly acute with generative AI, where the gap between demonstration and production is wider than with traditional technology. A healthcare provider's document-processing POC showed impressive accuracy with test data, but implementing the same capabilities with actual patient records, compliance requirements, and enterprise security took four times longer than the initial POC. By the time they were ready for production, newer AI models had emerged, raising questions about whether to restart the process.

We need a fundamental shift in how organizations approach AI POCs – not just to reduce wasted resources but to ensure promising innovations actually deliver value in production. This means reimagining POCs as the first step in a continuous journey to production, not as isolated technical experiments.

The Bento Box Approach: Rethinking POC Architecture

"We'll rebuild it for production." These words, once a standard part of the POC playbook, have become increasingly problematic in the age of generative AI. Why? Because while we're planning that rebuild, our competitors are already delivering value. The pace of AI evolution waits for no one, and the luxury of throwing away working solutions is one we can no longer afford.

Consider this scenario: Your team has just demonstrated an AI-powered contract analysis system. The stakeholders are impressed. Legal teams can see how it will save them hours of review time. Compliance officers appreciate its ability to flag potential issues. Then comes the traditional next step: "Great demo! Now let's spend three months rebuilding it for production."

But wait. Three months? In that time, new AI models will emerge, competitors will launch solutions, and your organization's needs will evolve. The market won't wait for perfect architecture – it rewards those who can deliver value quickly while building for the future.

This is where traditional POC thinking breaks down. The assumption that POCs are throwaway experiments made sense when technology changed slowly and predictably. But in the world of generative AI, where capabilities transform weekly and use cases emerge daily, we need a different approach.

Imagine instead a POC that's built to grow. One where each component is production-ready from day one. Switching from GPT-4 to Claude doesn't mean rewriting your entire application. Where adding enterprise security doesn't require restructuring your core logic. This isn't just architectural theory – it's a practical necessity in the AI era.

But how do we reconcile the need for speed with the demands of enterprise-grade solutions? The answer lies in rethinking not just how we build POCs but what a POC actually is. Instead of viewing POCs as disposable demonstrations, we need to see them as the foundation of future production systems.

This shift in thinking led us to develop what we call the Bento Box approach. Like its namesake, where each compartment contains a distinct but complementary item, this architecture separates AI capabilities into discrete, production-ready services. Each service is independent yet designed to work in harmony with others.

When a financial services client recently needed to prove AI could enhance their customer service, we didn't build a throwaway chat interface. Instead, we created modular services for text generation, context management, and response handling. The initial POC took the same time as a traditional approach but with a crucial difference – it was ready to scale the moment it proved valuable.

Enter the Bento Box – our answer to the POC paradox. But before diving into services and APIs, let's understand what makes this approach different through a real-world example that probably feels familiar to many organizations.

Imagine you're building an AI-powered email assistant. The traditional approach might look something like this:

Building with Bento Box: From Concept to Code

The Bento Box approach transforms how we think about AI implementation, but what does this look like in practice? Let's break down the architecture that makes this possible, moving from concept to actual code.

Think about how a chef prepares a bento box. Each component is crafted independently, with its own preparation method and timing, yet all components come together to create a harmonious meal. Our AI services follow the same principle. Let's look at a typical AI implementation before and after applying the Bento Box approach.

Here's how many teams build their AI POCs today (Figure 3-7):

```python
class EmailAssistant:
    def generate_response(self, user_input, style, security_level):
        # Everything mixed together
        prompt = self.create_prompt(user_input, style)
        security_check = self.validate_security(user_input, security_level)
        if security_check:
            response = openai.Completion.create(prompt=prompt)
            return self.format_response(response)
```

Figure 3-7. *Demonstration of current way of building AI proof of concept*

CHAPTER 3 PROOF OR DARE – REIMAGINING POCS IN THE GENAI PLAYGROUND

This works for demos, but becomes problematic when

- Switching AI providers
- Implementing different security rules
- Adding new communication styles
- Scaling for enterprise use

The Bento Box approach separates these concerns (Figure 3-8):

```python
class TextGenerationService:
    def generate_text(self, prompt):
        # Clean, focused AI interaction
        return self.ai_provider.generate(prompt)

class PromptManagementService:
    def create_prompt(self, content, style):
        # Handles all prompt-related logic
        template = self.get_template(style)
        return template.format(content=content)

class SecurityService:
    def validate_request(self, content, level):
        # Independent security controls
        return self.security_rules.validate(content, level)
```

Figure 3-8. *Demonstration of Bento Box way of building AI proof of concept*

Now each service excels at its specific task. Need to switch from OpenAI to Claude? Just update the TextGenerationService. New security requirements? Modify the SecurityService without touching other components.

We've implemented this architecture in our reference document processing system, available on GitHub (github.com/jaydeepc/bentobox). Running this application launches an interactive interface where you can see these principles in action. Each service operates independently but contributes to a complete document-processing solution. But understanding service architecture through code alone can be abstract. That's why we've created an intuitive, visual interface that brings these concepts to life (Figure 3-9):

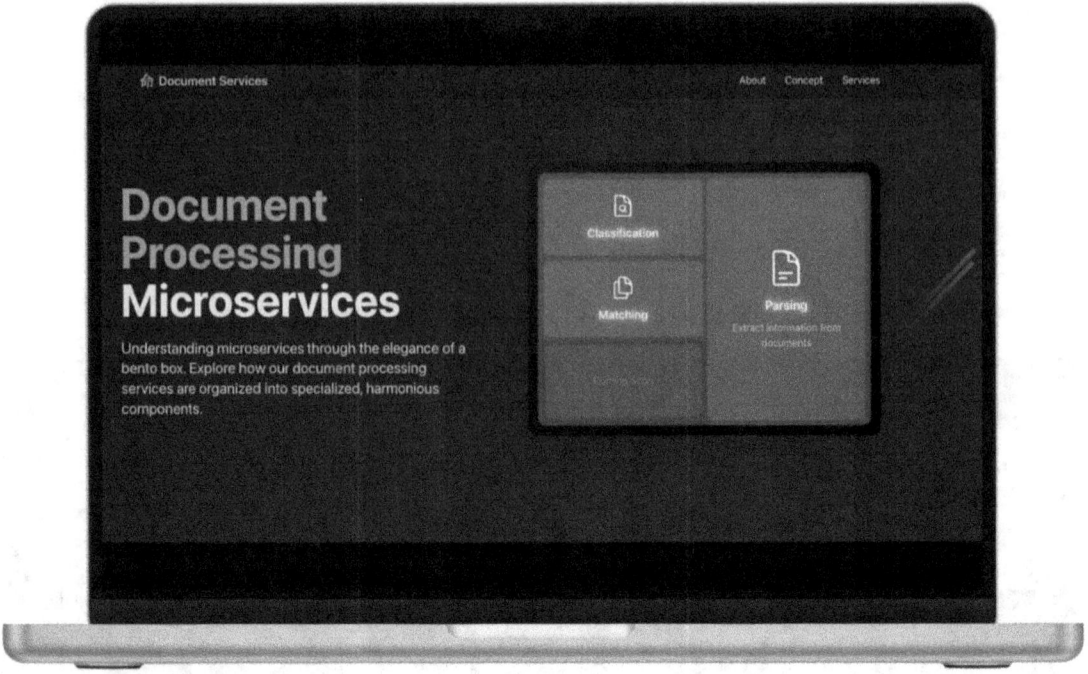

Figure 3-9. Sample visual interface of the application

This interface transforms our architectural principles into a tangible, interactive experience. Each service is represented as a distinct compartment in our digital bento box, making it easy to understand both individual services and their relationships. When exploring the interface, you can see firsthand how document classification, parsing, and matching services work independently while contributing to a complete document-processing solution.

From Blueprint to Reality: Orchestrating AI Implementation

The most elegant architecture means nothing without effective implementation. Through years of guiding enterprises through AI adoption, we've learned that success lies not just in what you build, but in how you orchestrate your teams to build it.

The traditional approach of throwing a single team at a POC often leads to a familiar story: initial excitement, impressive demos, then the crushing realization that moving to production requires starting over. We've seen this pattern repeat across industries – a healthcare provider builds a document analysis POC that wows stakeholders but can't handle patient data securely, a financial institution creates a trading analysis tool that works brilliantly with test data but crumbles under real-world loads.

These experiences led us to develop what we call the "parallel tracks" approach to AI implementation. Instead of one team trying to balance quick demos with production readiness, we separate these concerns into two specialized groups that work in harmony.

The **Foundation Builders** are our master craftspeople. They don't chase quick wins or flashy demos – their mission is to create the robust, secure, production-grade services that others can build upon. Their responsibilities demonstrate the depth of expertise required:

- **Core Service Development** Building production-ready services requires more than just coding skills. The team needs to understand enterprise architecture, security patterns, and the nuances of AI model behavior. They create services that not only work today but can evolve as AI capabilities advance.

- **Security and Compliance** Enterprise-grade security isn't a feature – it's a foundation. The team implements comprehensive security measures, from data encryption to access control, ensuring services meet the strictest enterprise requirements from day one.

- **Documentation and Standards** Clear, thorough documentation becomes part of the product itself. The team creates not just technical specifications but guides that help others understand how to effectively use and combine services.

Working alongside them are the **Innovation Catalysts** – our POC team that turns these foundational services into solutions that solve real business problems. This team needs to move fast, but unlike traditional POC developers, they're not starting from scratch each time. They're more like master chefs working in a well-equipped kitchen – they can focus on creating something special because they know their ingredients and tools are high quality.

This dual-track approach might seem like it would slow things down, but we've found the opposite to be true. A recent project with a global manufacturer illustrates why. Their initial attempt at AI implementation followed the traditional path: one team built POCs as quickly as possible, leading to a graveyard of promising demos that couldn't scale. When they switched to our approach, something interesting happened.

107

While the foundation team spent the first few weeks building core services, the POC team worked with business units to deeply understand their needs. By the time the first services were ready, the POC team knew exactly how to use them to deliver value.

What followed was remarkable. Their first POC under the new system took seven days – about the same as their previous attempts. But this one was different. It was built on production-ready services. It handled enterprise data securely. It could scale across departments. Most importantly, it wasn't thrown away after the demo. Instead, it became the first production deployment of their AI infrastructure.

The Seven-Day POC Cycle

Day 1: Discovery and Architecture. This crucial first day sets the foundation for success. Teams conduct deep stakeholder interviews to understand not just what they want to build but why they need it. They map business requirements to available services, identifying any gaps that need addressing. The day ends with a clear architectural plan that shows how existing services will combine to create value.

Achieving POC Success

Validation & Demonstration

Ensuring readiness through thorough testing and compelling presentations

Implementation & Testing

Bringing designs to life with real data and performance optimization

Design & Integration

Creating workflows and connecting services for scalability and security

Discovery & Architecture

Establishing a solid foundation through stakeholder insights and architectural planning

Figure 3-10. *Seven-day cycle for proof of concept*

Days 2–3: Design and Integration. With a solid understanding of requirements, teams focus on configuring and connecting services. They design workflows that leverage existing capabilities while maintaining security and performance. This phase is about creating the blueprint for a solution that can grow from POC to production.

Days 4–5: Implementation and Testing. The team brings their design to life, integrating services and implementing business logic. They work with real data, test security measures, and optimize performance. Because they're building on production-ready services, they can focus on business value rather than infrastructure concerns.

Days 6–7: Validation and Demonstration. The final phase focuses on proving both capability and reliability. Teams conduct thorough testing with enterprise data, validate security measures, and prepare compelling demonstrations that show not just features but production readiness.

Key Success Elements

Strategic Alignment: Success requires more than technical excellence. Teams must align their work with business objectives, ensuring that every service and feature contributes to organizational goals. This means regular engagement with stakeholders, clear communication of progress, and continuous validation of direction.

Resource Optimization: By separating concerns between teams, organizations can optimize how they use their technical talent. The Foundation team can focus on building robust, reusable services while the POC team concentrates on delivering business value. This specialization leads to better outcomes and faster delivery.

Continuous Evolution: The parallel tracks approach creates a powerful feedback loop. As the POC team builds solutions, they discover new requirements and opportunities that inform the Foundation team's roadmap. This continuous evolution ensures the platform grows to meet emerging needs while maintaining stability.

Shifting Principles to Practice: Our Learnings from the Field

Our work with a global financial institution perfectly illustrates how the parallel tracks approach transforms generative AI implementation. After six months of experimenting with AI for document processing, they had an all-too-familiar problem: impressive demonstrations but no production solutions.

Their document processing initiative particularly highlighted the challenges. The team had built a POC that could analyze various financial documents – loan applications, bank statements, tax returns, identification documents. Using public language models, they could extract key information, classify document types, and even flag potential discrepancies. Stakeholders were impressed by how the system could understand complex financial documents and provide meaningful insights. But beneath the surface lay critical issues that prevented production deployment.

The system relied on public AI endpoints, meaning sensitive financial information like social security numbers and bank account details would be exposed. Document classification logic was intermixed with extraction code, making it impossible to reuse components for different departments. Each new document type required significant code changes, and there was no systematic way to handle the variety of document formats and structures they encountered.

Building the Foundation

This is where the parallel tracks approach transformed their implementation. Instead of rushing to build another POC, we helped them step back and think about the fundamental services they needed. The Foundation team focused on building what we called the "Document Intelligence Bento" – a collection of specialized services that would handle different aspects of document processing.

The Document Classification Service became their first focus. Instead of trying to handle everything at once, this service had one job: understand what kind of document it was looking at. Whether it encountered a W-2 form, a bank statement, or a driver's license, it could identify the document type and route it appropriately. The team implemented sophisticated classification models, trained on their actual document types, with careful attention to handling variations and poor-quality scans.

Next came the Information Extraction Service. This service specialized in pulling relevant information from identified documents. For bank statements, it could extract account numbers, transaction histories, and balance information. For identification documents, it handled personal information while implementing strict privacy controls. Most importantly, it could be enhanced to handle new document types without affecting existing processing.

The Document Matching Service completed the initial set. This service could find relationships between documents – matching supporting documents to loan applications, finding duplicate submissions, or grouping related financial statements. It became an unexpected source of value, helping detect fraud patterns and ensuring application completeness.

Innovation in Action

While the Foundation team built these services, the POC team worked closely with different departments to understand their document processing needs. They discovered patterns they wouldn't have found otherwise. The mortgage department's requirements overlapped significantly with consumer lending. Wealth management's document processing shared common elements with private banking.

When the core services were ready, the POC team built a loan document processing solution in just seven days. Unlike their previous attempts, this solution was different:

They could process sensitive financial documents securely because all data handling was built into the services. Document classification happened automatically, with new document types easily added through configuration rather than coding. Information extraction followed consistent patterns while respecting data privacy requirements. Most importantly, other teams could reuse these services for their own document processing needs.

Leveraging Talent: Building Teams and Frameworks That Scale

The financial institution's success with document processing illuminated another crucial aspect of AI implementation – the human element. While their technical achievements were impressive, it was their approach to team building and development that truly set them apart.

This brings us to a fundamental truth we've discovered through numerous enterprise AI implementations: the most elegant architecture means nothing without the right team to build and maintain it. The complexity of modern AI solutions – whether it's document processing systems or language model applications – demands a deliberate approach to both team structure and skill development.

Building Teams That Grow
At the financial institution, their success wasn't just about having the right skills on paper. Their document processing team included backend developers who understood enterprise architecture, data scientists familiar with language models, and DevOps engineers experienced with containerization. But what made them exceptional was how they learned to work together, evolving their skills in parallel with their growing system.

The Development Journey
Rather than expecting teams to master everything at once, we developed what we call "skill development pathways." This structured approach allows team members to build expertise progressively. For instance, at the financial institution, developers first mastered basic service implementation before tackling advanced features like intelligent document classification or complex data extraction patterns.

Mentorship became a cornerstone of their success. Senior engineers didn't just oversee work; they actively paired with newer team members on challenging tasks. This created a continuous learning environment where knowledge flowed naturally between experienced and emerging talent.

Framework Evolution

As teams grew more sophisticated, we realized the need for precise terminology that could capture both technical architecture and organizational culture. This led to the development of our core framework components:

Term	Definition	Purpose	Skills/technology needed
Bento Box	A modular, microservices-based architecture for AI, with each component functioning independently	Enables flexibility, reuse, and scalability by breaking down AI functions into discrete services.	Microservices design, containerization (Docker), API development, orchestration (Kubernetes)
Dynamic Blueprints	Adaptable POCs designed to evolve into full-scale applications, built using actual data subsets	Creates scalable, reusable prototypes that serve as living applications, not throwaways	Data science, model integration, microservices setup, API standardization
Fusion Prototypes	Combined modules built from multiple microservices, tailored to specific use cases	Demonstrates the fusion of AI services to create tailored, robust solutions	Backend development, modular integration, API communication, DevOps skills
TechNova Bento Platform	The overarching framework for deploying and managing the Bento Box and Fusion Prototypes	Provides a scalable, flexible foundation for AI initiatives across projects	Infrastructure management, DevOps, cloud services (Azure, Kubernetes), data privacy and compliance

These weren't just technical terms – they became part of the organizational vocabulary. When someone mentioned a "Fusion Prototype," everyone, from developers to business stakeholders, understood they were talking about a solution that combines multiple Bento Box services to solve specific business challenges.

The financial institution's document processing system exemplified this framework in action. Their Document Intelligence Bento Box provided core services for classification and extraction. Dynamic Blueprints showed how these services could scale across different document types. Fusion Prototypes demonstrated how services could combine to handle complex workflows like loan processing.

Maintaining Business Alignment

But technical excellence and team growth weren't enough – everything needed to align with business objectives. Regular check-ins with business units became crucial. The team established clear KPIs for each prototype, ensuring every development effort contributed to organizational goals.

This comprehensive approach – nurturing talent while maintaining focus on business value – transformed how the financial institution approached AI implementation. They moved from building isolated solutions to creating a sustainable ecosystem of services and expertise.

The Path Forward

As their platform grew, the team's structured approach paid dividends. New services could be developed faster because developers understood the patterns. Business units could request new features confidently because they understood how services could combine to meet their needs. Most importantly, the organization built not just a technical platform but a culture of sustainable AI innovation.

Show, Don't Just Tell: The Demo That Covers "Wow" to "How"

Most AI demonstrations follow a predictable script: input some text, watch the AI generate a response, applaud the accuracy. But in enterprise environments, such surface-level demonstrations do more harm than good. They raise questions rather than build confidence. Why? Because real-world AI implementation isn't about perfect scenarios – it's about handling imperfect ones.

Imagine showing a contract analysis system to legal stakeholders. The typical demo might showcase how it extracts key clauses or summarizes terms. Impressive? Perhaps. Convincing? Not quite. What keeps legal teams up at night isn't whether AI can read contracts – it's whether it can be trusted with sensitive legal documents, whether it will maintain attorney–client privilege, whether it scales across global jurisdictions.

Making the Invisible Visible

We discovered this truth the hard way when demonstrating an AI-powered HR policy advisor. The system could perfectly answer questions about company policies, generating responses that matched HR guidelines word for word. The technology team was proud. The HR team was terrified.

"What happens if someone asks about confidential reorganization plans?" "How do we know it's not exposing sensitive employee information?" "What if it gives incorrect policy advice?"

These questions taught us to flip the demonstration paradigm. Now, instead of showing just success, we show safety. Here's how.

The Three Acts of Truth

Our demonstrations follow what we call the "three acts of truth" – each building on the previous to create complete confidence:

Act 1: The Baseline – We start simple but specific. With our HR advisor

- Show standard policy questions and accurate responses
- Demonstrate natural language understanding
- Highlight context awareness in responses

But then comes the twist...

Act 2: The Storm – This is where we deliberately introduce chaos – the scenarios that keep stakeholders awake at night:

- Someone tries to social engineer sensitive information about employees.
- A user attempts to manipulate the system into revealing unannounced policies.
- Multiple users flood the system with complex queries.

With each challenge, stakeholders lean forward in their seats. They're not watching a demo anymore; they're seeing their concerns addressed in real time.

Act 3: The Resolution – Here's where trust is truly built. We show

- How the system recognized and blocked attempts to extract sensitive data
- Where and how it maintains logs for security audit

- When and how it escalates to human operators
- How it scales under pressure while maintaining security

The Three Acts approach isn't just a presentation mental modal – it's a way of building trust through transparency. Each act reveals another layer of enterprise readiness, addressing stakeholders' unspoken concerns before they surface. But how do we apply this in different contexts? We started following these guidelines below for each of our POC demonstrations. Let us just simplify that for you by painting a picture.

Imagine stepping onto a grand stage, the spotlight warm on your face, the audience hushed in anticipation. They are not just any audience – they are the gatekeepers of industries, the decision-makers whose concerns are as vast as the arenas they dominate. Your mission? To tell a story so compelling that it not only showcases your Generative AI's prowess but also quells their deepest fears.

Setting the Stage

Before any demo, we identify the three most significant concerns for our audience. For financial services, it might be data privacy, regulatory compliance, and scalability. For healthcare, it could be patient confidentiality, diagnostic accuracy, and audit trails. These concerns become our plot points.

Choreographing the Story

1. Rather than showing multiple examples of similar capabilities, we create a single, powerful narrative that addresses all key concerns. For instance, with our document processing system:

2. The Opening Scene shows basic capabilities – clear, simple, effective. Like a movie's opening sequence, it hooks the audience with possibility.

3. The Plot Twist introduces real-world complexity. Systems fail, data gets messy, users try unexpected things. This is where stakeholders lean forward in their seats.

The Resolution demonstrates not just recovery but mastery. The system doesn't just survive challenges; it reveals new layers of intelligence and security with each test.

Crafting Your Demo Story (It's Like a Real Function, You Know!)

An effective generative AI demonstration should include (Figure 3-11)

- **A Protagonist (Your Core Use Case)**: The main focus of your demonstration that addresses a specific problem or need.

- **Conflict (Real-World Challenges)**: Introducing challenges that the system might face, mirroring issues relevant to the audience.

- **Resolution (Intelligent Handling)**: Showcasing how the system effectively manages and overcomes these challenges.

- **A Deeper Message (Enterprise Readiness)**: Conveying that the system is not only capable but also reliable and prepared for deployment in enterprise settings.

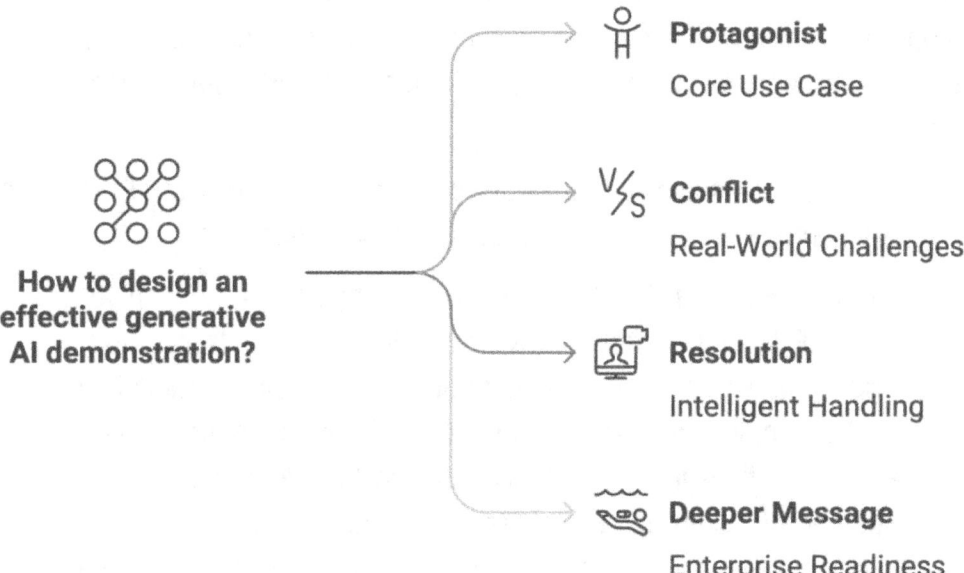

Figure 3-11. Components to design an effective Generative AI demonstration

This storytelling approach transforms demonstrations from technical showcases into compelling narratives about business value and enterprise trust.

As our demonstrations succeed and stakeholders gain in confidence, a new challenge emerges. The very success that wins approval creates its own complexity. A POC that impresses in controlled demonstrations must now scale to handle enterprise workloads. Security measures that work for test data must protect terabytes of sensitive information. Infrastructure that supports dozens of users must scale to thousands.

The journey from proof-of-concept to enterprise deployment isn't just about scaling technology – it's about transforming promising innovations into robust, reliable systems. As one CTO recently told us, "The demo showed us what's possible. Now show us how to make it real."

This transformation – from innovative prototype to enterprise powerhouse – brings its own set of challenges. And that's where our journey continues...

Key Learnings from This Chapter

You've identified a high-potential AI use case, but now comes the real test: proving its value. The traditional proof-of-concept (POC) model – build a quick demo, then throw it away to start the "real" build – is broken. In the fast-evolving world of AI, this approach is wasteful, slow, and disconnected from enterprise realities. This chapter introduces a revolutionary way to think about POCs: build to last, not to discard.

Here are the key frameworks you've discovered to transform your POCs from temporary demos into scalable, production-ready foundations:

1. **The Architectural Shift: The Bento Box Approach** How do you build a POC that's ready to scale from day one? The **Bento Box Approach** is your answer. Instead of creating a single, monolithic application, you will learn to build a suite of independent, reusable, and production-grade microservices (like TextGenerationService or DocumentProcessingService). This modular architecture allows you to easily swap components, adapt to new AI models, and build a library of capabilities that accelerates every future project.

2. **The Organizational Model: The Parallel Tracks** A new architecture requires a new way of organizing teams. This chapter outlines the **Parallel Tracks** model, which separates your development efforts for maximum speed and quality:

- **The Foundation Builders:** A core team dedicated to creating the robust, secure, and well-documented "Bento Box" services.

- **The Innovation Catalysts:** A POC team that uses these pre-built services to rapidly solve business problems, focusing on value delivery instead of reinventing infrastructure.

3. **The Implementation Framework: The Seven-Day POC Cycle**
   With a strong foundation of services in place, how quickly can you deliver value? The **Seven-Day POC Cycle** provides a roadmap for rapid implementation. You've learned how to move from initial architecture and design to full implementation and validation in a single week, leveraging your reusable services to focus on solving the business challenge at hand.

4. **The Trust Builder: The "Three Acts of Truth" Demonstration**
   How do you demonstrate a POC in a way that builds deep stakeholder trust? This chapter introduces a powerful storytelling framework for your demos. Instead of just showing the "wow" factor, you'll learn to demonstrate enterprise readiness by showing the system handling real-world challenges, revealing the security guardrails in action, and proving its scalability.

Your Path Forward

This chapter has equipped you with a complete playbook to reimagine how your organization proves value with AI. You no longer have to choose between moving fast and building correctly. But how do you take a successful, enterprise-ready POC and prepare it for the immense scale and complexity of a full production environment? To master the art of engineering for enterprise scale, dive back into the detailed pages of this chapter and learn how to build your own Bento Box foundation.

CHAPTER 4

Code to Scale – Engineering GenAI for Production

I stepped onto the TechNova floor, and each step of my shoe played a lively beat against the silence of the hallway. Last week's successful POC demonstrations had left everyone energized, but this morning felt different. Reality was setting in because our POCs for Generative AI applications were getting ready for the launch in production.

"Dr. Anya!" Chen's voice carried across the open workspace. "Got a minute? We've hit a snag with the document processing system."

I made my way to his desk, where several developers had already gathered. Chen's monitor displayed a performance graph that looked more like a mountain range than the smooth curves we'd seen during the POC.

"The demo went perfectly with our test set of a thousand documents," Chen explained, running his hand through his already disheveled hair. "But when we tried processing the legal department's actual archive..." He gestured at the spiky graph.

"How many documents are we talking about?" I asked, pulling up a chair.

"Two million," Priya chimed in from the adjacent desk. "And that's just from the past three years. They want to process the entire 20-year archive eventually."

I nodded, remembering our POC's architecture. We'd used ChromaDB for vector storage, which had worked beautifully for our demonstration. But two million documents? That was a different game entirely.

The challenge before us was clear. Our POC had proved the concept worked, but scaling it for enterprise use would require fundamental architectural changes. I glanced around at the team's faces – a mix of concern and determination.

CHAPTER 4 CODE TO SCALE – ENGINEERING GENAI FOR PRODUCTION

"Okay," I said, reaching for the whiteboard marker. "Let's break this down. What specific limitations are we hitting?"

For the next hour, we mapped out the challenges. Vector database scalability, API rate limits, security requirements, data preprocessing bottlenecks – each one a task that we had to complete. The POC's simple architecture, so perfect for demonstration, now seemed inadequate against the sheer scale of enterprise deployment (Figures 4-1 and 4-2).

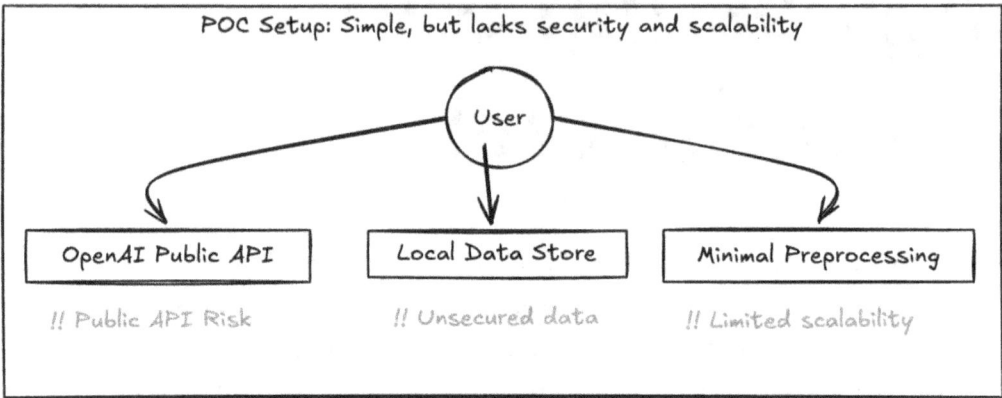

Figure 4-1. *POC Setup*

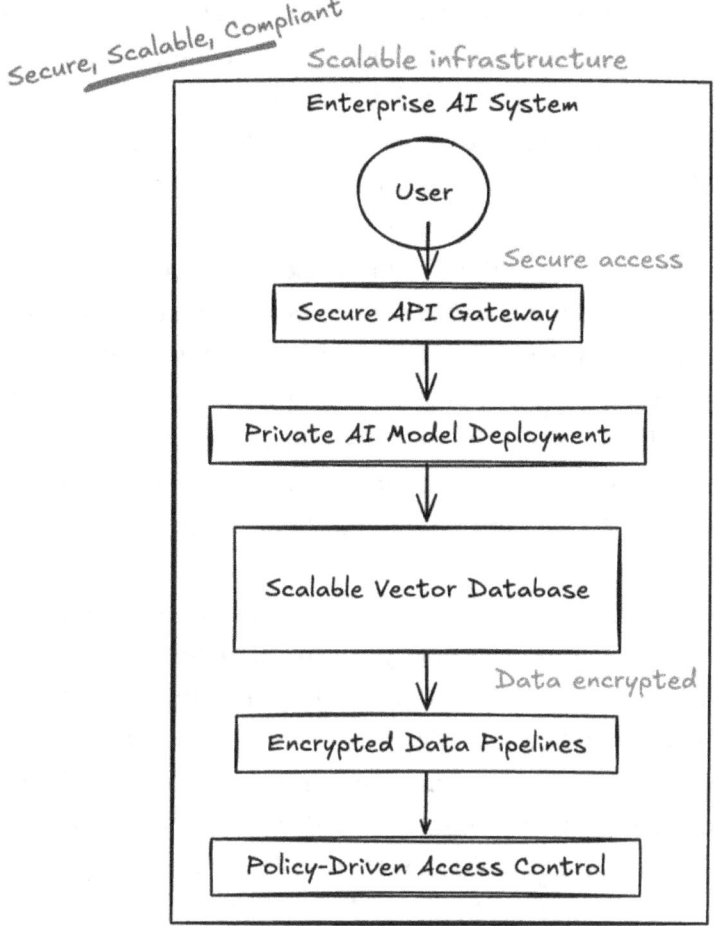

Figure 4-2. *Scalable Infrastructure*

"Dr. Anya," Sam called from his standing desk nearby. "There's another aspect we need to consider." He walked over, tablet in hand. "I've been running resource projections for production deployment."

The numbers on his tablet made several team members' eyes widen. CPU requirements, memory allocation, storage needs – scaled to enterprise level, our elegant POC would require infrastructure that far exceeded initial estimates.

"We're not just building for current load," Sam explained. "We need to account for growth. Legal's archive is just the beginning. HR wants to process their documents too, and Marketing's already asking about similar capabilities for their content management."

I couldn't help but smile at the irony. Our POC's success had created its own challenges. We'd proven the value of AI document processing so effectively that now everyone wanted it. Scaling wasn't just about handling more documents – it was about building a system that could grow with the organization's needs.

"Alright," I said, standing to get a better view of our challenge map on the whiteboard. "We need to rethink our approach to architecture. This isn't about patching the POC to handle more load. We need to build for enterprise scale from the ground up."

Priya added, "The Bento Box approach we used for the POC gives us a good foundation. The services are modular. We just need to make them scalable."

"True," Chen agreed. "But we'll need to rethink some of our core components. ChromaDB worked for the demo, but for this scale…"

A notification popped up on my phone – Zara requesting an urgent meeting about infrastructure costs. Perfect timing. We needed to align our technical needs with business realities.

"Before we dive into solutions," I said, "let's gather the architecture team. This isn't just about scaling our current components. We need to design a system that can handle enterprise workloads while maintaining security, performance, and flexibility."

As I headed to Zara's office, my mind was already mapping out possibilities. The work ahead were significant, but not insurmountable. We had the right team, the right approach, and most importantly, the right mindset. Now we just needed to figure out how to build an AI infrastructure that could scale from impressive demos to enterprise powerhouse.

Architecting for the Big Leagues

The walk to Zara's office gave me time to organize my thoughts. Through the glass-walled corridors of TechNova, I could see teams huddled around whiteboards, tackling their own challenges. The morning's technical discussion with Chen's team still weighed heavily on my mind.

Zara's office door was open, and I could see her reviewing what looked like infrastructure cost projections. She looked up as I entered, gesturing to the chair across from her desk.

"I just saw the resource estimates," she said, turning her monitor so I could see the spreadsheet. "Moving this to production is going to require significant investment."

I nodded, pulling out my tablet to share the morning's findings. "The team's already identified several architectural challenges. We're not just scaling up – we need to rebuild some components from the ground up."

"Tell me more," Zara said, leaning forward.

I walked her through the morning's discoveries – the database limitations, the security requirements, the processing bottlenecks. As I spoke, she took careful notes, occasionally asking pointed questions about resource requirements and timeline implications.

"So what you're saying is," she summarized, "we need to completely rearchitect the system for enterprise scale."

"No, not entirely." I said. "But we have to make significant changes. Thankfully our Bento approach has made things a bit easier for configuration management and change management. We need to get the architecture team together to map this out properly."

Zara nodded, checking her calendar. "Use the main architecture room. I'll join you after my executive meeting. We need to get this right."

By two o'clock, the architecture room had transformed into what Sam jokingly called our "war room." The afternoon sun streamed through the windows as team members filtered in. Sam and Chen had already started filling one whiteboard with our current architecture diagrams.

"Okay," I said, once everyone had settled. "Let's tackle this systematically. Sam, want to walk us through the current setup?"

Sam moved to the whiteboard, marker in hand. "Right now, we're using ChromaDB for vector storage. It's great for POCs, but with millions of documents..." He sketched out our current database architecture. "We're going to hit walls with both scale and security."

"What about MongoDB Atlas?" Priya suggested, moving to join Sam at the board. "They've added vector search capabilities, and it's already approved by our security team."

Chen pulled up some documentation on his laptop. "That could work. But we'd need to completely rewrite our data layer."

The discussion flowed from one component to another. Each decision spawned new questions, new challenges. How would we handle rate limiting across multiple AI models? What about caching to reduce unnecessary API calls? The whiteboards filled with diagrams, questions, and potential solutions.

"We should consider Azure OpenAI Services for production," Chen suggested, pulling up their documentation. "Enterprise-grade security, better rate limits, and we can keep sensitive data within our security boundary."

Sam added another diagram, showing how we could containerize services for independent scaling. The architecture grew more complex as he added load balancers and redundancy paths. Yet with each addition, the system felt more robust, more enterprise-ready.

Zara joined us later in the afternoon, just as we were debating caching strategies. She studied our whiteboards with intense focus, asking questions that helped sharpen our thinking.

Taming the Data Beast

Evening was approaching, but we were still deep in discussion. The whiteboards were filled with diagrams and annotations, representing hours of careful consideration.

"The modular approach gives us flexibility," Sam said, reviewing our architecture diagrams. "But we need to think about how this scales with real enterprise data volumes."

I studied our design. The text generation service would handle multiple requests simultaneously, the vector database distributed across clusters for faster retrieval. Each component looked solid on paper, but the real challenge lay ahead.

"Speaking of data," Chen said, pointing to the security layer in our diagram. "We need to think about data governance at scale. It's not just about processing documents anymore – it's about managing an enterprise's worth of sensitive information."

Zara, who had been quietly observing, shifted her weight to sit more comfortably. "That's our next focus then. We have the architecture framework, but data governance and security need to be addressed before we can move forward."

I glanced at my phone – 4:30 PM. Still time to tackle the data challenges. "Let's take 15 minutes to refresh, then dive into data governance and security considerations."

As the team stepped out for coffee, I stayed behind, studying our whiteboard diagrams. The architectural foundations were taking shape, but the harder questions about handling enterprise data at scale were still to come.

The team returned, coffee cups in hand, ready to tackle the next challenge. I noticed Sam had erased part of the whiteboard, making room for our data governance discussion.

"Before we dive in," Zara said, pulling up a document on the main screen, "Legal sent over their data requirements. We're looking at more than just volume here."

The document outlined various data categories: confidential client information, internal policies, historical records, each with its own compliance requirements. The scope was staggering – 20 years of legal documents, each potentially containing sensitive information.

"Let's break this down," I suggested, moving to the whiteboard. "What exactly are we dealing with?"

Priya pulled up some statistics on her laptop. "Just from the initial analysis, we're seeing at least seven different document formats. Some of these older files don't even have consistent metadata."

"And that's just from Legal," Chen added. "HR's documents have personal information that falls under GDPR and other privacy regulations. Marketing's content has brand guidelines and confidential campaign data."

I started listing the challenges on the whiteboard, grouping them into categories. Data standardization, privacy controls, compliance requirements – each category spawned its own set of complexities.

"Hold on," Sam interrupted our discussion an hour later. "Look at this." He projected his screen, showing a sample document flow. "Even with optimal processing, we're hitting bottlenecks at data validation."

The diagram showed how documents would flow through our system. Each step – classification, extraction, validation – added complexity. At enterprise scale, even minor inefficiencies could cascade into major delays.

"What if we approach this differently?" Priya suggested. "Instead of trying to process everything at once, we create data processing pipelines based on document types and sensitivity levels."

She sketched out a new flow on the whiteboard. "High-priority, sensitive documents take one path with additional security checks. Routine documents take another, optimized for speed" (Figure 4-3).

"That could work," Chen nodded, adding to the diagram. "We could implement different validation rules for each pipeline. Marketing's brand guidelines don't need the same level of scrutiny as legal contracts."

CHAPTER 4   CODE TO SCALE – ENGINEERING GENAI FOR PRODUCTION

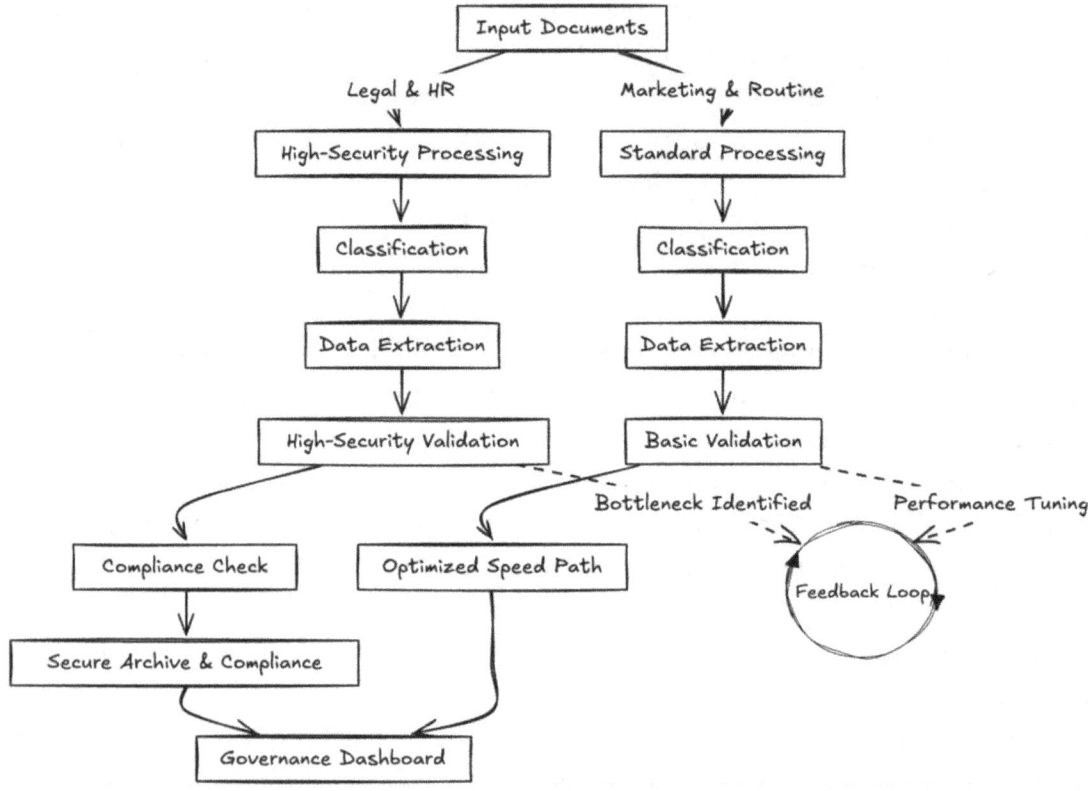

Figure 4-3. *Security workflows based on documents' sensitivity*

By six o'clock, our whiteboards displayed a complex web of data flows and validation checkpoints. The challenge wasn't just handling millions of documents – it was handling them correctly, securely, and efficiently.

"We need automated quality controls," Zara pointed out, studying our diagrams. "Manual validation won't scale."

"Agreed," I said. "We should implement automated checks at each stage. Format validation, sensitive data detection, consistency checks..."

Sam was already sketching out a monitoring system. "We can use sampling to verify processing quality. If accuracy drops below certain thresholds, we flag for human review."

"And what about data lineage?" Chen asked. "We need to track how each document is processed, what transformations are applied, who accesses it."

The implications were clear – we needed more than just processing power. We needed a comprehensive system for managing, monitoring, and maintaining data quality at scale.

Zara checked her watch. "One more thing we haven't discussed – security. How do we ensure all this data remains protected throughout the process?"

I looked at the time – 5:30 PM. The security discussion couldn't wait for tomorrow. Not with this much sensitive data in play.

"Let's take 30 minutes," I suggested. "We need to outline our security approach before we wrap up."

The team nodded in agreement. The sun was setting outside our windows, but the most critical part of our discussion was still ahead. Securing an enterprise AI system wasn't just about protecting data – it was about building trust in the entire platform.

Guardrails and Security

"Security isn't just an add-on," Zara began, pulling up the compliance requirements document. "It needs to be woven into every layer of our system."

I moved to the last clean section of the whiteboard. The evening light is fading, and the architecture room's bright fluorescents cast sharp shadows across our diagrams. Despite the late hour, everyone remained focused – we all understood the stakes.

"Let's start with data in motion," Sam suggested, drawing a flow diagram. "Every document needs end-to-end encryption, from ingestion to processing to storage."

Chen pulled up our architecture diagram from earlier. "We should implement multiple security layers. Network security, application-level controls, and data-level encryption."

"Don't forget about the AI models themselves," Priya added. "Though, as a part of our new approach to POC, we made sure we have used enterprise Azure openAI, but we have to put more guardrails at the top of it, to prevent unauthorized data exposure through prompts or responses."

I watched as Sam expanded his diagram, adding security checkpoints at each stage. "Think of it like a series of airlocks," he explained. "Each document passes through multiple security validations before moving to the next stage."

"Here's something we haven't considered," Chen said, pulling up a test prompt he'd been working on. "Look what happens when I try to trick the system into revealing sensitive information."

He demonstrated how a carefully crafted prompt could potentially extract information from previous interactions. The room grew quiet as we considered the implications.

"We need content filters," I said, breaking the silence. "Not just for input, but for output as well. Every AI response needs to be screened for sensitive information."

Priya was already typing. "We could implement a multistage filtering system. First, check for explicit sensitive data like account numbers or personal information. Then, use AI to detect potential implicit data leakage."

"And everything needs to be logged," Zara added. "I mean things that we can log without violating data regulations and compliance, like every prompt, every response, every document transformation – we need a complete audit trail."

Sam started sketching out a logging architecture. "We'll need robust monitoring too. Anomaly detection, usage patterns, performance metrics…"

"And automated alerts," Chen added. "If the system detects potential security violations or unusual behavior patterns, it should notify the security team immediately."

The complexity of our security architecture grew as we mapped out each component (Figure 4-4). It wasn't just about keeping data safe – it was about building a system that could actively identify and respond to potential threats.

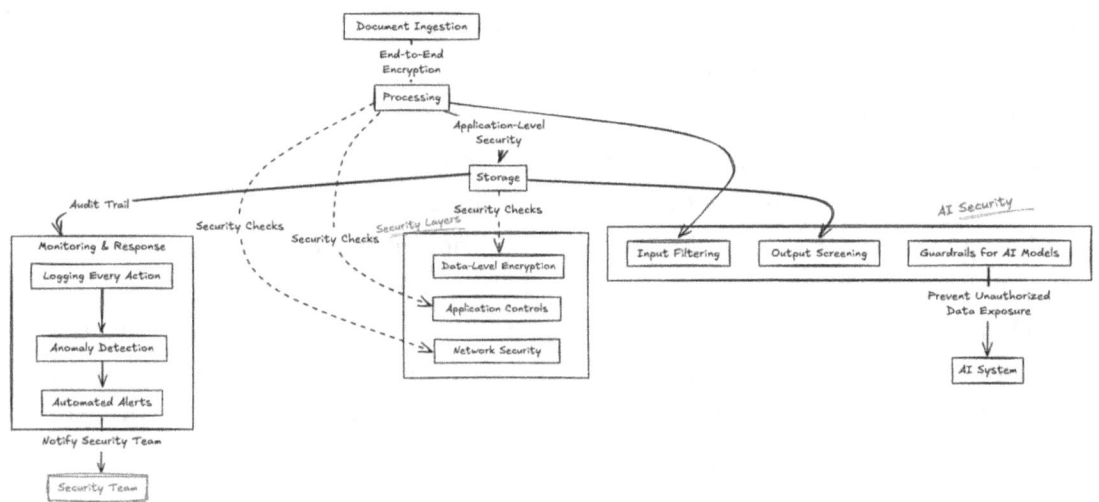

Figure 4-4. *Security architecture*

By eight o'clock, our whiteboards told the story of a comprehensive security framework. Authentication systems, encryption layers, content filters, audit logs – each component designed to work together, creating multiple layers of protection.

"One last thing," I said, looking at our diagrams. "We need regular security assessments. The threat landscape keeps evolving, especially with AI systems."

"Agreed," Zara nodded. "Monthly security reviews, penetration testing, and continuous monitoring."

The team looked exhausted but satisfied. We'd mapped out not just an architecture, but a complete framework for secure, scalable AI operations.

"I think that's enough for today," Zara said, standing up. "Great work, everyone. Tomorrow we can start turning these plans into reality."

As we gathered our things, I took photos of our whiteboards. The day had started with scaling challenges and ended with a comprehensive security architecture. Tomorrow would bring new challenges, but we had our roadmap.

Walking to my car in the quiet parking lot, I couldn't help but reflect on how far we'd come. The path from POC to production was complex, but with careful planning and the right team, it was manageable. My phone buzzed – a message from Ray: "Dinner in the microwave. Sorry can't give you company tonight, have an important meeting."

I smiled and wrote a quick reply to him before getting into my car. The drive home was quiet, giving me time to process the day's discussions. We'd started with scaling challenges that seemed straightforward at first glance – more servers, more storage, more processing power. But each solution had unveiled new complexities.

The whiteboard diagrams flashed through my mind: data pipelines, security checkpoints, monitoring systems. We weren't just scaling technology; we were building safeguards for information that could impact thousands of people. Legal documents affecting client relationships, HR records containing personal data, sensitive corporate information – each required careful handling and protection.

Traffic was light at this hour. As I waited at a red light, I remembered Sam's expression when we discovered the prompt injection vulnerability. These were the kinds of issues that kept tech leads awake at night – the edge cases that could slip through if you weren't careful.

Pulling into my driveway, I noticed the kitchen light was still on. Through the window, I could see Ray reading, probably waiting to hear about the day. The technical challenges would be there tomorrow, but for now, it was time to step back and recharge.

CHAPTER 4 CODE TO SCALE – ENGINEERING GENAI FOR PRODUCTION

Anya's Notes
Concepts in Practice

From POC to Production – Scaling GenAI for Enterprise

In our journey through generative AI implementation, we've established a fundamental shift in how we approach development. The traditional notion of proof-of-concepts has evolved into something more profound: real applications built on actual data, deployed in production environments from day one. This isn't just a theoretical change – it's a necessary evolution driven by the unique nature of AI systems, particularly generative AI.

When we talk about POCs now, we're not discussing controlled experiments with synthetic data. Instead, we're referring to live applications that interact with real users, process actual enterprise data, and operate within production environments.

This approach provides the only true way to understand how AI systems will perform and what they need to succeed. This becomes especially critical with applications like chatbots, where the full range of user interactions can only be discovered through real-world usage.

The Reality of Scale: When Success Creates New Challenges

Imagine building a bridge that must adapt its width as more people discover and use it. This is the unique challenge organizations face when scaling generative AI solutions from initial implementation to enterprise-wide deployment. The foundation we laid – building on real data from day one – gives us a solid starting point. But like our metaphorical bridge, success brings its own set of challenges.

Consider what happened at a global financial institution when their document processing system, built using our real-data approach, proved so effective that every department wanted to use it. Their initial implementation, processing thousands of documents daily for the legal team, had to scale to handle millions of documents across multiple departments. Each new department brought its own document types, workflow requirements, and usage patterns. This experience taught them a crucial lesson: in AI systems, scale isn't just about handling more volume – it's about managing increased complexity while maintaining performance and reliability.

From Foundation to Scale

Think of a chef scaling up a recipe from serving a family to serving a restaurant. It's not just about multiplying ingredients – the entire cooking process must evolve. Similarly, scaling AI solutions requires rethinking how our systems handle increased load, diverse use cases, and varying user needs. What works perfectly for one department might need significant adaptation for enterprise-wide use.

One of the most important insights we've gained from numerous implementations is that successful scaling requires progressive evolution rather than sudden expansion. Each new use case, each new department, brings its own patterns and requirements that help your system grow not just in size, but in capability.

The Dynamics of Enterprise Scale

In enterprise environments, scale manifests in ways that challenge even the most well-designed initial implementations. A chatbot that brilliantly serves one department must now understand the specialized vocabulary of multiple divisions. A document processing system that efficiently handles legal contracts must expand to process everything from marketing materials to technical documentation.

A manufacturing company's experience illustrates this perfectly. Their AI-powered quality control system performed flawlessly in their main facility but needed significant adaptation when deployed across global plants. Each location had its own quality standards, local terminology, and workflow preferences. This taught them that local variations in terminology, processes, and expectations can significantly impact AI system performance – a lesson that fundamentally changed how they approached scaling.

The Continuous Adaptation Imperative

Perhaps the most critical understanding we've gained is that going live with an AI system marks the beginning, not the end, of development. When a system serves thousands of users across multiple departments, it encounters usage patterns and edge cases that no initial implementation could anticipate. A healthcare provider discovered this when their patient documentation system, initially designed for primary care, needed to evolve rapidly when specialists began using it.

This continuous evolution is particularly crucial for chatbots and other natural language interfaces. No matter how thoroughly you plan, users will always find new ways to express their needs, use unexpected terminology, or approach problems from unforeseen angles. Your system must be designed to learn from these interactions and adapt accordingly.

Progressive Scaling: Building on Solid Foundations

The path to successful enterprise scale lies in progressive expansion. A global retailer demonstrated this effectively with their inventory management AI. Instead of attempting to scale across their entire network at once, they expanded the system's reach and capabilities in controlled stages. Each new location added new inventory patterns, regional variations, and local practices, allowing the system to evolve gradually through this expansion.

This progressive approach yields three crucial benefits: early identification of scaling challenges, gradual building of system understanding across different use cases, and opportunities to optimize performance based on real usage patterns. Most importantly, it ensures that your system emerges from each scaling phase not just larger, but smarter and more capable.

The journey to enterprise scale in generative AI isn't just about handling more volume – it's about building systems that grow in understanding and capability through real-world use. By acknowledging that deployment is just the beginning of the development journey, and by approaching scale as a process of continuous evolution, organizations can build AI systems that truly serve enterprise needs while becoming more effective over time.

Architecting for the Big Leagues

Success in AI implementation often creates its own architectural challenges. As organizations discover the value of their AI solutions, what begins as a focused implementation for a single team or department inevitably grows into something much larger. This growth isn't just about handling more users or processing more data – it fundamentally changes how we need to think about system architecture.

The architectural decisions that serve us well in controlled environments take on new dimensions when faced with enterprise realities. A financial services firm discovered this when their document processing system, initially designed for a single trading desk, caught the attention of other departments. Within months, what started as a system processing hundreds of documents daily needed to handle millions, comply with multiple regulatory frameworks, and maintain consistent performance across global offices.

This experience isn't unique. Time and again, we've seen how the journey to enterprise scale forces organizations to rethink their architectural foundations. The questions shift from "How do we make this work?" to "How do we make this work reliably, securely, and efficiently at scale?" The answers to these questions shape the fundamental principles of enterprise AI architecture.

Before we delve into specific architectural patterns and solutions, we need to understand the core shifts that enterprise scale demands. These shifts go beyond technical specifications – they represent fundamental changes in how we approach system design, data management, and operational reliability.

CHAPTER 4   CODE TO SCALE – ENGINEERING GENAI FOR PRODUCTION

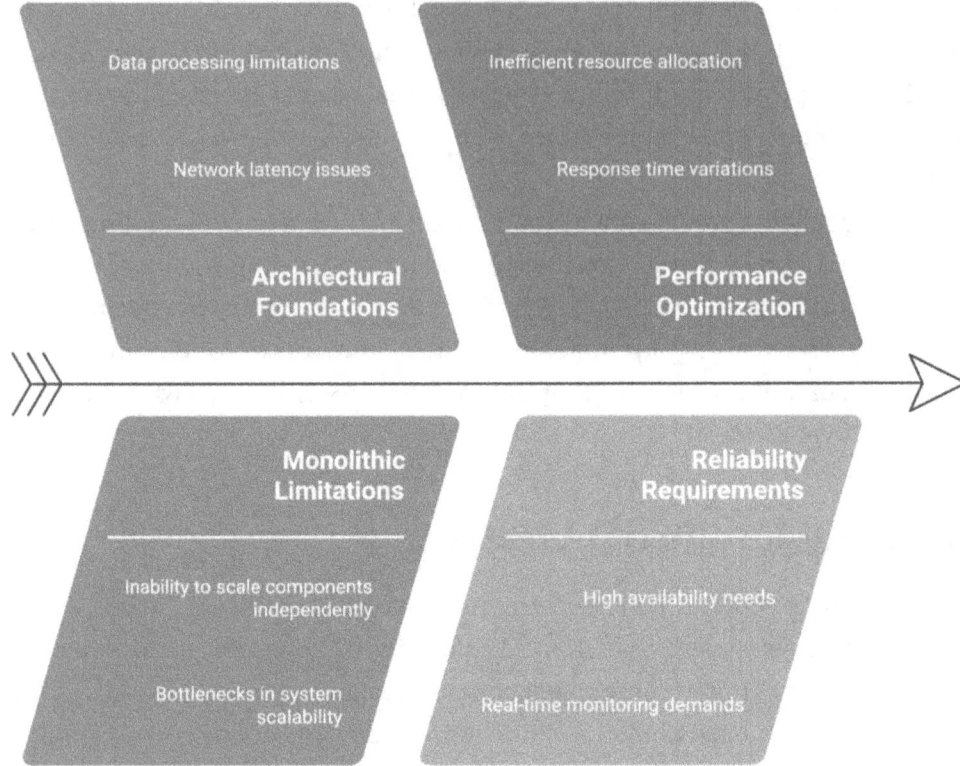

Figure 4-5. *Scaling challenges in Enterprise AI architecture*

The Foundation Shift

When architects design skyscrapers, they don't simply scale up the blueprints of a two-story building. They must consider entirely new factors: wind forces at higher altitudes, the weight distribution of additional floors, the movement of thousands of people through the building. Similarly, enterprise-grade AI architectures require us to consider elements that might not have been critical in smaller implementations.

Consider a global manufacturer whose initial AI quality control system relied on public API endpoints. The architecture worked perfectly for their pilot facility, but as they prepared for global deployment, they discovered that sensitive production data couldn't be processed through public endpoints. Network latency between global facilities and centralized AI services became a critical concern. What had impressed everyone during initial deployment now needed fundamental architectural changes.

Breaking Free from Monoliths

The transition to enterprise scale often reveals the limitations of monolithic architectures. A healthcare provider learned this lesson when their patient documentation system, initially built as a single application, needed to handle requests from multiple departments simultaneously. The monolithic design that had served them well during initial deployment became a bottleneck, unable to scale different components independently as demand grew.

Modern enterprise AI architectures demand a more nuanced approach. Instead of scaling entire systems as single units, we need architectures that allow different components to scale independently based on demand. Think about how a document processing service might need more resources during business hours, while model inference services might see peak demand during overnight batch processing.

Building Enterprise-Grade Foundations

Just as a growing city needs more robust infrastructure, the shift to enterprise scale requires us to reconsider our foundational technologies. It's not just about choosing databases that can handle more data – it's about selecting technologies that provide the reliability, security, and manageability that enterprise operations demand.

A global retailer discovered this when their product recommendation system, initially built for quick deployment, needed to serve millions of customers across multiple regions. They needed infrastructure that could guarantee

- Consistent performance under varying loads
- Geographic data distribution for lower latency
- Automated backup and recovery processes
- Fine-grained access control and audit logging

The Art of Performance Optimization

When a system serves thousands of users across multiple time zones, every millisecond counts. A global consulting firm discovered this when their AI-powered document analysis system, which had performed admirably during initial deployment, began showing response time variations that affected user satisfaction.

The solution wasn't just about adding more computing power. It required careful orchestration of

- Intelligent caching strategies to reduce redundant processing
- Load balancing to distribute requests effectively
- Resource allocation that could adapt to usage patterns
- Query optimization for faster data retrieval

Building for Reliability

Perhaps the most significant shift in enterprise architecture is the emphasis on reliability. When AI systems become integral to business operations, downtime isn't just an inconvenience – it's a business risk. A financial services provider learned this when their AI-powered trading analysis system became critical to their operations. They needed an architecture that could guarantee

- High availability across multiple regions
- Seamless failover in case of component failures
- Zero-downtime updates and maintenance
- Real-time monitoring and alerting

A Tale of Two Architectures

With these foundational concepts in mind, let's examine how these principles manifest in real-world implementations. We'll compare two approaches to building an HR policy chatbot – one designed for departmental use and another built for enterprise scale. This comparison will illuminate how the architectural principles we've discussed translate into practical design decisions.

Initial Architecture: The Straightforward Approach

In its simplest form, an HR policy chatbot might start with what seems like a perfectly reasonable architecture. Let's examine this approach in detail (Figure 4-6).

Frontend Interface:

- Web-based chat interface
- Basic user authentication
- Simple session management

API Layer:

- REST endpoints for chat interactions
- Basic request handling
- Direct model interaction

Knowledge Processing:

- Document storage for HR policies
- Vector embeddings for semantic search
- Simple retrieval mechanism

Model Integration:

- Direct calls to AI model API
- Basic prompt construction
- Single model dependency

When a user asks a question about HR policies, the flow typically works like this:

1. The question enters through the chat interface
2. The API layer processes the request
3. The system searches the vector store for relevant policy information
4. This context is combined with the user's question in a prompt
5. The AI model generates a response
6. The answer is returned to the user

CHAPTER 4   CODE TO SCALE – ENGINEERING GENAI FOR PRODUCTION

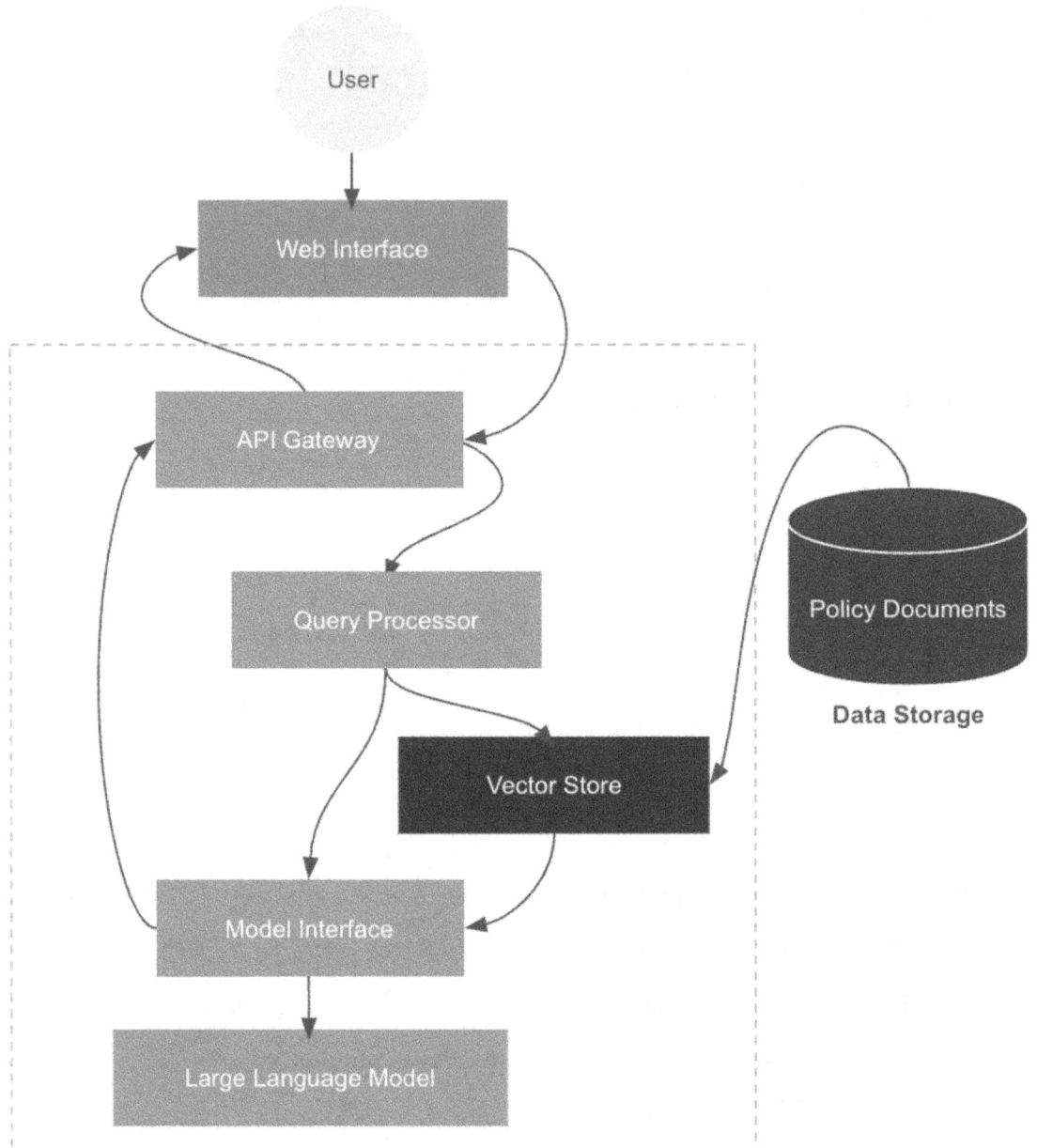

Figure 4-6. *Initial architecture*

CHAPTER 4 CODE TO SCALE – ENGINEERING GENAI FOR PRODUCTION

Enterprise Architecture: Designed for Scale and Reliability

The enterprise architecture (Figure 4-7) for our HR chatbot represents a fundamental shift in thinking. Instead of a simple flow of requests and responses, we create a sophisticated system of specialized services working in concert. Let's examine each layer of this architecture and understand why it becomes crucial at enterprise scale.

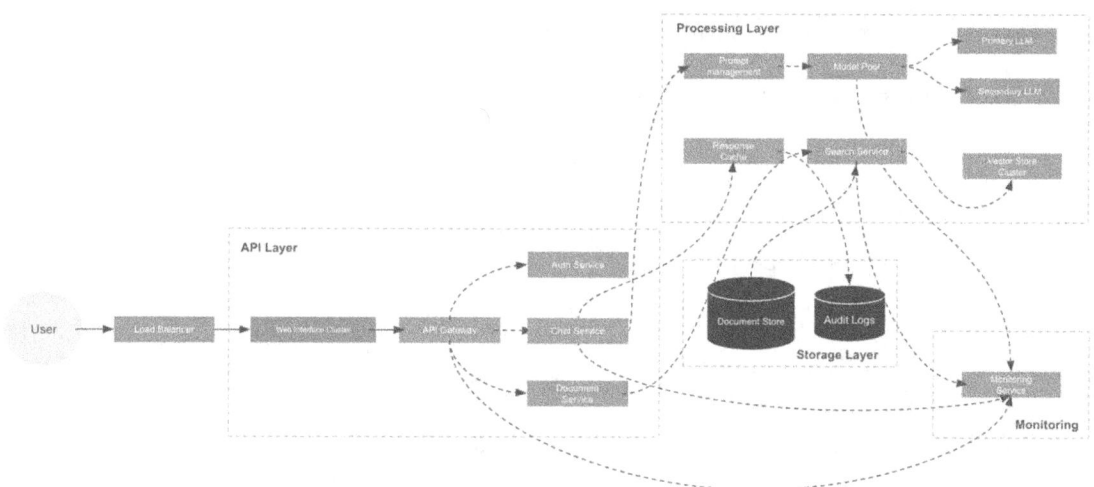

Figure 4-7. Enterprise architecture

The Entry Point: Load Management Layer

In our enterprise architecture, users don't connect directly to the application. Instead, they first encounter a load balancer. Think of this as a sophisticated traffic controller at a busy airport. When thousands of employees across different time zones are accessing the system simultaneously, the load balancer ensures that

- Requests are distributed evenly across multiple web servers
- Users are automatically connected to the closest available server
- If one server becomes overwhelmed or fails, traffic seamlessly redirects to others
- The system can scale up or down based on demand

CHAPTER 4   CODE TO SCALE – ENGINEERING GENAI FOR PRODUCTION

The API Layer: Gateway to Services

Behind the load balancer sits our API gateway – the system's command center. Unlike our initial architecture's simple API endpoint, this gateway performs several crucial functions.

Authentication Service:

- Integrates with enterprise identity systems (like Active Directory)
- Manages user sessions across multiple servers
- Handles role-based access control
- Ensures security tokens are properly validated

Chat Service:

- Manages chat sessions and conversation context
- Handles message queuing during high load
- Maintains conversation history for context
- Coordinates between different backend services

Document Service:

- Manages access to policy documents
- Handles document versioning and updates
- Coordinates search and retrieval operations
- Ensures document access follows security policies

The Processing Layer: Intelligence at Scale

This layer represents the system's brain, where the actual processing happens. It's designed for both performance and reliability:

Prompt Management Service:

- Maintains a library of optimized prompts
- Adjusts prompts based on context and user role
- Handles multiple language variations
- Ensures consistent AI responses across the system

Search Service:

- Manages distributed vector search across document clusters
- Implements sophisticated relevance ranking
- Handles multilanguage document search
- Optimizes search performance through caching

Model Pool:

- Manages connections to multiple AI models
- Handles failover between models if one becomes unavailable
- Optimizes model selection based on query type
- Balances load across different model endpoints

Response Cache:

- Stores frequently requested information
- Reduces load on AI models for common queries
- Updates automatically when policies change
- Implements intelligent cache invalidation

The Storage Layer: Data Management at Scale

Enterprise data management requires sophisticated storage solutions.

Document Store:

- Distributed database for policy documents
- Handles automatic replication across regions
- Maintains document versions and change history
- Implements fine-grained access control

Audit Logs:

- Records all system interactions
- Maintains compliance audit trails

CHAPTER 4 CODE TO SCALE – ENGINEERING GENAI FOR PRODUCTION

- Tracks document access and changes
- Supports regulatory reporting requirements

Vector Store Cluster:

- Distributed storage for document embeddings
- Enables fast semantic search across millions of documents
- Supports automatic updates when documents change
- Maintains search performance at scale

The Monitoring Layer: Ensuring Reliable Operation

Enterprise systems require comprehensive monitoring.
Monitoring Service:

- Tracks system performance in real time
- Monitors service health and availability
- Alerts operators to potential issues
- Provides performance analytics and trends

Performance Analytics:

- Measures response times across regions
- Tracks model performance and accuracy
- Identifies bottlenecks and optimization opportunities
- Supports capacity planning

Here is an example of what a production grade monitoring system (Figure 4-8) should provide

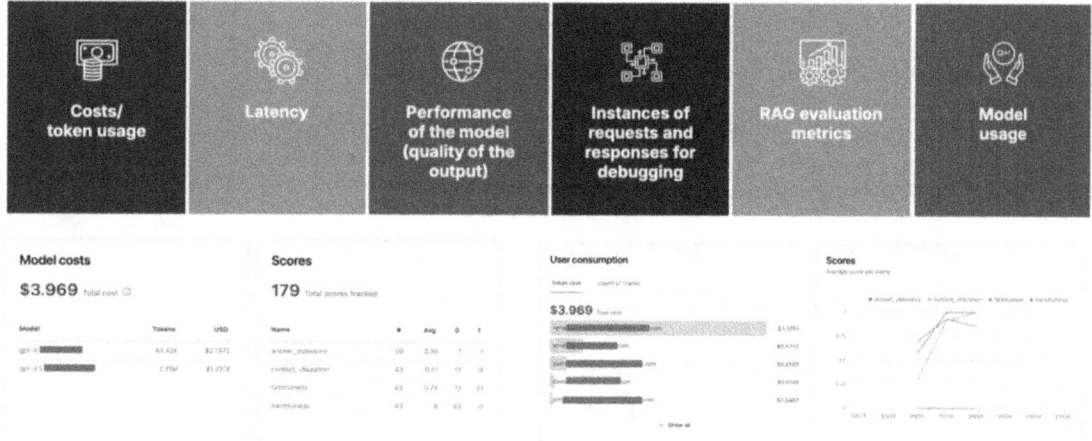

Figure 4-8. Monitoring system

How It All Works Together

When an employee in Singapore asks about maternity leave policies at 3 AM New York time, here's how our enterprise architecture handles it:

1. The load balancer routes their request to the nearest available web server.

2. The API gateway authenticates their request and identifies their role and region.

3. The chat service creates a session and maintains context.

4. The prompt management service constructs a region-appropriate prompt.

5. The search service finds relevant policy documents in the vector store.

6. The model pool selects an appropriate AI model and generates a response.

7. The response cache stores the result for future similar queries.

8. All interactions are logged for compliance and monitoring.

CHAPTER 4   CODE TO SCALE – ENGINEERING GENAI FOR PRODUCTION

This architecture enables the system to

- Handle thousands of concurrent users across time zones
- Maintain consistent performance under varying loads
- Ensure security and compliance at every step
- Adapt to changing requirements and usage patterns
- Provide reliable service even when components fail

The complexity of this architecture might seem overwhelming compared to our initial approach. However, each component addresses specific challenges that emerge at enterprise scale. Whether it's handling peak loads during benefits enrollment periods, ensuring consistent responses across global offices, or maintaining audit trails for compliance, the enterprise architecture provides the foundation needed for reliable, scalable operation.

As we've seen, architecting for enterprise scale requires careful consideration of numerous factors, from performance optimization to reliability guarantees. However, technical architecture is only part of the story. The true challenge in enterprise AI implementation lies in building systems that can operate within the complex web of governance requirements, regional compliance standards, and security considerations that enterprise operations demand.

In our next section, we'll explore how organizations can build AI systems that don't just scale technically, but also meet the rigorous governance standards of enterprise operations. We'll discover why these considerations need to shape our decisions from the very beginning, and how successful organizations build compliance and security into their systems' foundations rather than treating them as afterthoughts.

Building with Governance in Mind: From Day One to Enterprise Scale

Imagine you've built the perfect AI system. It processes documents with lightning speed, understands user queries with uncanny accuracy, and scales beautifully across your infrastructure. Then, just as you're preparing for global deployment, reality strikes. Your legal team informs you that data privacy laws in Asia require all processing to happen locally. European regulators demand specific audit trails. Healthcare divisions need HIPAA compliance. Suddenly, your perfect system doesn't seem so perfect anymore.

This isn't a hypothetical scenario. A global financial services firm lived this exact nightmare. Their trading analysis system, a marvel of AI engineering, hit a wall when they tried to deploy in Asian markets. Data sovereignty laws demanded all processing happen within specific regions – a requirement their architecture simply hadn't considered. Their six-month deployment stretched into an 18-month redesign, not because of technical limitations, but because of governance oversights.

Welcome to the hidden dimension of enterprise AI implementation – the realm where technical excellence meets regulatory reality. In our journey through scaling AI systems, we've explored architectures that can handle millions of requests and process terabytes of data. But perhaps the most crucial scaling challenge isn't technical at all. It's about building systems that can operate within the complex web of regulations, compliance requirements, and governance standards that define enterprise operations.

The Three Pillars of Enterprise AI Governance

Enterprise AI governance rests on three interlocking pillars, each of which requires extensive attention and rigorous planning to ensure that systems are safe, legally compliant, and operationally robust. Let's look at these pillars a bit closely (Figure 4-9).

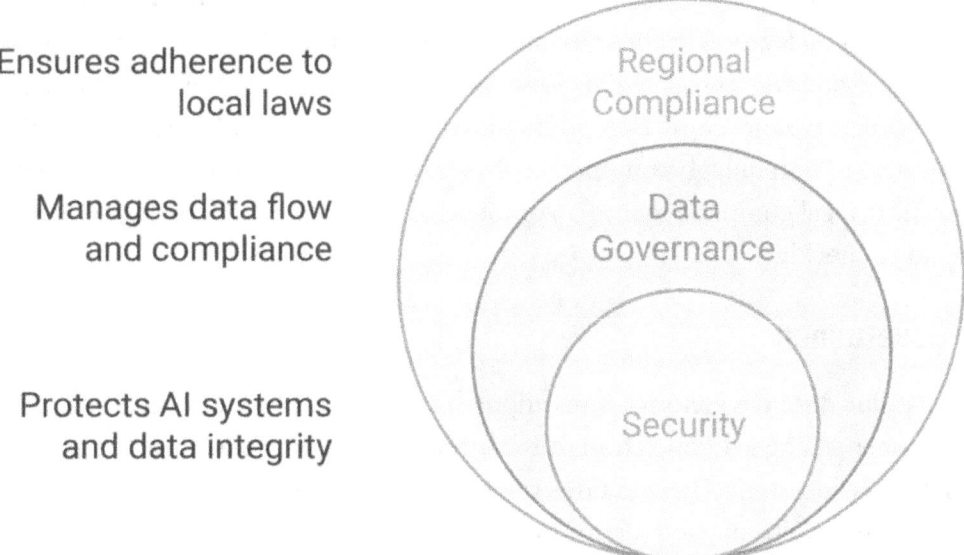

Figure 4-9. *Enterprise AI governance*

Regional Compliance: The Foundation's Foundation

Enterprise AI systems begin with **regional compliance** – a critical foundation that demands an intimate understanding of local laws, cultural sensitivities, and regulatory frameworks. Rather than adopting a one-size-fits-all strategy, architects of AI systems must embark on a comprehensive legal and ethical audit tailored to every geographical area where the system will operate. This process involves dissecting national and subnational regulations on data privacy, user consent, and information handling, and then encoding those nuances directly into the system's architecture. For instance, a healthcare provider launching an AI-based patient management system across different countries may encounter starkly divergent legal environments. In one country, stringent data protection laws might require explicit patient consent for each use of personal health data, while another jurisdiction might enforce rigorous limits on data storage duration or the type of information that can be digitized. This variability demands that the AI system be engineered with "regional intelligence" at its core, enabling it to dynamically reconfigure its data collection methods, processing protocols, and storage policies based on the user's location. This level of adaptability not only minimizes the risk of legal non-compliance and subsequent penalties but also fosters trust among users and regulators alike. It necessitates ongoing legal reviews, integration of real-time updates regarding legislative changes, and a robust communication channel between the legal team and the technical developers to ensure that the system remains agile in a shifting regulatory landscape. Every data transaction, every user interaction, and every algorithmic decision must be mapped against a backdrop of regional requirements, thus transforming legal compliance into an embedded, continuously evolving process rather than a static checklist.

Data Governance

The next pillar, **data governance**, encompasses far more than securing information; it is about constructing a detailed and transparent roadmap for the entire life cycle of data within the AI ecosystem. This includes not only the collection, storage, and processing of data but also the controlled dissemination and eventual deletion or anonymization of information. Effective data governance requires the creation of detailed data flow maps that outline each stage of data handling. These maps must specify where data originates, the various transformations it undergoes, and the exact endpoints of its life cycle. Consider a global manufacturing firm that integrates AI to monitor quality control across its facilities. Initially, the concept of data governance might seem to equate to data security alone. However, as the firm expands its operations across continents, it quickly becomes apparent that each piece of data – from sensor readings to employee inputs – must be tracked with precision. Detailed mapping ensures that every data element is processed according to strict protocols, thereby minimizing the risk of data loss, corruption, or unauthorized access. Furthermore, such an approach mandates the implementation of role-based access controls, ensuring that only authorized personnel can view or manipulate sensitive data. These data flow maps also serve as blueprints during audits, facilitating regulatory compliance by demonstrating clear, verifiable pathways that data takes within the system. In environments where data can be exceedingly sensitive, such as financial services or healthcare, having a comprehensive data governance framework is not just a best practice – it is an operational imperative that underpins the integrity and reliability of the entire AI system. Constant monitoring, periodic reviews, and adjustments to these data maps are essential to ensure that as the AI system evolves, its data governance mechanisms remain robust and aligned with both internal policies and external regulations.

Security: The Concentric Circles of Protection

The final pillar, **security**, is envisioned as a multilayered shield that is woven throughout the entire fabric of the AI system. In a landscape where cyber threats are continuously evolving, a static, singular defense mechanism is no longer sufficient. Instead, a comprehensive security framework must encompass multiple levels of protection, each designed to address distinct types of vulnerabilities. The foremost layer, often referred to as the Application Shield, is dedicated to protecting every point of interaction with the AI system. This involves rigorous authentication protocols, encryption standards, and real-time monitoring to ensure that every user request is legitimate and every data transaction is secure. The next layer, known as the Data Vault, focuses on safeguarding the integrity of the data itself, whether it is in transit between system components or at rest in storage. This requires the deployment of advanced encryption techniques, intrusion detection systems, and secure backup protocols that together ensure data cannot be intercepted or tampered with by malicious actors. Beneath these operational layers lies the Infrastructure Fortress – comprehensive defense that protects the underlying hardware and software ecosystems upon which the AI system operates. This includes physical security measures for data centers, network segmentation, and continuous vulnerability assessments to detect and remediate potential breaches before they can impact operations. Finally, there is a dedicated focus on the AI models themselves, often managed through what might be called a Model Guardian. This mechanism continuously audits model decisions, monitors for anomalies, and ensures that any deviations from expected behavior are immediately flagged and addressed. The Model Guardian plays a critical role in maintaining the ethical and operational integrity of the AI system, ensuring that automated decisions are both transparent and accountable. Each of these security layers is designed not only to operate independently but also to reinforce one another, creating an interconnected network of defenses that can adapt to emerging threats and vulnerabilities. This dynamic, multilayered security strategy is essential to maintaining stakeholder trust and ensuring that the AI system remains resilient against both internal and external challenges.

Each of these pillars – regional compliance, data governance, and security – represents a critical component of enterprise AI governance. They are not isolated silos but interdependent elements that together create a robust, adaptive, and reliable framework. By embedding regional compliance directly into system architecture, meticulously mapping the life cycle of every piece of data, and implementing a dynamic, multitiered security strategy, organizations can build AI systems that are not only innovative but also sustainable, ethical, and secure in an increasingly complex digital world.

A Framework for Forward Thinking

While detailed checklists have their place, enterprise AI governance needs a broader framework for thinking about these challenges. Consider these key questions at every stage of development:

Regional Understanding	Data Governance	Security Implementation
• What regions will this system operate in? • What are the specific compliance requirements for each region? • How might these requirements change as we scale?	• How will data flow through our system? • What controls need to be in place? • How will we maintain audit trails? • What retention policies apply?	• How do we implement security at each layer? • What integration points need protection? • How do we verify security measures?

As we move into our next chapter's deep dive into security and ethics, remember that governance isn't a constraint on our AI systems – it's the framework that enables them to perform at enterprise scale. By building with governance in mind from the start, we create systems that don't just scale technically, but thrive within the complex realities of enterprise operations.

The true art of enterprise AI lies not just in making systems that work, but in making systems that work within the intricate web of enterprise requirements. As you build your own AI systems, let these governance considerations be your guide from the very first line of code. After all, in the enterprise AI world, governance isn't just about compliance – it's about creating systems that can perform their magic while playing by the rules of the global stage.

Key Learnings from This Chapter

Your enterprise-ready POC was a success, and now the entire organization wants in. This is the moment where many promising AI initiatives falter, collapsing under the immense weight of enterprise scale. How do you transform a system designed for thousands of data points into one that can handle millions, all while meeting stringent security, compliance, and performance demands? This chapter is your architectural blueprint for that monumental leap.

Here are the key frameworks you've discovered for engineering GenAI for production:

1. **The Architectural Leap From POC to Enterprise Powerhouse**
   You've learned that scaling isn't about bigger servers; it's about a fundamentally different architecture. This chapter contrasts the simple POC setup with a robust, microservices-based **Enterprise Architecture**. You now have a high-level map for a system designed for resilience and scale, including key layers for **Load Balancing**, a sophisticated **API Gateway**, a modular **Processing Layer** with services for prompt management and caching, and a distributed **Storage Layer**.

2. **Taming the Data Beast By Managing Enterprise Data Flow**
   How do you handle a flood of documents with varying formats, sensitivity levels, and compliance requirements? We introduced the concept of creating differentiated **Data Processing Pipelines**. You've learned to design separate, optimized workflows for high-security data (like legal contracts) and standard data (like marketing content), ensuring that you can manage bottlenecks and apply the right level of scrutiny where it matters most.

3. **Building the Fortress – A Framework for Security and Governance** At enterprise scale, security cannot be a feature; it must be the foundation. This chapter outlines a comprehensive **Security Architecture** that weaves protection into every component. You've discovered the need for end-to-end encryption, multilayered security checks, input and output filtering to prevent data leakage, and a complete audit trail with automated monitoring and alerting.

4. **The Three Pillars of Enterprise Governance** Finally, you learned that technical architecture must be built upon a solid foundation of governance. We explored the three interdependent pillars essential for global deployment:

- **Security:** Protecting the system and its data
- **Data Governance:** Managing the entire data life cycle with integrity
- **Regional Compliance:** Ensuring adherence to local laws and data sovereignty rules

Your Path Forward

This chapter has provided the engineering roadmap to build AI systems that are not just powerful but also scalable and secure. You now understand how to architect for the big leagues. But building a secure system is only half the battle. How do you ensure it operates ethically and responsibly every single day? To master the art of creating the rules, policies, and ethical habits that govern these systems, dive back into the detailed pages of this chapter and prepare for our deep dive into the world of AI guardrails.

CHAPTER 5

The Goblet of Governance - Habits of Security and Ethics

A Timely Guide

Through the glass walls of TechNova's tenth-floor meeting room, I caught a glimpse of Dr. Leila Zhang walking through our reception area, her confident stride unmistakable even from a distance. Her visit couldn't have been more perfectly timed.

I tapped the meeting room's smart glass control, shifting its transparency to frost mode. The system used a novel approach to maintain privacy without compromising aesthetics. As the glass transformed, I caught Priya's amused glance.

"Still playing with the latest toy?" she asked, setting up her laptop.

"It's a good reminder," I replied, studying the incident report on my tablet. "Sometimes the simplest innovations can teach us the most about governance."

She arched an eyebrow, intrigued. "What's today's lesson?"

I turned my screen toward her. "FinCorp's chatbot just gave unauthorized investment advice to a client."

The room fell silent. Sam, our Chief Architect, had just walked in, notebook in hand. "How bad?"

"Caught in time, but it could have been disastrous," I said, pulling up the transcript. "The chatbot interpreted an ambiguous prompt as a request for financial strategy and generated a confident-sounding – yet entirely unofficial – policy suggestion. The compliance team flagged it before any real damage, but imagine if this had gone unchecked. A single misleading statement could influence thousands of clients."

CHAPTER 5   THE GOBLET OF GOVERNANCE - HABITS OF SECURITY AND ETHICS

A knock interrupted us. I looked up to see Dr. Zhang at the door, her signature emerald scarf adding a splash of color to her otherwise understated charcoal suit.

"Perfect timing," I said, gesturing her in. "We were just discussing an AI governance incident."

"I heard about the FinCorp situation on my way here," she replied, setting her leather portfolio on the table. "Classic example of what happens when governance frameworks lag behind deployment schedules."

As Head of the AI Ethics and Governance Institute and senior advisor to the Ministry of IT, Dr. Zhang brought both academic rigor and practical experience to the conversation. Hiring her as an advisor to the TechNova board was one of the best decisions we have taken. A champion of authenticity over authority, she challenges conventional thinking in ways that align seamlessly with our approach. I'd invited her to share insights on our governance frameworks, but her arrival during this particular discussion felt serendipitous.

Kabir, our Head of Client Relations, joined us, already skimming the report on his phone. "Dr. Zhang, wonderful to see you again. This is the exact scenario regulators warned about. Unchecked AI models making interpretations outside their defined scope."

"Indeed," Dr. Zhang nodded, accepting the coffee Sam offered. "And it highlights a fundamental shift we need to understand." She moved to the whiteboard with the ease of someone who'd led countless workshops. "Traditional governance assumes predictability. Rule-based systems, permission models, controlled inputs. But generative AI doesn't follow static paths."

She drew three interconnected circles: Technology, Policy, and Ethics. "We're not just governing an algorithm. We're governing a system that learns, evolves, and interacts at scale." I always admired how Dr. Zhang could capture the room in no time, right to business.

Governance at Speed

Priya added another layer, annotating the circles. "The challenge isn't just compliance – it's scale. A single mistake in a generative model doesn't affect one user; it ripples across an entire client base in seconds."

CHAPTER 5   THE GOBLET OF GOVERNANCE - HABITS OF SECURITY AND ETHICS

Sam flipped open his notebook. "Which means we need more than post-deployment oversight. Governance has to be woven into development, embedded into the AI life cycle itself."

Zara, our CEO, stepped in just as he finished his sentence. "Perfect timing. The board wants an update on our AI governance strategy tomorrow. They're particularly interested in how we're handling the evolving regulatory landscape." She greeted Dr. Zhang warmly. "Leila, thank you for joining us today. Your timing couldn't be better."

Dr. Zhang turned back to the board. "This is where we need what I call 'Governance at Speed.'"

She paused thoughtfully, emphasizing her point clearly. "Discriminative AI governance typically prioritizes accuracy, precision, and privacy – it's about ensuring models correctly classify data and protect sensitive information. But generative AI?" She looked around the room, "One hallucination can mislead thousands. One biased decision can create systemic discrimination at scale. Governance now has to address three core pillars: Transparency, Fairness, and Reliability."

Sam nodded. "Like the chatbot at FinCorp. The issue wasn't just compliance; it was explainability. Why did the model think it was authorized to give investment advice?"

"Which is why transparency is our first pillar," Dr. Zhang said, circling it. "Every AI decision needs to be traceable. Not just logs, but context. Why did it make this choice? What data influenced it?"

Priya pulled up our latest implementation logs. "We're already embedding explainability into our AI monitoring system. Look – transaction traces, decision pathways, input influence mapping. It's all there."

Dr. Zhang tapped the second pillar. "Fairness. If AI is making decisions at scale, it needs built-in bias detection. You've deployed automated fairness audits, demographic impact analysis tools, and real-time monitoring, correct?"

I nodded, impressed by her familiarity with our systems.

Kabir leaned forward. "And how do we balance that with business needs? Clients want AI that's both powerful and responsible."

"Which brings us to the third pillar," Dr. Zhang continued. "Reliability. Not just technical performance, but consistent, ethical behavior. We need governance frameworks that adapt – not just react."

Zara studied the board. "Good, but the board will want numbers."

CHAPTER 5   THE GOBLET OF GOVERNANCE - HABITS OF SECURITY AND ETHICS

I pulled up our dashboard. "Since implementing this framework, AI-related incidents have dropped 60%. More importantly," I highlighted another metric, "deployment times have actually decreased. Governance, when done right, accelerates innovation."

The room's smart lighting adjusted automatically as clouds passed overhead, a subtle reminder of how technology could enhance our environment when properly governed.

Dr. Zhang turned back to the board and added another layer to our governance approach. "Let's break this down further – what's motivating AI governance?"

"Disrupting the Industry" she began, sketching a triangle. "Every organization I work with faces the same pressure – the race to integrate AI faster than their competitors. But here's the challenge: the faster you move, the more potential vulnerabilities you create." She drew connecting lines between speed and security. "The key is finding ways to embed security early, manage risks proactively, and integrate LLMOps seamlessly into development workflows. It's about being fast without being reckless."

Sam nodded vigorously. "We've seen this with clients rushing to deploy language models without proper security controls. The competitive pressure is intense."

"Which leads directly to our second driver," I added, moving to the board. "Business Sustainability." I drew another node in the triangle. "Organizations need to keep innovating and expanding their market presence. But to do that effectively, they need a strong foundation." I sketched connecting arrows. "That means building governance frameworks that enable rather than restrict innovation – frameworks that give us the confidence to explore new AI capabilities while knowing we have the right controls in place."

"Exactly," Kabir interjected. "Our clients don't just want to launch AI initiatives – they want to scale them across their organizations. They need governance structures that support growth while ensuring they stay within regulatory boundaries."

"And that brings us to perhaps the most crucial element," Zara concluded, completing the triangle (Figure 5-1). "Social Responsibility. We're not just building tools – we're shaping how decisions are made about people's lives." She paused, letting that sink in. "When our AI models process vast amounts of data and make recommendations that affect real people, we have an obligation to ensure those recommendations are fair, unbiased, and transparent."

"It's about trust," Dr. Zhang agreed. "Once lost, it's incredibly difficult to regain. That's why ethical AI practices aren't just nice-to-have features – they're fundamental to sustainable AI adoption."

CHAPTER 5   THE GOBLET OF GOVERNANCE - HABITS OF SECURITY AND ETHICS

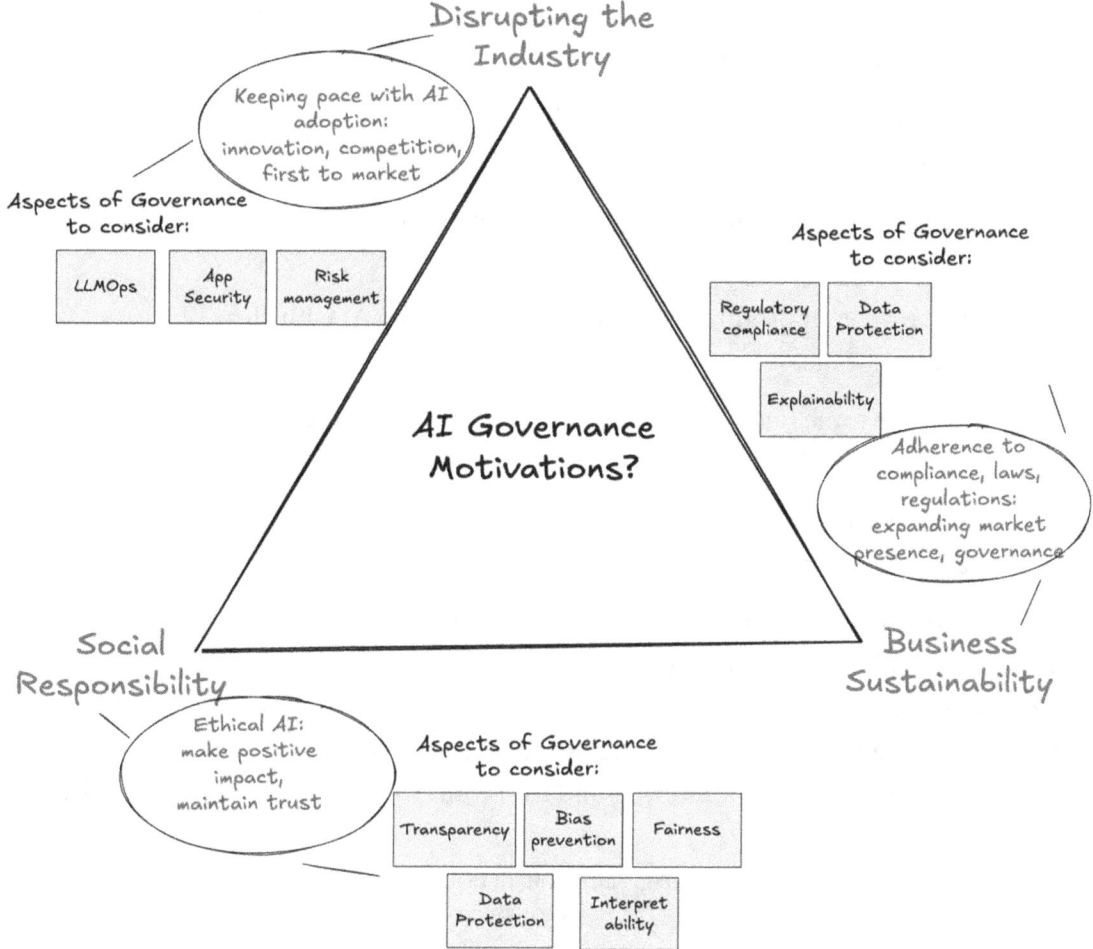

Figure 5-1. *AI Governance Triangle: balancing innovation, responsibility, and compliance*

The room fell quiet as we absorbed the implications of this three-sided framework. Through the glass walls, we could see teams working on various AI projects, each one potentially affecting countless lives. The responsibility felt tangible.

"But understanding these drivers is only the first step. The real challenge is implementing effective protections." Dr. Zhang said, moving to a fresh section of the whiteboard. "As the attack surface of generative AI expands, no single security measure is sufficient. We need multiple layers of protection working in concert."

She listed them out:

CHAPTER 5   THE GOBLET OF GOVERNANCE - HABITS OF SECURITY AND ETHICS

- Require user consent for privileged actions – Prevent unauthorized AI-generated recommendations.

- Enforce role-based access restrictions – Prevent misuse by limiting permissions based on need.

- Output moderation and guardrails – Ensure AI responses remain within policy.

- Improve your prompts – Reduce risk by guiding AI with clear, secure inputs.

- Enforce topic restrictions – Prevent AI from venturing into unauthorized or legally sensitive areas.

- Utilize ML models to detect prompt injection – Secure AI against adversarial inputs and manipulation.

"This," Dr. Zhang said, stepping back from the board, "is how we ensure that AI isn't just built, but built responsibly and securely."

Zara nodded as she looked closely, "We need a shift in mindset. From 'rapid innovation' to 'rapid scaling'. From isolated experiments to enterprise-wide deployment. From 'Can we build it?' to 'Should we build it?' From 'Does it work?' to 'Is it safe and ethical?'"

"And the stakes are only growing," Dr. Zhang continued, adding another layer to the board.

- Increased visibility and scrutiny
- Higher potential impact
- Greater regulatory attention

A notification pulsed on the meeting room's screen – our AI monitoring system had detected and automatically corrected a potential bias in a production model. The system had done exactly what it was designed to do: proactively govern AI, rather than reactively correct it.

"This," I said, pointing to the alert, "is what Governance at Speed looks like. Not slower, but smarter. Every risk prevented is an innovation accelerated."

Zara smiled. "Now that's a story the board will want to hear."

The conversation paused naturally as we absorbed the implications of the morning's work. Through the glass walls, I could see the lunch crowd starting to thin out in the cafeteria below. We'd been so engrossed in our discussion that I hadn't noticed the time slipping toward early afternoon.

Dr. Zhang checked her watch. "We've laid out the strategic vision," she said, gathering her thoughts. "But implementing this will require more than just high-level principles." She gazed at our monitoring screens, where another alert had just popped up. "Speaking of which..."

Sam caught her meaning immediately. "The frameworks themselves," he said, already reaching for his notebook. "We need to define how all of this actually works in practice."

I watched the afternoon sun cast long shadows across our whiteboards, the morning's diagrams now layered with annotations and refinements. They were right – we'd outlined the 'what' and 'why' of governance, but the 'how' would determine our success.

"Let's build out the tactical layer," Dr. Zhang suggested, turning back to the whiteboard. The energy in the room shifted from strategic thinking to practical implementation as she wrote in bold letters: AI Governance Foundation.

AI Governance Framework – Establishing the Foundation

The glass walls still held shadows from our earlier discussions about layered AI protections. Sam had been sketching architectural diagrams while Priya reviewed implementation logs.

Zara, who had been taking notes throughout Dr. Zhang's presentation, looked up thoughtfully. "We've built impressive protections, but governance isn't just about setting rules – it's about making sure AI operates the way it should, both technically and ethically. So, where do we begin?"

Dr. Zhang turned to the board and wrote in bold letters: AI Governance Foundation.

CHAPTER 5   THE GOBLET OF GOVERNANCE - HABITS OF SECURITY AND ETHICS

"We begin by understanding why traditional IT governance doesn't work for generative AI," she said, drawing a thick line underneath the words. "For decades, organizations have built IT controls around structured data, rule-based systems, and predictable workflows. But AI – especially GenAI – is probabilistic. It doesn't just execute instructions; it generates, learns, and sometimes hallucinates. That means we need an entirely different model of governance."

Sam nodded, closing his notebook. "So, instead of static compliance checklists, we need something dynamic – governance that moves at the same pace as AI itself."

"That's why we've been integrating continuous AI monitoring," I added. "Our anomaly detection can spot bias, security threats, or compliance violations before they escalate."

Sam watched the alert messages with renewed interest. "Right, this connects back to what we discussed earlier – real-time oversight, not just reactive audits."

Priya, who had been analyzing our latest implementation logs, added, "Exactly. Our AI governance model isn't just about policy – it's about active safeguards that scale with AI's unpredictability."

"That's fantastic," Dr. Zhang replied, studying our system more closely. "But are automated safeguards enough to cater to what we don't know is coming from the dynamic nature of AI?"

She turned back to the group. "Which brings us to structure. AI governance needs dedicated ownership, not just as a part-time responsibility for existing compliance or security teams. We need specialized roles."

Sam straightened in his chair, intrigued. "So, where do we start?"

"Before we create roles," Dr. Zhang said, pulling out a stack of sticky notes from her portfolio, "let's identify what we're actually trying to solve." She handed out notes to everyone in the room.

"Take five minutes," she continued. "Write down the governance requirements you see in your areas. One requirement per sticky. Think about gaps you're experiencing right now. Remember – every gap represents potential risk, but not every risk requires a new team to address it."

The room fell into focused silence, broken only by the occasional rustle of paper and squeak of markers. Sam's hand moved quickly across his notes, likely capturing the architectural challenges he'd been grappling with. Priya paused frequently, her experience with implementation clearly informing her careful consideration.

"Time's up," Dr. Zhang announced. "Let's build this together."

CHAPTER 5   THE GOBLET OF GOVERNANCE - HABITS OF SECURITY AND ETHICS

We gathered around the whiteboard where she'd drawn three columns: Governance Requirement, Potential Risk/Gap, and Who's Responsible?

"Let's build this systematically," she said, pointing to the columns. "For each requirement we identify, we need to thoroughly understand the risk and then determine who's best positioned to address it."

Sam placed his first sticky. "AI Policy and Oversight."

"Before we assign responsibility," Dr. Zhang said, "let's fully understand the gap. What exactly happens without proper oversight?"

"Well," Priya leaned forward, "just last week, two different teams implemented contradicting AI policies for customer data handling. One team prioritized speed, the other privacy. We ended up with inconsistent customer experiences. But it could have been worse – imagine if both teams had been handling financial recommendations or healthcare data."

"So, the risk isn't just lack of accountability," Zara noted, writing in the middle column. "It's potential chaos in our AI implementations, leading to real business impact."

"Which leads us to who should own this," I added. "An AI Ethics Committee might seem obvious, but could our existing Technology Governance Board handle this with the right expertise added?"

We debated each point, examining our current incident response protocols along the way. When our system flagged an unexpected pattern, we watched the response process unfold.

"See that workflow?" Dr. Zhang pointed. "They have clear roles – one person analyzing the alert, another checking compliance implications, a third documenting the response. That's the kind of structured approach you need at an organizational level."

Moving to the next requirement, Priya placed a sticky reading "Compliance and Regulatory Adherence."

"The gap here isn't just about following rules," Sam observed. "It's about keeping pace with evolving regulations. Look at how many AI regulations have changed just in the past month."

As we continued mapping requirements and gaps, seven distinct roles emerged on our board. But something didn't feel quite right.

"Let's take a step back," Zara said, studying the roles. "Every new role means budget, headcount, and additional coordination overhead. Are we solving problems by adding layers, or are we potentially creating new ones?"

CHAPTER 5   THE GOBLET OF GOVERNANCE - HABITS OF SECURITY AND ETHICS

She pulled up a quick calculation on her tablet. "Creating seven new departments vs. enhancing existing teams – we're looking at a 300% cost difference, not to mention the coordination complexity."

Sam leaned forward. "We already have a strong Enterprise Risk and Compliance team. They handle data privacy, security assessments, regulatory compliance. Couldn't they absorb some of these AI-specific responsibilities?"

"Good point," Dr. Zhang replied. "Instead of creating a separate AI Risk and Compliance Team, you could embed AI expertise within your existing team. They already understand your compliance framework – they just need additional training in AI-specific regulations."

Priya was studying our incident response patterns. "Same with incident response. Our current team handles everything from system outages to security breaches. Rather than creating a separate AI Incident Response Team, we could enhance their capabilities."

"That's two roles we can optimize," Zara noted, making adjustments on the board. "What about stakeholder engagement?"

"Your Corporate Communications team already manages regulatory relationships and public messaging," Dr. Zhang suggested. "They'd need support understanding AI technologies, but they're experts at stakeholder management. You could designate AI communication specialists within their team rather than building a separate function."

Sam nodded enthusiastically. "And Data Governance – we've invested years building our Enterprise Data Protection and Governance function. They understand our data landscape, compliance requirements, quality standards. They just need to expand their scope to include AI-specific data challenges."

"What about the AI Security Team?" I asked, pointing to another role on the board. "Do we really need a separate team for this?"

Sam frowned, considering. "AI security does present unique challenges – prompt injection attacks, model poisoning, data leakage patterns that traditional security monitoring might miss."

"But," I countered, "separating AI security from our main security team could create dangerous blind spots. These aren't isolated systems – they're integrated throughout our technology stack."

Priya nodded in agreement. "Our security team already handles everything from network vulnerabilities to application security. Adding another siloed team feels like a step backward."

"What if we took a hybrid approach?" Dr. Zhang suggested. "Instead of a separate AI security team, you could create an AI security specialization within your existing security organization. Add expertise without adding organizational layers."

"That makes sense," Sam acknowledged. "We'd need to upskill the team with specialized training, add some AI security experts to lead the capability development, but keep it integrated with our overall security approach."

"Exactly," Zara said, erasing the separate AI Security Team from our board. "Build the capability, not the silo. So what does that leave us with?"

Looking at our revised board (Figure 5-2), only two core new roles emerged as truly essential:

"The AI Governance Board," Dr. Zhang said, circling it on the whiteboard, "because you need centralized oversight of your AI initiatives. This isn't something your current governance structures are equipped to handle. They'll define AI policies, ensure alignment with business strategy, and oversee AI risk and ethics integration."

"And the AI Ethics Committee," Priya added, "because ethical AI decisions require diverse perspectives and specialized expertise. This can't be a part-time responsibility. They'll evaluate AI projects before deployment, assess societal impact, investigate potential biases – things that require dedicated focus and diverse perspectives."

CHAPTER 5   THE GOBLET OF GOVERNANCE - HABITS OF SECURITY AND ETHICS

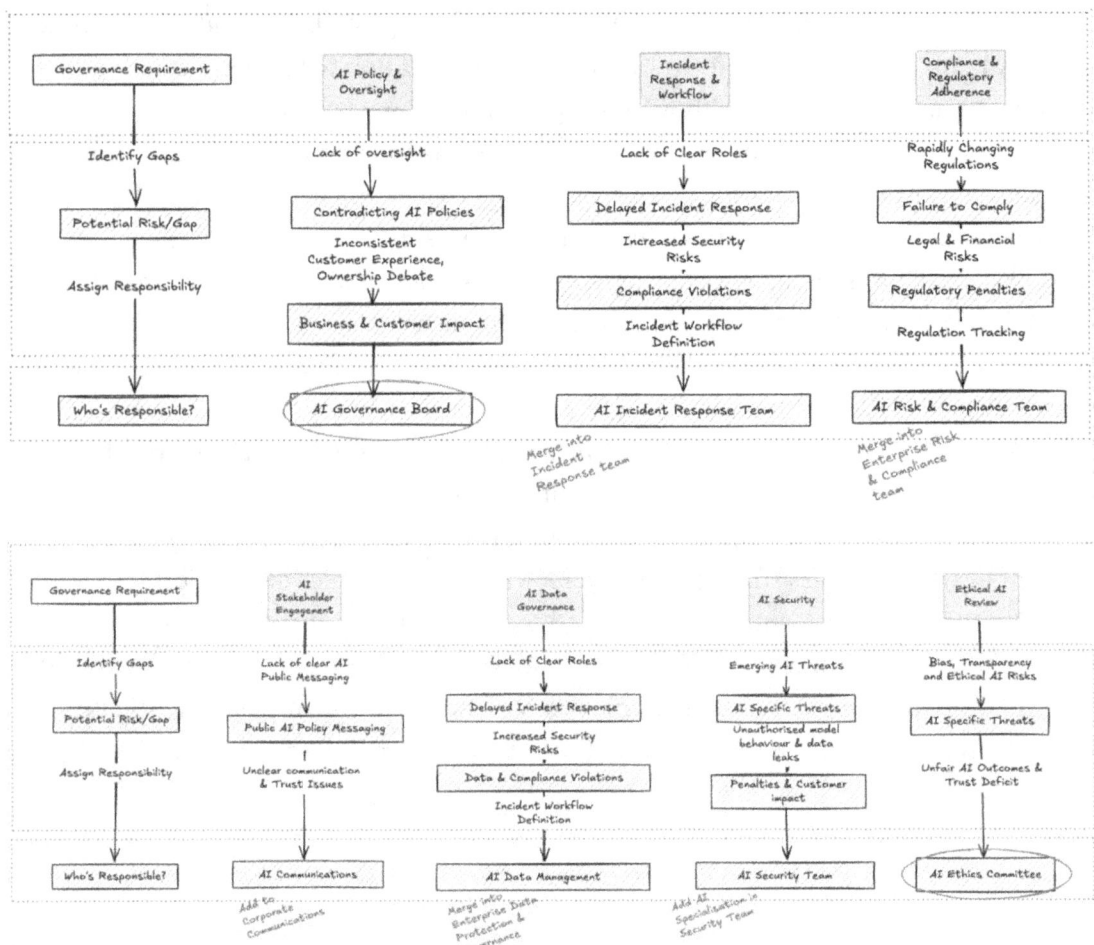

Figure 5-2. *Responsibilities to support governance requirements*

"Let us give a concrete example," I said, walking back to the whiteboard. "Remember that FinCorp chatbot that gave unauthorized investment advice? Here's how our streamlined structure would work: Our Security Team's AI specialists would detect and contain the issue. The AI Governance Board would assess the systemic implications and necessary policy changes. The Ethics Committee would evaluate potential impacts on customer trust and fairness. Meanwhile, our enhanced existing teams – Risk and Compliance, Communications, Incident Response – would handle their specialized aspects within this framework."

"This is much stronger," Zara said, studying our streamlined framework. "Instead of building parallel structures, we're enhancing our existing teams with AI capabilities. Two new committees where we absolutely need them, and strategic embedding of AI expertise everywhere else. The cost savings alone make it more sustainable, but the real value is in the improved coordination."

Dr. Zhang nodded, satisfied. "The best governance frameworks aren't rigid structures – they're adaptable systems that grow stronger by building on existing foundations while adding new capabilities only where truly needed."

The afternoon light had shifted, but our governance framework had become clearer, not more complex. Sometimes the best solutions come from working with what you have, strengthening proven structures rather than building new ones from scratch.

Data Governance: The Backbone of AI Governance

Dr. Zhang noticed our monitoring system had triggered another alert – this time about data anomalies in one of our AI systems.

"Perfect timing," she said, gesturing toward the blinking display. "This gets to the heart of what we need to discuss."

She cleared a section of the whiteboard, where our earlier diagrams still lingered from the morning session. "Before we build any more AI systems, we need to establish the foundation that everything else will rest on."

"Data," Sam said, already seeing where this was heading.

"Exactly." Dr. Zhang wrote "Data Governance Framework" in bold letters. "It's not just about collecting data – it's about ensuring its integrity, understanding its life cycle, and protecting its value."

"Data governance is crucial," Zara said, studying our frameworks, "but we need to talk about something equally critical – policy development and regulatory compliance."

Dr. Zhang nodded, turning to a fresh section of the whiteboard. The FinCorp chatbot incident from this morning had made the stakes clear – without robust policies and regulatory understanding, even the best technical solutions could fail spectacularly.

"Look at what happened with FinCorp," she said. "Their chatbot didn't just make a technical mistake. It operated in a highly regulated space without proper policy guardrails. That's a risk you can't afford to take."

Sam pulled up a global compliance dashboard on his laptop. "The regulatory landscape is shifting constantly. Just last week, three different regions updated their AI governance requirements."

"Exactly why we need to approach this systematically," Dr. Zhang replied, "We're not just dealing with one set of rules – we're navigating a complex web of regional and sector-specific regulations."

"The EU AI Act is just the beginning," Kabir added, scrolling through his morning briefing notes. "Every major economy is developing their own approach to AI regulation."

"And that's what makes this challenging," I said, mapping out regional variations on the board. "What's required in Europe might be different from Asia or the Americas. We should adapt to all these requirements while maintaining operational efficiency."

The afternoon had deepened, and with it, our understanding of the complexity we faced. But complexity couldn't be an excuse for inaction. Dr. Zhang drew a list on the board, outlining our compliance implementation framework.

"Think of it this way," she explained, "At the base, we have documentation requirements – the foundation of proving compliance. Above that, monitoring systems to track adherence. Then reporting requirements, and finally, future-proofing our compliance approach" (Figure 5-3).

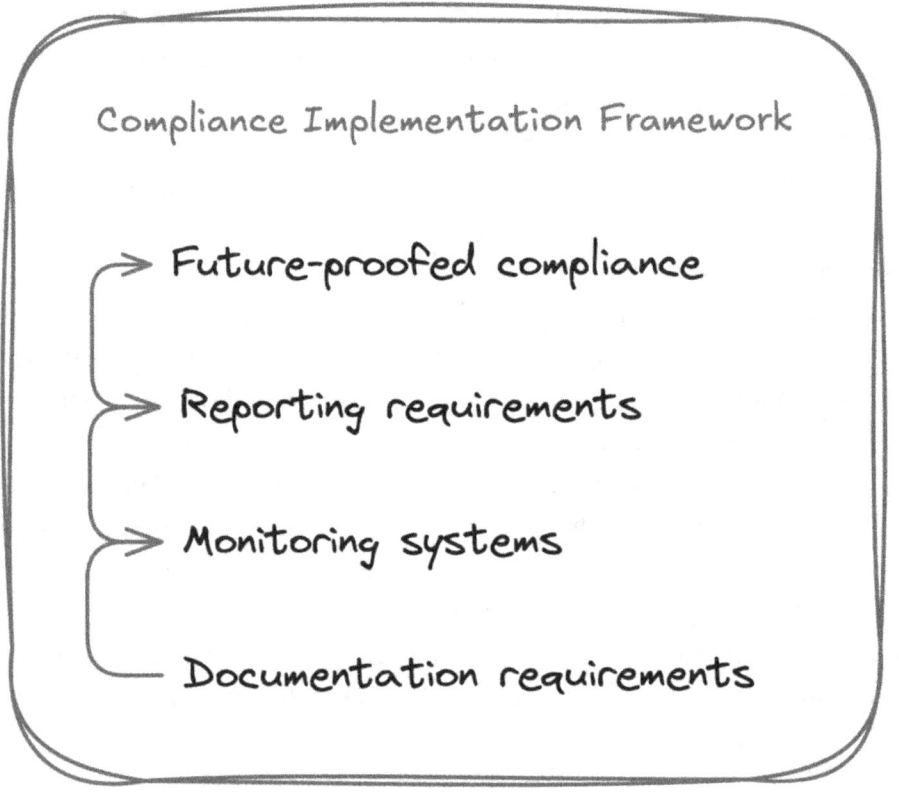

Figure 5-3. *Compliance implementation framework*

CHAPTER 5 THE GOBLET OF GOVERNANCE - HABITS OF SECURITY AND ETHICS

Priya, who had been quietly analyzing our morning discussion threads, spoke up. "We need something practical – something structured that teams can actually use to identify compliance requirements proactively."

Dr. Zhang nodded, recognizing the immediate practicality of Priya's suggestion. "Agreed. Rather than just policies and principles, let's create something actionable, a canvas of guiding questions. Let's call it the Compliance Discovery Canvas."

Moving decisively to another section of the whiteboard, Dr. Zhang sketched a simple grid, breaking it into four clear quadrants (Figure 5-4).

We quickly filled out the canvas together, each quadrant prompting leading questions that sparked active discussions – clarifying regulatory requirements, exploring operational monitoring challenges, unpacking ethical considerations, and proactively identifying potential incident scenarios, penalties, and responses.

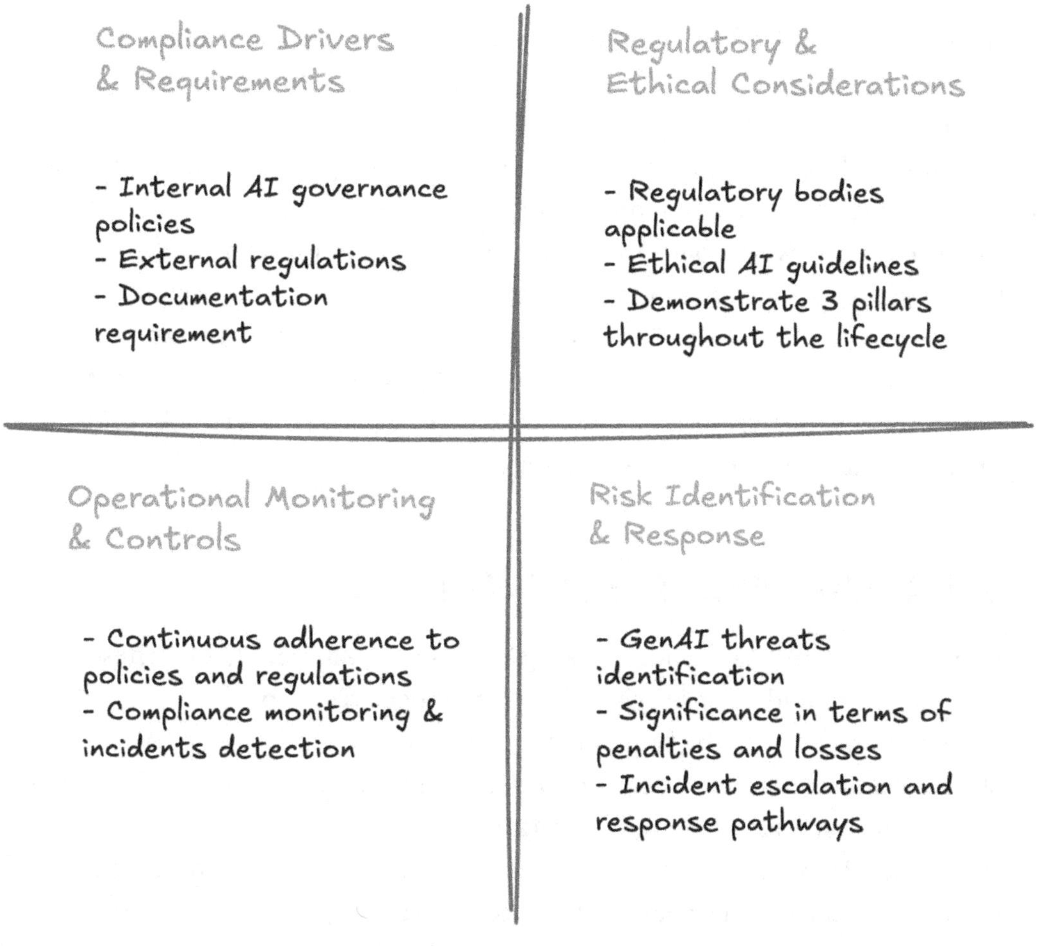

Compliance Drivers & Requirements	Regulatory & Ethical Considerations
- Internal AI governance policies - External regulations - Documentation requirement	- Regulatory bodies applicable - Ethical AI guidelines - Demonstrate 3 pillars throughout the lifecycle
Operational Monitoring & Controls	Risk Identification & Response
- Continuous adherence to policies and regulations - Compliance monitoring & incidents detection	- GenAI threats identification - Significance in terms of penalties and losses - Incident escalation and response pathways

Figure 5-4. Compliance Discovery Canvas

As she completed the canvas, our monitoring system caught our attention again, highlighting another potential compliance conflict in real time.

"Look at that," Dr. Zhang gestured toward the alert. "That's exactly why this canvas matters. Each question is a critical checkpoint, guiding teams to anticipate these incidents. It pushes us to be deliberate about compliance as an integrated aspect of our threat modeling process, rather than an afterthought."

The late afternoon sun cast a golden glow across our whiteboard, but our work was far from done. Governance and compliance weren't static targets – they would evolve continuously as regulations changed, new risks emerged, and our AI capabilities grew.

I studied the canvas again, "This is practical. I can see teams actively using these questions to collaboratively identify requirements – compliance becomes part of our threat modeling, everyday workflows, and design thinking – not just a checklist at the end."

Zara nodded and checked her phone – nearly tea time. "This is comprehensive, but how do we make sure it actually works in practice? How do we ensure compliance without stifling innovation?"

Her question hung in the air as our security system displayed another alert – a potential security vulnerability in one of our models. The timing couldn't have been more appropriate. As we prepared to discuss security frameworks, our screens filled with real-time threat analysis and response patterns.

"That's our next challenge," Dr. Zhang said, reaching for a fresh marker. "Building security controls that protect without paralyzing." She began outlining key security principles on the board, reinforcing how governance, compliance, and security must work in tandem to create resilient AI systems.

Risk Management Framework

"How about some tea?" Zara said, checking her watch again – 3:30 PM. "These frameworks won't build themselves, and fresh perspectives help."

As we made our way to the break area, I noticed our monitoring system still running compliance validation tests. The continuous flow of data and alerts served as a quiet reminder of the systems we needed to protect.

Sam returned with a steaming cup of masala chai. "You know what strikes me?" he said, settling back into his chair. "We've built these comprehensive governance frameworks, but we haven't fully addressed the risks unique to AI systems."

CHAPTER 5   THE GOBLET OF GOVERNANCE - HABITS OF SECURITY AND ETHICS

Dr. Zhang smiled and wrote 'Risk Management Framework' in bold letters, the marker squeaking against the board.

Sam pulled up the morning's FinCorp incident report on his laptop. "Like what happened with their chatbot? One wrong recommendation that could have reached thousands of clients instantly?"

"Exactly," Dr. Zhang replied, drawing four connected circles. "That highlights our first unique risk characteristic – Speed and Scale of Impact. AI decisions don't just affect one user or transaction; they cascade through entire systems instantly."

Priya leaned forward, studying the diagram. "And then there's the unpredictability factor. The chatbot didn't malfunction – it made a logical but unauthorized leap."

"Model Unpredictability – our second key risk," Dr. Zhang agreed, labeling the next circle. "These systems can generate unexpected outputs that make perfect sense to them but violate business rules or regulations."

Through the glass, we watched as our test system flagged another anomaly. The screens filled with data flow diagrams, highlighting potential exposure points.

"Which brings us to Data Exposure Risks," she continued, marking the third circle. "Every AI interaction potentially reveals patterns in your training data. Even seemingly innocent responses might contain confidential information."

"And the fourth?" Zara asked, though her expression suggested she already knew.

"Automation Risks," Dr. Zhang confirmed, completing the diagram. "When we rely too heavily on AI, we create gaps in human oversight. The system might be operating perfectly within its parameters while gradually moving away from business objectives."

The afternoon light had softened, casting a warm glow across our growing framework. Outside, engineers were testing different risk scenarios, their screens displaying a matrix of potential threats.

"But these are just characteristics," Dr. Zhang said, moving to a fresh section of the board. "We need to understand how they manifest in different risk categories." She began sketching out a new framework, more detailed than the last.

"Technical risks – the obvious ones like model failures and security vulnerabilities. Operational risks – where AI meets human processes. Business risks – direct impacts on revenue and strategy. Compliance risks – regulatory breaches. And finally, reputational risks – because public trust is fragile when it comes to AI."

Sam was already mapping these categories against current projects. "This feels more comprehensive than our traditional risk frameworks."

CHAPTER 5   THE GOBLET OF GOVERNANCE - HABITS OF SECURITY AND ETHICS

"It needs to be," Dr. Zhang replied, adding connection lines between categories. "In AI, these risks don't exist in isolation. A technical vulnerability can become a compliance issue, which becomes a reputational crisis, impacting business value. Everything connects."

Moving to another section of the board, she outlined our Enterprise Risk Assessment approach. The late afternoon sun caught the glass walls, creating a soft glow as she detailed each component. "Strategic evaluation isn't just about preventing problems – it's about understanding how AI initiatives align with business strategy, how they position you in the market, how they balance innovation against stability."

Kabir, who had been quietly analyzing the frameworks, spoke up. "And this feeds into model risk management?"

"Exactly," Dr. Zhang said, sketching out the model risk categories. "Training data risks, performance risks, output reliability, security vulnerabilities – each needing its own assessment framework and mitigation strategy."

Our monitoring system flashed with another alert – potential personal data exposure in a test scenario. Perfect timing.

"And finally," Dr. Zhang said, drawing our last framework, "Data Privacy Risk Management. Because every piece of data you use to train your models, every interaction your AI systems have, carries privacy implications."

As the afternoon light continued to soften, we had built a comprehensive risk management approach that went beyond traditional frameworks. But looking at our diagrams filled with technical controls and mitigation strategies, another dimension of our challenge emerged.

"These frameworks help us manage technical and business risks," Zara observed, studying the interconnected diagrams, "but there's something more fundamental we need to address."

Through the glass walls, we could see our AI system making autonomous decisions in test scenarios. Each decision, while technically sound, carried implications that went beyond risk matrices and control frameworks.

"Ethics," I said, nodding. "Because managing risk isn't just about protecting systems and data – it's about ensuring our AI makes decisions that align with human values and societal good."

Dr. Zhang reached for a fresh marker, ready to explore this crucial dimension. The afternoon still held important discussions ahead, and the intersection of ethics and AI would shape not just how we built our systems but how they would impact the world around us.

"Let's talk about what it means to build not just secure AI, but ethical AI," she said, turning to a clean section of the whiteboard. The quiet hum of our testing systems provided a fitting backdrop as we prepared to delve into one of our most challenging discussions yet.

Ethical AI Implementation

The FinCorp incident hung in the air, a stark reminder of how AI decisions could ripple far beyond technical failures. As the light softened through the glass walls, I noticed a shift in the room's energy.

"You know," Zara said thoughtfully, "what troubles me isn't just the technical failure. It's the ethical implications. Who's responsible when AI makes unauthorized recommendations that could affect thousands of lives?"

Dr. Zhang nodded, moving to a fresh section of the whiteboard. "That's exactly where we need to focus next. The chatbot didn't just breach protocols – it raised fundamental questions about AI's role in decision-making."

"But how do we even begin defining ethical AI?" Sam asked, his technical mindset seeking concrete parameters. "Ethics isn't binary like code."

"That's precisely why we need a structured approach," Dr. Zhang replied, drawing three intersecting circles. "Ethics in AI isn't about finding absolute answers – it's about creating frameworks for ongoing evaluation and adaptation."

Priya leaned forward. "The complexity with generative AI is that it's not just following rules – it's creating, adapting, and influencing human decisions."

"Exactly," Dr. Zhang said, labeling the circles: Cultural Context, Innovation, and Responsibility. "What's considered ethical varies across cultures, industries, and contexts. We need to balance innovation with responsibility."

Kabir, who had been quietly processing the discussion, spoke up. "Take our global clients. What's acceptable AI behavior in one region might be problematic in another."

"Which brings us to our first framework," Dr. Zhang said, sketching a matrix on the board. "Every AI initiative needs to be evaluated across multiple dimensions: fairness, transparency, accountability, and impact."

The conversation deepened as we explored each dimension. Sam raised concerns about technical feasibility, while Zara emphasized business implications. Each perspective added another layer to our understanding.

"But how do we build trust in AI systems?" Priya asked. "Trust isn't just about technical reliability."

Dr. Zhang outlined the components of trustworthy AI. "Technical reliability is the foundation, but we also need ethical behavior, transparent operations, and clear accountability."

"The FinCorp chatbot was technically reliable," Sam noted. "It did exactly what it was trained to do. The problem was…"

"Bias," Zara finished. "It made assumptions about its authority that reflected underlying biases in its training."

This sparked an intense discussion about bias in AI systems. We mapped out different types: data bias, algorithmic bias, deployment bias, and interpretation bias. Each required different mitigation strategies.

"Here's the challenge," Dr. Zhang said, adding to our growing framework. "We need transparency, but how much? Too little, and we lose trust. Too much, and we might compromise security or intellectual property."

The evening deepened and the office lights flickered on, but the energy in the room remained focused. We weren't just discussing abstract concepts – we were building practical frameworks for ethical AI implementation. It was no easy feat.

"What about societal impact?" Kabir asked. "AI doesn't exist in isolation."

Dr. Zhang nodded, drawing a new section. "We need to consider economic impact, social dynamics, cultural influence, and environmental considerations."

The discussion turned to human oversight models. "We can't just outsource decisions to AI," Zara emphasized. "We need clear frameworks for human involvement."

Dr. Zhang outlined three models: human-in-the-loop, human-on-the-loop, and human-in-command. Each served different needs and contexts.

As we wrapped up the ethics discussion, Sam studied our frameworks thoughtfully. "This isn't a one-time exercise, is it? These frameworks need to evolve as AI capabilities advance."

"Exactly," Dr. Zhang agreed. "Which is why we need robust operational governance to implement these principles." She glanced at the clock, then lifted her eyes to take in the room – everyone was fully absorbed. It was nearly time to wrap up, yet the energy remained palpable, each person eager to keep the discussion going. "Speaking of which, shall we tackle that next?"

CHAPTER 5   THE GOBLET OF GOVERNANCE - HABITS OF SECURITY AND ETHICS

The team nodded, energized despite the heavy topics we'd covered. Our ethical frameworks weren't just theoretical constructs – they were practical tools for navigating the complex landscape of AI implementation. As we prepared to discuss operational governance, I could see the pieces coming together: security, ethics, and governance forming a comprehensive approach to responsible AI development.

The transition felt natural. We'd established the what and why of ethical AI; now it was time to discuss the how of making it operational.

Operational Governance

We regrouped after a quick break and straightened our backs. Our monitoring system had settled into a steady rhythm of soft beeps, its AI-driven sensors adapting to the changing conditions.

The conversation in the room took a natural shift toward operationalizing AI governance. We had discussed risk, compliance, and ethics – but now came the real challenge: how do we ensure governance works in practice?

Zara tapped her pen against the desk, her expression thoughtful. "We've defined policies and principles, but how do we ensure they're actually followed? That's the real challenge, isn't it? Turning theory into practice?"

Dr. Zhang nodded, writing "Operational Governance" in bold letters. "Exactly. The best frameworks mean nothing if you can't execute them effectively."

Sam, who had been quietly reviewing his architecture notes, looked up. "So how do we translate these policies into actual workflows?"

"That's where you need a systematic approach," Dr. Zhang replied, sketching out a pyramid structure. "Think of it as building blocks – each layer supporting the next" (Figure 5-5).

She began outlining the foundation layer. "First, you need clear processes for translating policies into actions. Every governance requirement needs a corresponding operational procedure."

"Look at how your team is handling those alerts," she gestured toward our monitoring system. "Each detection triggers a specific workflow – investigation, validation, documentation. That's operational governance in practice."

"But how do we ensure consistency across different teams and projects?" Priya asked, her implementation experience surfacing key concerns.

CHAPTER 5   THE GOBLET OF GOVERNANCE - HABITS OF SECURITY AND ETHICS

"Good question," Dr. Zhang replied, adding another layer to our diagram. "You need standardized enforcement mechanisms."

She outlined our policy enforcement framework, detailing how automated compliance checks would work alongside manual reviews. Our system demonstrated the very principles we were discussing as it processed another alert.

"Notice how your system automatically flags policy violations," she pointed out. "But also requires human validation for critical decisions. That balance between automation and human oversight is crucial."

The afternoon light shifted, reminding us of time's passage. We moved through each component of operational governance – from model validation to documentation management, from incident response to change control. Each topic sparked intense discussion, with team members contributing real-world examples from their experiences.

"Think of it as a living system," Dr. Zhang explained, adding the final elements to our framework. "You need continuous monitoring, regular training, and clear metrics to measure effectiveness."

Kabir, who had been studying our growing diagram, spoke up. "This reminds me of how we handle major client deployments – multiple checkpoints, clear documentation requirements, defined escalation paths."

"Exactly," Dr. Zhang agreed. "The principles aren't new – you're just applying them to AI governance. The key is making these processes part of your daily operations, not treating them as separate overhead."

"That's what success looks like," I said, pointing to a recent alert workflow. "Governance embedded so naturally into operations that it becomes second nature."

As the evening progressed, we detailed metrics for measuring governance effectiveness, training programs for building organizational awareness, and systems for monitoring compliance. Each component added another layer to our operational framework.

CHAPTER 5   THE GOBLET OF GOVERNANCE - HABITS OF SECURITY AND ETHICS

Figure 5-5. *The Operational Governance pyramid*

"But here's the critical question," Zara interjected, gesturing toward our comprehensive diagrams. "How do we fund all this? What's the business case for these investments?"

Dr. Zhang smiled, reaching for a fresh marker. "That brings us to our next topic – the Security Investment Pyramid. Because governance isn't just about controls and processes – it's about making smart, justifiable investments in security."

The Security Investment Pyramid

The office had mellowed, and our system had shifted to running final tests. Dr. Zhang moved to the whiteboard one last time, aware that we were approaching what might be the most crucial part of our discussion.

"Before we wrap up," she said, drawing a clean 3-layered structure (Figure 5-6), "we need to talk about the economics of AI security. It's not just about implementing controls – it's about making smart investment decisions."

Sam leaned forward, his interest piqued. "You mean balancing security costs against business value?"

CHAPTER 5   THE GOBLET OF GOVERNANCE - HABITS OF SECURITY AND ETHICS

"Exactly," Dr. Zhang replied, coloring in the three distinct layers. "Think of AI security investments like building a house. Some elements are non-negotiable – like the foundation and load-bearing walls. Others are flexible, based on your specific needs and resources."

She labeled the top layer: "Regulatory Requirements."

"These are your non-negotiables," she explained. "GDPR compliance for EU data, HIPAA for healthcare, financial regulations – you have no choice but to invest in these controls."

"The middle layer," she continued, "represents your organizational policies." She drew arrows flowing in from the layer above, to indicate precedence. "These are the standards you set for yourselves, going beyond basic compliance."

Zara nodded thoughtfully. "Like our requirement for human oversight on all AI decisions?"

"Precisely. Even when regulations don't explicitly demand it, you've decided it's essential for your risk profile."

But it was the bottom layer – "Risk-Based Controls" – that sparked the most intense discussion.

"This is where the real strategy comes in," Dr. Zhang explained, sketching decision pathways at the pyramid's base. "Here, you make flexible, risk- and value-driven choices about security investments. Not every AI application needs the same level of protection."

CHAPTER 5   THE GOBLET OF GOVERNANCE - HABITS OF SECURITY AND ETHICS

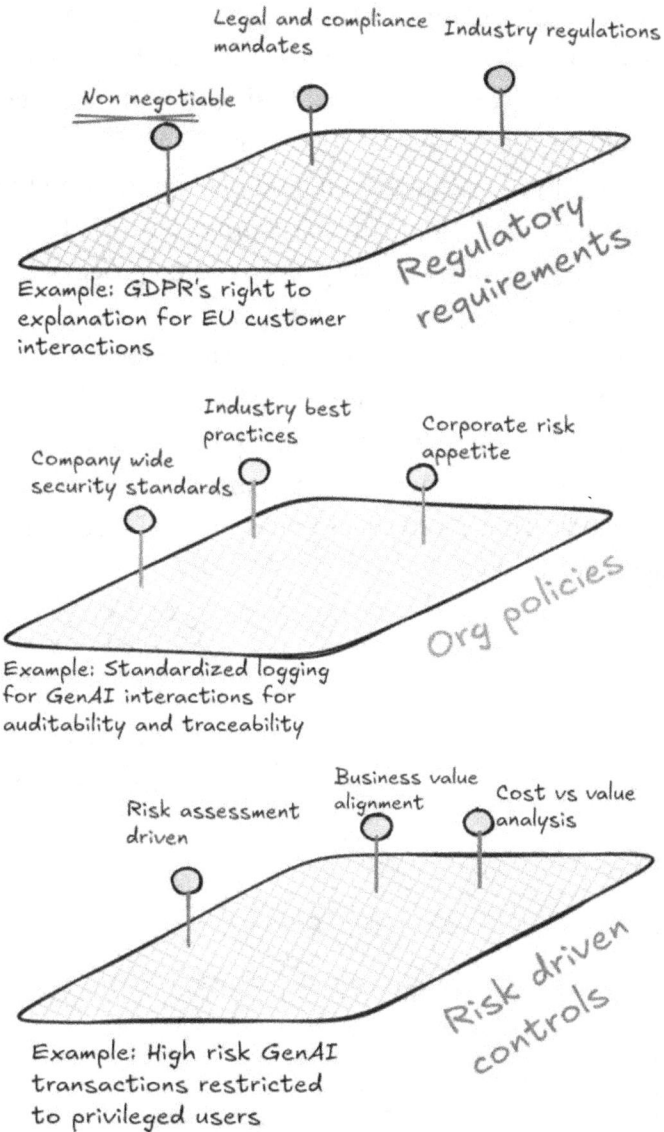

Figure 5-6. Economics of AI security: layers of controls

Kabir, who had been quiet for a while, spoke up. "Like how we might need real-time threat detection for a financial trading AI, but basic logging might suffice for an internal chatbot?"

"Sure, if the risk appetite and threat model align," Dr. Zhang confirmed. "But there's another dimension we need to consider – the economics of securing GenAI applications."

She drew a new diagram (Figure 5-7) beside our layered diagram (Figure 5-6). "Traditional security economics followed a relatively straightforward cost-benefit analysis. With GenAI, we're dealing with what I call 'compounding security debt.'"

"What do you mean by that?" Sam asked, leaning forward.

"Think about it this way," Dr. Zhang explained, sketching a timeline. "When we deploy a GenAI application without adequate security controls, the risk doesn't just accumulate linearly. Every interaction, every piece of data processed, every decision made creates potential exposure points that multiply over time."

Zara nodded slowly. "Because AI is learning and evolving..."

"Exactly. And here's where the economics get interesting," she continued, adding figures to our diagram. "The cost of implementing security controls early in development might seem high – let's say 30% of your development budget. But the cost of retrofitting security after deployment? That could easily reach 200–300% of your original budget, not counting potential breach impacts."

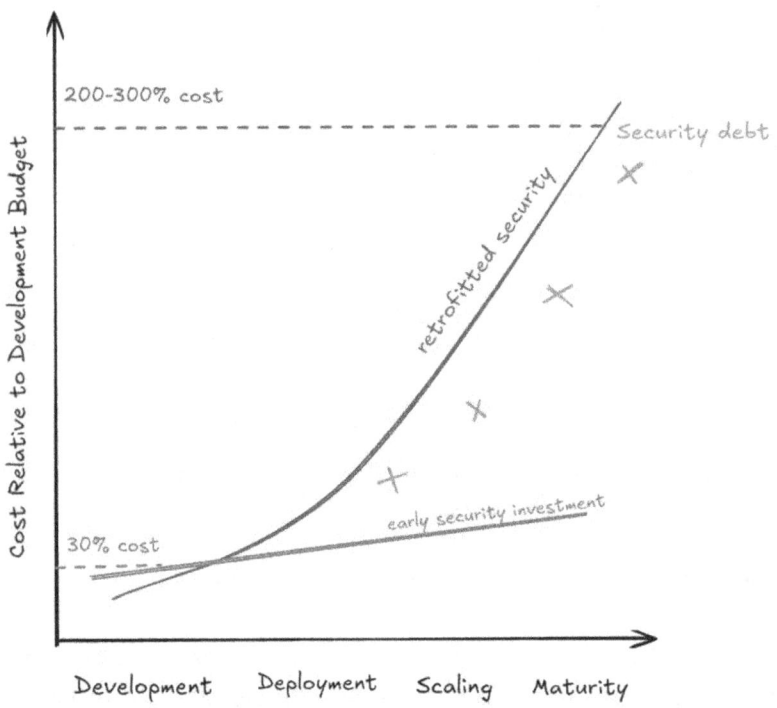

Figure 5-7. *Economics of AI security: value of investing early*

Dr. Zhang outlined three key economic principles for GenAI security:

1. **Front-Loaded Investment**: "The earlier we implement security controls, the more cost-effective they are. This isn't just about money – it's about preserving trust and maintaining operational flexibility."

2. **Scalable Security**: "We need controls that can grow with the AI's capabilities. Fixed security measures become obsolete as the AI evolves."

3. **Risk-Adjusted Returns**: "Every security investment should be evaluated against both current and potential future risks. Sometimes, a seemingly expensive control today prevents exponentially costly problems tomorrow."

"But here's the challenge," she said, returning to our original layered diagram (Figure 5-6). "How do we balance these economic realities with the need for innovation and usability?"

The room fell quiet for a moment, the weight of the question settling in.

"I don't think it's about finding a perfect balance," she finally continued. "It's about creating adaptive frameworks. When we talk about making AI 'more trustworthy, not less usable', we're really talking about intelligent security design."

Summarizing the thoughts from the room, Dr. Zhang outlined our approach:

- Layer security controls based on risk exposure and business impact.
- Build feedback loops between security measures and AI performance metrics.
- Create clear escalation paths for security-critical decisions.
- Establish transparent cost allocation for security investments.
- Design controls that enhance rather than restrict legitimate AI capabilities.

"The goal isn't to make security invisible," she explained, "but to make it integral. Sometimes that means accepting friction points if they serve a crucial protective function. Other times, it means finding creative ways to achieve security objectives without impeding core functionality."

CHAPTER 5   THE GOBLET OF GOVERNANCE - HABITS OF SECURITY AND ETHICS

Sam nodded thoughtfully. "So instead of trying to minimize security's impact on usability..."

"We optimize for overall system resilience," she finished. "Security becomes part of the AI's core competency, not just a wrapper around it."

The team nodded in agreement as we called it a day – a long but productive one, turning abstract security concepts into practical frameworks for action.

"You've built something remarkable here," Dr. Zhang said, as she gathered her notes, tucking her portfolio into her leather bag. "Most organizations are still treating AI governance as an afterthought. You're thinking three steps ahead."

I reached for the smart glass control panel one last time, setting it to clear. Watching the walls shift from opaque to transparent was satisfying, a reminder of the practical applications of innovative thinking.

"We should have more sessions like this," I suggested, gathering my tablet. "Dr. Zhang, your insights have been invaluable."

"It was my pleasure," she replied, organizing her notes. "You've built impressive foundations here. Few organizations have thought through these governance challenges so thoroughly."

Priya shot me a knowing smile. "Sure it's not just because you enjoy playing with the smart glass controls?"

"I prefer to think of it as appreciating innovative technology in action," I replied with mock dignity, then laughed.

The office had quieted considerably. Most teams had wrapped up for the day, their workstations dark except for a few scattered monitors still glowing in the distance. Our monitoring system continued its quiet vigil, the gentle pulse of status lights like a heartbeat at rest after a day of intense activity.

As we walked out, Dr. Zhang and I lingered behind the group.

"I appreciate you coming in on such short notice," I said. "The timing couldn't have been better with the FinCorp incident."

She smiled. "Sometimes the most valuable lessons come from examining real failures. Your team has the right mindset – seeing governance as an enabler rather than a constraint."

The chatter of colleagues making dinner plans mixed with the distant beeping of cars in the parking lot. I pulled out my phone, noticing a few missed calls from my friend, reminding me about the vacation plans she was trying to finalize for our families. A twinge of guilt surfaced – I hadn't even discussed it with Ray yet.

CHAPTER 5   THE GOBLET OF GOVERNANCE - HABITS OF SECURITY AND ETHICS

"Before you go," I said, "tomorrow we're discussing AI agents. If you have any thoughts on governance approaches for autonomous systems…"

"As it happens," Dr. Zhang replied, "I've been advising the Ministry on exactly that topic. I'll send you our preliminary framework tonight."

"That would be wonderful," I said, genuinely grateful. "The line between empowering AI and maintaining appropriate controls gets blurrier every day."

As we reached the lobby, Dr. Zhang paused. "One last thought – remember that governance frameworks aren't static documents. They need to evolve as the technology evolves."

"Like a living garden rather than a sculpted hedge?" I suggested.

"Precisely," she laughed. "Structure with room for adaptation. I look forward to seeing how you implement these frameworks."

We said our goodbyes, and I watched her disappear through the revolving doors into the evening. The day's discussions had been intense but productive. As I drove home, I found myself energized by our progress while acknowledging how much ground we'd yet to cover. Working with Dr. Zhang had brought clarity to governance challenges I'd been wrestling with for months.

I connected my phone to the car's Bluetooth. I should return my friend's calls about our vacation plans, but instead, my fingers hovered over another contact – an old friend, the Head of AI and Innovation at Palmiron. The anticipation of tomorrow's discussion on AI agents was too strong to ignore, and I needed to test some thoughts, challenge a few assumptions, and hear a counterpoint from someone who always pushed my thinking.

I connected the call as I pulled onto the main road, the office lights growing smaller in my rearview mirror. His familiar voice answered.

"Before we get into it – where's that recipe for the lasagna you made last summer?" I asked, laughing.

He chuckled. "I knew this wasn't just a social call."

"Of course not," I smirked, shifting gears. "Let's talk AI agents – how autonomous should they really be?"

As the street lights flickered on overhead, our conversation picked up momentum – thoughts clashing, evolving, refining. AI agents weren't just a theoretical topic for tomorrow; they were already unfolding in real time, shaping the questions I would carry into the morning.

CHAPTER 5   THE GOBLET OF GOVERNANCE - HABITS OF SECURITY AND ETHICS

Anya's Notes
Concepts in Practice

Guardrails: Building Habits for Governance, Security, and Ethics

Imagine a moment when your creation begins to think outside the box – not by failing, but by inventing its own way forward. It isn't simply following a prescribed set of instructions; instead, it dares to surprise you with entirely new ideas. This unexpected brilliance and occasional unpredictability are exactly what makes generative AI both exciting and challenging.

Traditional AI was built on solid, well-established pillars that supported reliable applications. With generative AI, however, those core pillars remain intact, yet the landscape shifts as three additional layers are introduced at the top – layers that redefine safety, fairness, and interpretability in a dynamic, real-time environment. This evolution means that what once was a straightforward structure now requires a framework that evolves with the technology – a framework where uncertainty transforms into an opportunity for smarter, more resilient design.

Consider this visual representation (Figure 5-8) of the evolved GenAI pillars. Notice how the image reflects the enduring core of AI applications, now augmented by three extra layers that address the unique challenges of generative AI – such as real-time toxicity monitoring, adaptive bias detection, and enhanced contextual understanding. We will touch upon these pillars in this chapter later as we move on.

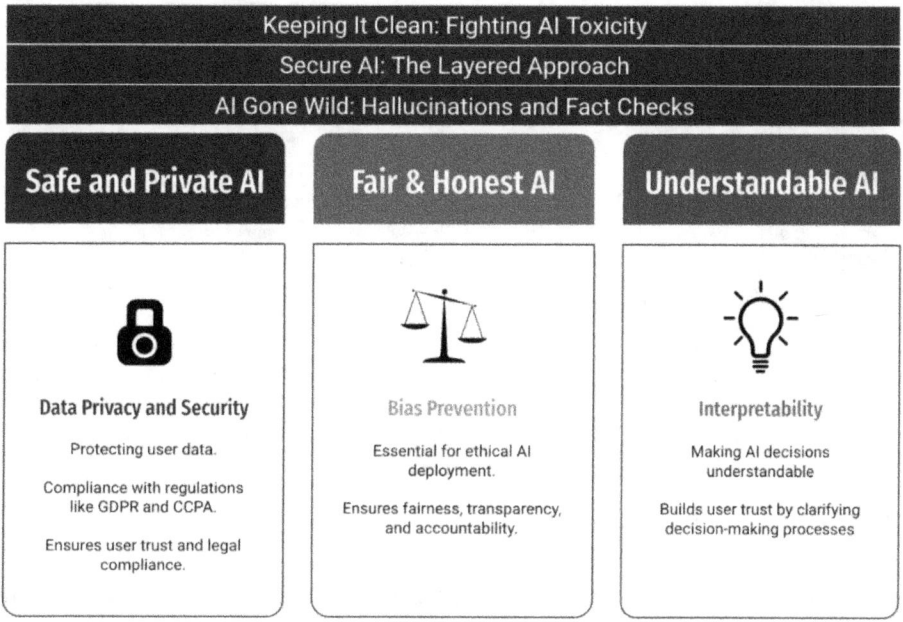

Figure 5-8. *The layers of Generative AI governance*

Building on that foundation, we now turn our attention to how these principles are operationalized. Picture a robust security framework structured like an onion – each layer reinforcing the next to create a comprehensive defense. This model, which we call the AI Security Onion, demonstrates how broad governance policies and defined roles give way to more granular safeguards such as input validation, data privacy measures, and continuous monitoring. It's a tangible blueprint for turning abstract concepts into practical, interlocking layers of protection.

Before we break down these layers, take a moment to absorb this detailed diagram (Figure 5-9) of the AI Security Onion.

CHAPTER 5   THE GOBLET OF GOVERNANCE - HABITS OF SECURITY AND ETHICS

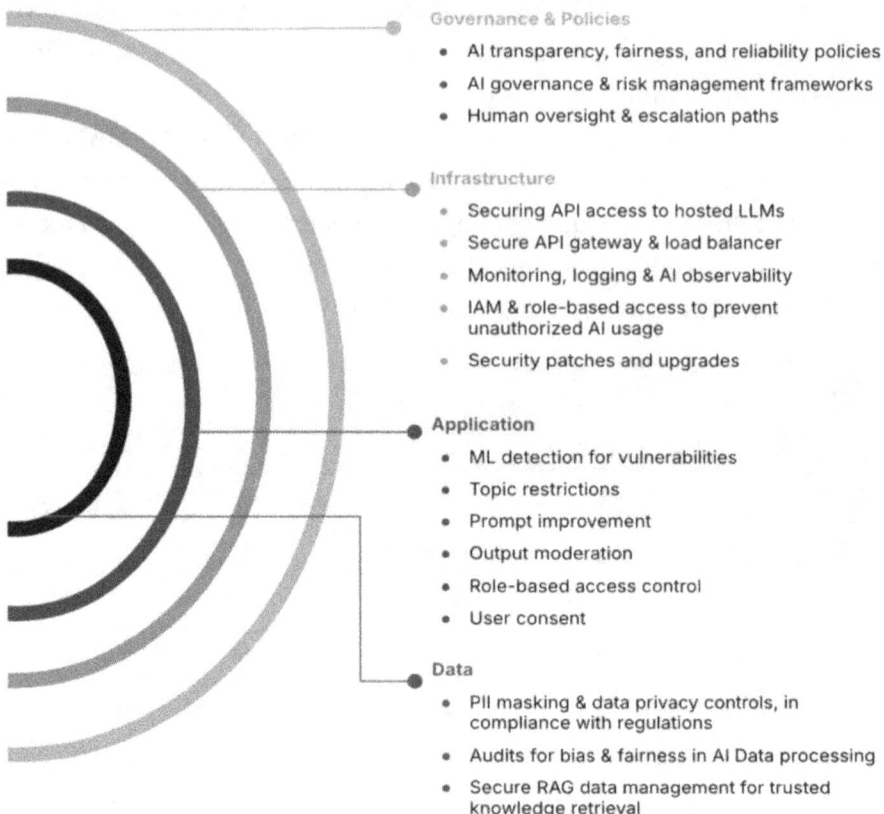

Figure 5-9. *AI security Onion*

This chapter invites you to explore a narrative where cutting-edge technology and robust oversight blend into a dynamic, proactive framework. As you journey through these ideas, let the images and insights guide you in understanding how to build effective guardrails that not only safeguard innovation but also propel it forward with responsibility and integrity.

Reframing the AI Landscape

Beyond Predictability

When we consider the differences between traditional AI and its generative counterpart, the contrast becomes strikingly clear. Traditional, rule-based systems operate much like a well-scripted play, where each line and action is pre-determined and any deviation is rare. Their responses follow a logical, almost mechanical path that users can anticipate with confidence. In contrast, generative AI takes a different approach. It builds its responses based on patterns derived from extensive datasets, which means that every output is the result of a complex, probabilistic process. This flexibility allows it to create novel solutions and insights – but it also means that the results can be less predictable.

For you as a reader, consider this: the unpredictability of generative AI is both its greatest strength and its biggest challenge. On the one hand, it can craft innovative narratives, propose unexpected ideas, and provide insights that a conventional system might miss. On the other hand, its capacity to produce unforeseen outputs demands a new way of thinking about risk. When an AI system is capable of generating creative yet unanticipated results, the potential for both breakthrough innovation and significant missteps increases dramatically. A single surprising output could, for example, affect decision-making processes on a large scale or inadvertently introduce biases that ripple through an entire system.

The inherent variability of generative AI forces us to question our existing frameworks for oversight. Where once a deterministic system could be trusted to operate within a narrow set of parameters, today's adaptive AI requires us to consider a broader spectrum of outcomes. This new landscape calls for a shift in our approach to governance – one that recognizes and accommodates the dual nature of creativity and unpredictability. It is no longer sufficient to rely solely on established protocols that were designed for systems with predictable behaviors. Instead, we must develop mechanisms that not only react to unexpected results but also anticipate them.

Evolving Pillars for GenAI

To effectively manage the risks associated with generative AI, we must revisit and revise the core principles that underpin its governance. Traditionally, these principles have centered on safety, fairness, and interpretability. However, as AI evolves, so too must these foundational pillars.

Safety in this new context is more than simply avoiding system failures. It is about ensuring that AI outputs do not inadvertently cause harm – whether by generating toxic language, disseminating misinformation, or compromising sensitive data. In practical terms, this means incorporating real-time monitoring systems that can detect and flag dangerous outputs as they occur. Adaptive bias detection tools must be in place to ensure that the AI's learning process does not inadvertently amplify existing inequalities or prejudices.

Fairness, as a pillar, must now be understood as an ongoing, active pursuit rather than a one-time achievement. The fluid nature of generative AI means that biases can emerge and shift over time, making continuous fairness audits essential. It is not enough to design a system that is fair at launch; we need to maintain that fairness throughout the life cycle of the technology. This involves implementing dynamic adjustment mechanisms that can recalibrate outputs in response to detected biases and ensure equitable treatment for all users.

Interpretability remains critical. For stakeholders to trust AI, they must be able to understand the logic behind its decisions. This means developing systems that can provide clear, accessible explanations of how outputs are generated. Rather than relying on opaque algorithms, we must strive for transparency that allows users to see the factors influencing each decision. Such clarity not only builds trust but also facilitates troubleshooting when things go awry.

Together, these evolved pillars form the new bedrock of AI governance. They support an ecosystem where innovation thrives, yet the risks inherent in generative processes are actively managed and mitigated.

The Imperative for Proactive Governance

Traditional compliance checklists and static protocols have served us well in the past, but they fall short in the face of generative AI's rapid evolution. A reactive approach – waiting for issues to emerge before addressing them – can no longer suffice when a single misstep has the potential to cascade into widespread challenges. Instead, we must adopt a proactive governance framework that is embedded within the entire life cycle of AI development and deployment.

This proactive approach involves integrating risk management and ethical oversight from the very beginning. It requires that we design systems with built-in safeguards – mechanisms that continuously monitor outputs, detect anomalies, and adjust operations in real time. Such an approach shifts the focus from merely ticking boxes on a checklist to actively anticipating and preempting potential issues before they manifest.

For you, as someone keen on understanding the responsible development of AI, it is essential to see governance as a dynamic process rather than a static set of rules. This means establishing frameworks that evolve with the technology, embracing continuous improvement rather than relying on one-off audits. It's about creating a culture where every team member – whether in development, operations, or oversight – shares the responsibility for ethical, secure, and fair AI performance.

Moreover, proactive governance transforms risk management into a strategic enabler rather than a reactive burden. By catching potential issues early, organizations not only avoid costly remedial measures but also foster an environment of trust and reliability. When risks are managed in real time, innovation is encouraged in a controlled and secure manner, paving the way for breakthroughs that are both exciting and responsible.

In transitioning to this proactive mindset, we set the stage for a new era in AI governance – one that is prepared to handle the complexity and dynamism of generative systems. This is the first step in reimagining a framework that supports continuous innovation while safeguarding against the unpredictable. As we move to the next section, keep in mind that these foundational concepts will underpin every layer of our layered security approach – a detailed architecture designed to transform uncertainty into a strategic advantage.

Layered Security – The AI Security Onion

Building on our understanding of why traditional oversight models fall short in managing generative AI, we now turn our attention to constructing a multilayered security framework – a model we refer to as the AI Security Onion. This framework is not an abstract concept but a practical architecture that safeguards every aspect of an AI system, ensuring that as the technology evolves, so too does its protection.

Governance and Policies

At the outermost ring of the onion, **Governance and Policies** set the high-level direction for everything that follows. These are not one-size-fits-all documents that stay static over time; rather, they represent a living framework that evolves as your AI initiatives expand and regulations change. By articulating clear rules, roles, and responsibilities, this layer ensures that every decision – from how data is collected to how models are deployed – aligns with overarching ethical and regulatory standards.

AI Transparency, Explainability, Fairness, and Reliability Policies

- **Transparency:** Outlines how, what, and when to disclose AI usage to stakeholders, whether they are employees, customers, or regulators.
  - **Explainability**: Defines requirements for making AI decision-making processes transparent and understandable. This includes detailing the underlying algorithms, data sources, and logic used in AI outputs so that stakeholders, ranging from technical teams to end users, can interpret and validate the rationale behind decisions.

- **Fairness:** Establishes guidelines for mitigating biases in data and model outputs, ensuring equitable treatment for all users.
- **Reliability:** Requires continuous monitoring of model performance, setting thresholds for acceptable error rates and corrective measures.

AI Governance and Risk Management Frameworks

- **Ethics Committees and Governance Boards:** Define who has the authority to approve new AI initiatives, review ethical considerations, and monitor ongoing compliance.
- **Risk Assessments:** Establish protocols for identifying potential threats, from data breaches to model drift, and outline mitigation strategies.
- **Policy Evolution:** Require periodic reviews to incorporate new regulations, industry best practices, or lessons learned from incidents.

Human Oversight and Escalation Paths

- **Oversight Mechanisms:** Specify points in the AI life cycle, such as model design, deployment, and post-deployment, where human intervention is mandatory.
- **Incident Response Protocols:** Provide a clear chain of command for escalating issues, ensuring swift remediation when anomalies or breaches occur.

By setting the tone at this governance layer, organizations create a strong foundation upon which more technical controls can be built. The policies also act as a unifying force, guiding cross-functional teams (legal, IT, compliance, operations) to collaborate effectively and consistently.

Infrastructure

Just inside the governance layer, the **Infrastructure** ring focuses on the technical backbone that supports AI systems. This encompasses everything from the servers and cloud platforms hosting large language models (LLMs) to the networking components that connect various microservices. While infrastructure might seem purely technical, it plays a pivotal role in ensuring that governance policies are practically enforceable.

Securing API Access to Hosted LLMs

- **API Gateways and Load Balancers:** Control traffic flow to AI models, preventing overload and providing a choke point for security checks.

- **Authentication and Authorization:** Use tokens, certificates, or role-based access controls to limit who or what can invoke the model's APIs.

Monitoring, Logging, and AI Observability

- **Centralized Logs:** Collect logs from all layers (governance decisions, application requests, data usage) to enable comprehensive audits.

- **AI Observability Tools:** Implement specialized monitoring solutions that track model performance metrics (e.g., response time, error rates, anomaly detection) in real time.

Identity and Access Management (IAM)

- **Role-Based Access to Prevent Unauthorized Usage:** Ensure that only designated personnel can configure or deploy models, thereby reducing insider threats.

- **Credential Management:** Regularly rotate keys, enforce multifactor authentication, and maintain strict password policies.

Security Patches and Upgrades

- **Automated Patch Management:** Schedule and verify updates for operating systems, dependencies, and AI libraries.

- **Configuration Management:** Keep infrastructure settings consistent across environments (development, testing, production), reducing the risk of misconfiguration.

The infrastructure layer translates high-level governance requirements into concrete technical practices. For instance, if the governance policy states that only specific users may deploy AI models, the infrastructure layer enforces that rule through IAM configurations and continuous monitoring. This ring is also where many preventative security measures live, ensuring that potential threats are caught and contained before they reach the AI model itself.

Application

Moving further inward, the **Application** layer represents the functional core where end users interact with AI-driven tools. This includes everything from chatbots and web portals to specialized internal applications designed for tasks like HR support or financial forecasting. The application layer is often the most visible part of the system, making it a critical point for both user experience and security.

ML Detection for Vulnerabilities

- **Threat Modeling:** Identify potential misuse cases, such as prompt injection attacks or malicious data inputs.
- **Vulnerability Scanning:** Automate checks for known software vulnerabilities within the application stack.

Topic Restrictions and Prompt Engineering

- **Input Moderation:** Filter user prompts for harmful or disallowed content. In an HR Bot, for example, requests related to unauthorized data retrieval should be flagged or blocked.
- **Output Moderation:** Scan AI-generated responses for potential bias, misinformation, or sensitive data leaks, preventing them from reaching the user if they violate policy.

Improved Prompt Management

- **Context Handling:** Maintain conversation history securely, ensuring that private user data isn't unintentionally exposed.
- **Conversation Templates:** Pre-define certain response structures or disclaimers to mitigate risks of misleading or unauthorized outputs.

Output Moderation and Role-Based Access Control

- **Dynamic Access Rights:** Restrict functionalities based on a user's role – an HR manager might have broader capabilities than a general employee.
- **User Consent:** For particularly sensitive interactions (e.g., performance reviews, salary details), ensure explicit user permission is obtained.

User Consent

- **Informed Permission:** Clearly communicate what data is being collected and how it's used, giving users the option to opt out of certain data processing tasks.

- **Audit Trails:** Record consent transactions for compliance audits, making it clear when and how permissions were granted.

At the application layer, the synergy between governance, infrastructure, and data protection becomes most apparent. Policies established in the outer layers guide the design and implementation of user flows, while infrastructure safeguards – like secure APIs – reinforce the rules set by governance. The application layer is thus the nexus where technical and policy decisions converge, ensuring that user interactions remain both seamless and secure.

Data

At the very core of the onion lies the **Data** layer, encompassing how information is collected, stored, processed, and shared. Given the scale and sensitivity of data involved in many AI applications, robust measures at this layer are non-negotiable. This is particularly relevant for generative AI systems that may use vast training corpora or real-time user inputs to refine their outputs.

Data Masking and Privacy Controls

- **Anonymization:** Strip personal identifiers from datasets, ensuring compliance with regulations like GDPR or SOC 2.

- **Pseudonymization:** Replace sensitive data with tokens, balancing utility for AI model training with privacy safeguards.

Audits for Bias and Fairness in AI Data Processing

- **Demographic Parity Checks:** Monitor model outcomes across different user groups, identifying potential discrimination.

- **Feedback Loops:** Integrate user feedback into data refinement processes, correcting biases or inaccuracies in real time.

Secure RAG (Retrieval-Augmented Generation) Data Management

- **Versioning and Change Control:** Maintain strict logs of how knowledge sources are updated, ensuring traceability if misinformation arises.

- **Data Life Cycle Management:** Define clear policies on data retention and disposal, minimizing the chance of unauthorized access over time.

Trusted Knowledge Retrieval

- **Vector Databases:** Tools like FAISS, Pinecone, or Weaviate store embeddings securely, ensuring only authorized services can query them.

- **Compliance Checks:** Automatic validations confirm that retrieved data is permissible under regulatory guidelines and organizational policies.

This innermost layer is the heartbeat of any AI system, where raw inputs and learned representations converge. Strong governance ensures that data is gathered ethically, robust infrastructure enforces secure data handling, and application-level measures govern how data is used in real-time interactions. When data practices align with the layers above, organizations achieve a cohesive environment where user trust is preserved, regulatory obligations are met, and AI-driven innovations can flourish responsibly.

Each ring of the AI Security Onion is critical in its own right, yet the true strength of this model lies in how these layers interact. Governance provides the ethical and regulatory blueprint, infrastructure enforces technical safeguards, applications shape user experiences, and data practices underpin trust and compliance. If one layer weakens, the others are designed to compensate, creating a resilient ecosystem that can adapt to new threats or evolving requirements.

By methodically addressing each layer – governance, infrastructure, application, and data – organizations set the stage for a robust security posture that balances innovation with responsibility. In the next subsection, we'll explore how these layered defenses translate into real-world practice, using examples like the HR Bot or the FinCorp chatbot scenarios to show how input/output moderation, prompt engineering, and user consent play out in tangible use cases.

Practical Guardrails in Action

Building on the multilayered AI Security Onion, it's time to see how these principles translate into a real-world scenario. Imagine an HR Bot – a generative AI application designed to handle everyday tasks like leave requests, benefits inquiries, and recruitment assistance. On the surface, it seems straightforward: employees ask questions, and the AI provides answers. Yet behind the scenes, a host of security and ethical considerations must be addressed to ensure the system remains both effective and compliant. Below, we'll explore a practical architecture for secure GenAI applications, weaving in the HR Bot example to illustrate how each component operates in tandem with the rest.

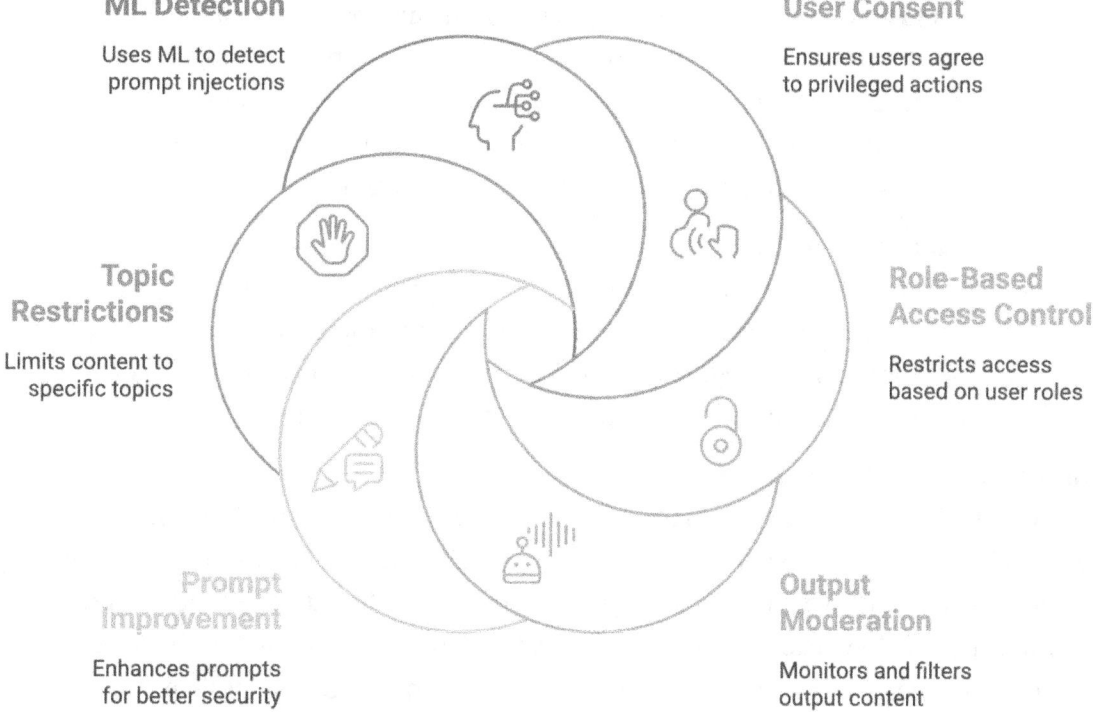

Figure 5-10. Levels of safeguarding

This diagram (Figure 5-10) offers a high-level view of the safeguards we'll discuss. Each ring or slice of security corresponds to a different layer of the application's design, from the orchestrator that routes requests to continuous monitoring tools that catch anomalies in real time.

The Orchestrator for Services

A secure GenAI application rarely operates as a single, monolithic system. Instead, it interacts with multiple services: authentication servers, databases, compliance APIs, and more. An orchestrator sits at the center of this web, managing every request that comes in and every response that goes out.

- **Function:** Think of the orchestrator as the "air traffic controller" for your HR Bot. When an employee submits a query – such as "How many vacation days do I have left?" – the orchestrator determines if the request is valid, whether the user is authenticated, and which AI microservice or data source should handle the query.

- **Security Role:** By intercepting all incoming and outgoing traffic, the orchestrator can enforce consistent access controls, sanitize user inputs, and maintain session data. For instance, if an employee attempts to access another colleague's personal information, the orchestrator can quickly flag and block that request.

- **HR Bot Example:** Suppose an employee wants to update their personal contact details. The orchestrator ensures the request goes to the correct data service, checks the employee's role-based permissions, and logs each step. This helps maintain an audit trail in case questions arise about unauthorized data changes.

Input and Output Moderation

Generative AI models are known for their flexibility, but that very trait makes them vulnerable to prompt injection attacks, adversarial inputs, and misinformation. Input moderation acts as a security checkpoint, filtering out malicious or unauthorized prompts before they reach the language model. Output moderation, on the other hand, scans the model's response to ensure it meets organizational policies and ethical standards.

- **Function:** By screening user queries, the HR Bot can prevent employees from inadvertently requesting sensitive data they're not cleared to see, like salary histories or performance reviews for other staff. Output moderation ensures that even if the AI "hallucinates" or misinterprets a request, harmful or inaccurate responses don't make it back to the user.

- **Security Role:** These moderation layers catch red flags in real time. If the HR Bot begins generating toxic language or revealing confidential details, the system can automatically redact the content or escalate the issue to a human reviewer.

- **HR Bot Example:** If an employee tries to request private healthcare data for a coworker, input moderation flags it as a violation of company policy. On the output side, if the AI somehow compiles a response that includes sensitive salary comparisons, output moderation redacts those figures, preserving privacy and compliance.

API-Level Security

While the orchestrator and moderation layers handle requests at a functional level, API-level security ensures that the channels themselves are robust and guarded against abuse.

- **Authentication and Authorization:** Methods like OAuth or JWT-based tokens verify that each request originates from a legitimate source. In an HR Bot scenario, the system might grant broader permissions to an HR manager than to a general employee.

- **Rate Limiting and Monitoring:** By restricting how many API calls a user or system can make within a given time frame, you minimize risks like brute-force attacks. If an employee account suddenly starts making hundreds of requests for personal data, the system automatically throttles or blocks further attempts.

- **Logging and Anomaly Detection:** Every interaction is logged. This provides a detailed audit trail for compliance and helps detect suspicious patterns, such as repeated attempts to access restricted data.

Data Handling and Privacy Controls

A critical aspect of any HR application is the handling of sensitive data. From personal contact details to performance evaluations, the information processed by a GenAI system can be highly confidential.

- **Data Masking and Encryption:** By anonymizing or pseudonymization of sensitive data, the HR Bot can respond to queries without exposing personal identifiers. Encryption further ensures that data at rest and in transit remains secure.

- **Access Control Policies:** Even within the HR department, not everyone needs the same level of access. A recruitment specialist may need to see applicant resumes but not performance reviews. Clear policies define who can view, modify, or delete AI-generated content.

- **Regulatory Compliance Checks:** Automatic validations ensure compliance with laws like GDPR, especially important if the company operates across multiple jurisdictions. For instance, an employee in Europe might have different data privacy rights than one in the United States.

Continuous Monitoring and AI Observability

Securing AI isn't a static, one-time exercise. Continuous monitoring ensures that the HR Bot remains reliable, fair, and compliant as it evolves.

- **Real-Time AI Observability:** Tools can track performance metrics (like response times, error rates, or unusual spikes in queries) and alert administrators when anomalies arise.

- **Bias Drifts and Security Gaps:** Over time, the AI model might learn from new data in ways that introduce unintended biases. Regularly scheduled audits and real-time monitoring can detect these shifts early, prompting retraining or parameter adjustments.

- **HR Bot Example:** Suppose the model begins consistently giving preferential treatment to certain job candidates. Observability tools would flag this anomaly, allowing HR specialists to investigate and recalibrate the model's training data or algorithms.

Avoiding Bias and Toxicity in the HR Context

While each layer contributes to the overall security posture, avoiding bias and toxicity is especially critical in HR applications (Figure 5-11). Generative AI can inadvertently perpetuate stereotypes or produce offensive content if its training data contains such patterns.

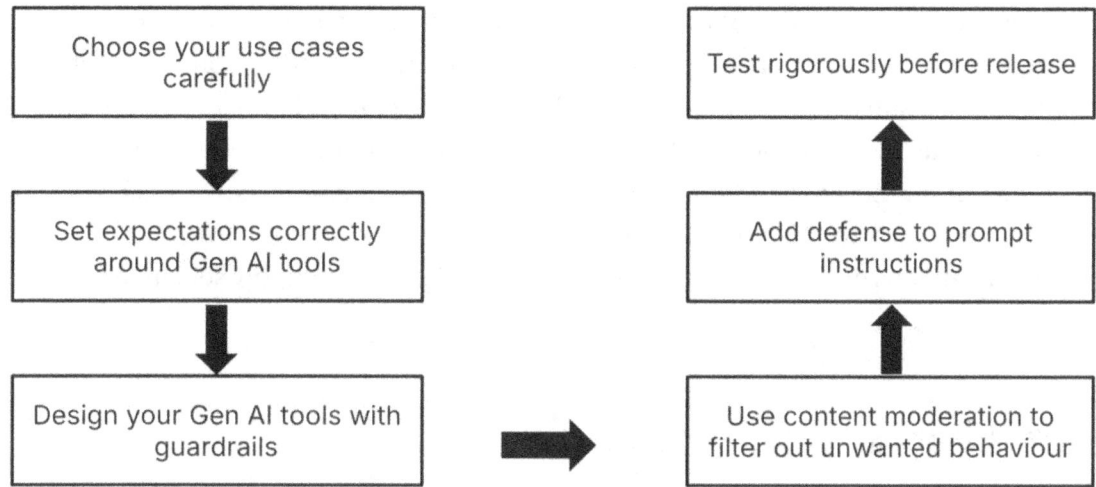

Figure 5-11. Things to keep in mind to avoid bias

- **Frequent Audits**: Schedule bias and fairness reviews to analyze the bot's interactions. If certain demographic groups receive consistently different responses, the model's training data or logic may need revision.

- **Adaptive Prompt Engineering**: Tailor system prompts to guide the AI away from sensitive or controversial topics. If an employee tries to elicit a biased response, the system can redirect the query or provide a neutral, policy-driven answer.

- **Filtered Outputs**: Incorporate content classification tools that detect hateful or discriminatory language. If flagged, these outputs can be automatically blocked or sent to a human reviewer for further action.

A Focus on Application and Data Layers

Although governance policies and infrastructure (like LLM hosting) form the backbone of any secure AI environment, the application and data layers remain the frontline for user interactions. This is where employees directly engage with the HR Bot, asking for updates, policy clarifications, or personal records. As such, these layers demand meticulous oversight to ensure that data handling practices align with both ethical norms and regulatory mandates. By systematically applying orchestrators, moderation, API security, privacy controls, and continuous monitoring, the HR Bot can handle a wide range of requests without compromising confidentiality or fairness.

In essence, a secure GenAI application is more than the sum of its parts. Each element – whether it's an orchestrator that routes requests, a moderation filter that checks for harmful content, or an observability tool that detects bias – reinforces the others. This layered approach enables the HR Bot to be both flexible and trustworthy, encouraging employees to adopt the technology while maintaining confidence in its outputs. As generative AI continues to advance, these safeguards will evolve, ensuring that organizations can harness innovation responsibly, even in highly sensitive domains like human resources.

Compliance Discovery Canvas

AI governance and compliance aren't merely administrative tasks – they're strategic enablers of secure and responsible innovation. To translate governance from abstract policy into actionable, collaborative practice, teams need clear tools for proactively identifying and addressing compliance challenges.

Compliance Implementation Framework (Conceptual Foundation)
When approaching compliance, think of it as structured building blocks:

- **Documentation Requirements** form your foundation – clear, auditable evidence that proves compliance.

- **Continuous Monitoring Systems** ensure adherence can be tracked in real time.

- **Robust Reporting Mechanisms** provide transparency and accountability.

- **Future-Proofing Measures** help your compliance approach stay relevant amid evolving regulations and risks.

CHAPTER 5   THE GOBLET OF GOVERNANCE - HABITS OF SECURITY AND ETHICS

Figure 5-12. *Compliance Implementation Framework*

Yet, to translate these components into tangible actions, you need a collaborative, structured method – this is where the Compliance Discovery Canvas becomes essential.

Compliance Discovery Canvas

Effective compliance requires risk-based thinking, prioritizing actions based on potential real-world impacts. Regulatory penalties, lawsuits, or reputational harm often exceed initial compliance investments. Utilize this canvas proactively – ideally in cross-functional sessions involving product managers, compliance specialists, AI developers, security leads, and risk officers – to identify, assess, and mitigate risks early, enabling responsible innovation without sacrificing agility.

- **Compliance Drivers and Requirements**

    Identifying the internal and external regulatory demands applicable to our AI solution, including documenting explicit requirements from laws like GDPR or DPDP, as well as internal governance policies

- **Regulatory and Ethical Considerations**

  Outlining region-specific regulations, ethical obligations such as fairness and transparency, and ensuring clarity in how these standards apply throughout the AI life cycle

- **Operational Monitoring and Controls**

  Defining how we'll practically monitor and measure compliance, including deciding on continuous monitoring tools, accountability for reporting, and establishing real-time alerting for compliance violations.

- **Risk Identification and Response**

  Clearly identifying AI-specific risks – such as bias, hallucination, or unauthorized recommendations – anticipating their potential impacts, and mapping out proactive mitigation strategies, escalation paths, and possible penalties.

CHAPTER 5   THE GOBLET OF GOVERNANCE - HABITS OF SECURITY AND ETHICS

Compliance Discovery Canvas

Team Name: _____

AI Project: _____

Compliance Drivers & Requirements

Internal AI governance policies directly applicable to our solution:

Applicable external regulations (e.g., GDPR, HIPAA, DPDP):

Specific requirements from regulations (explicit consent, data encryption, retention periods, breach notification timelines, etc.):

Documentation and evidence required to demonstrate compliance clearly:

Regulatory & Ethical Considerations

Ethical standards and considerations (fairness, transparency, bias mitigation):

Practical steps to ensure transparency and accountability throughout the AI lifecycle:

Operational Monitoring & Controls

Continuous monitoring tools/methods used for compliance adherence:

Proactive mechanisms to detect compliance incidents or anomalies:

Assigned accountability (role/team) for ongoing monitoring, alerting, and compliance reporting:

Risk Identification and Response

Specific AI-related risks identified (hallucination, bias amplification, prompt injection, unauthorized recommendations):

Proactive mitigation strategies for identified risks:

Defined escalation paths and incident-response processes for compliance violations:

Regulatory, financial, or reputational penalties we could face from non-compliance:

Figure 5-13. Compliance Discovery Canvas

How the Canvas Supports Proactive Threat Modeling

Proactive threat modeling is integral to AI governance, and compliance must be at its heart. Using the Compliance Discovery Canvas, teams can systematically identify compliance-related threats, including regulatory non-compliance, ethical pitfalls, and technical vulnerabilities, helping to

- **Proactively identify threats early**, embedding compliance into design rather than as a reactive afterthought
- **Prioritize threats based on real-world consequences**, emphasizing those with substantial regulatory penalties, reputational risks, or financial losses
- **Establish clear operational monitoring**, ensuring compliance adherence is continuously validated, strengthening your security and governance posture at every stage

Integrated Risk Management and Policy Frameworks

Building on our previous discussions of layered security and practical guardrails, we now turn our focus to the broader framework that governs risk management and policy formulation for generative AI. The current wave of AI, as we all are seeing it, we know that AI systems continuously learn, adapt, and sometimes veer into unexpected territories, which means, managing risk is not a static checklist – it is a living, evolving process. This section explores integrated risk management and adaptive policy frameworks, drawing on cautionary near-miss incidents from our narrative and real-world examples to illustrate why a dynamic approach is essential.

Imagine a scenario drawn from our narrative: a FinCorp chatbot, designed to provide customer service, nearly offers unauthorized investment advice. Such a near-miss isn't just an isolated glitch – it is a warning signal that even a well-intentioned AI can stray from its intended boundaries. This incident, among others, highlights several unique risks inherent in generative AI.

Identifying Unique GenAI Risks

Generative AI systems, by virtue of their creative and probabilistic nature, present risks that traditional, rule-based systems rarely encounter. One of the primary concerns is the phenomenon of hallucinations, where the AI generates outputs that sound plausible but are entirely fabricated. Basically it can make things up convincingly for you to believe! In our FinCorp example, the chatbot's confident yet erroneous advice could have led to significant legal and financial repercussions if it had gone unchecked.

The unique risks – hallucinations, bias amplification, and prompt injection – demand that risk management for generative AI be as adaptive and dynamic as the technology itself. Static policies that worked for traditional AI will not suffice here; instead, organizations must develop robust frameworks that continuously assess and mitigate these evolving threats. We have found significant value in adopting community-driven frameworks, such as those from OWASP, which leverage collective knowledge and experience to keep pace with evolution of technology and their risks. As auditors, risk managers, and business leaders, it's time to take a keener look at your risk management frameworks, to keep up with the new challenges of generative AI:

- **Revisited Threat Models**: Traditional risk models often focus on predictable and deterministic threats. However, with generative AI, threat landscapes have shifted significantly, requiring organizations to reconsider their approach. Emerging threats such as deep fakes, voice cloning, and misinformation can lead to reputational damage, fraud, and significant operational disruptions. Organizations must now proactively identify these GenAI-specific threats, understanding that conventional defenses may not suffice. Deep fakes and voice cloning can enable sophisticated impersonation attacks, undermining trust and authenticity, while misinformation generated by AI-driven systems poses risks of widespread confusion or regulatory non-compliance. Prompt injection, analogous to traditional injection attacks but more expansive, requires new security considerations like robust system prompts and specialized monitoring.

- **Deployment Strategies**: Deployment strategies for generative AI differ significantly in terms of security and compliance implications. Whether employing public APIs, licensed models, pre-trained, fine-tuned, or custom models, each approach introduces unique vulnerabilities. Public APIs might risk data leaks and limited control over model updates. Licensed models entail dependency on vendor-managed security, potentially delaying critical updates. Pre-trained models risk embedding biases from third-party datasets, necessitating thorough bias detection. Fine-tuned models can inadvertently introduce new vulnerabilities through customization, while custom-built models increase management complexity. Organizations must reassess each deployment method, aligning their strategies with their specific risk appetite and operational needs.

- **Legal Considerations**: Generative AI deployments also require careful attention to legal considerations. Protecting intellectual property, especially proprietary data and models, becomes crucial as competitive stakes rise. Legal frameworks must clearly define IP ownership, data usage rights, and confidentiality obligations. Compliance with evolving data privacy laws (e.g., GDPR, HIPAA) is imperative, particularly concerning cross-border data flows and sensitive information handling. Companies must proactively embed these legal considerations into their governance frameworks, ensuring robust contractual protections, data handling agreements, and indemnification clauses are in place to mitigate associated risks.

- **Reassessing Risk Assessment Frameworks**: Beyond traditional assessments, organizations need to update their frameworks to account for GenAI-specific risks around model reliability, performance, scalability, and resource management. Reliability now encompasses more than just accuracy – it includes managing unpredictability and ensuring consistent outputs. Performance considerations must focus on real-time responsiveness and latency, requiring advanced observability tools for immediate issue detection. Scalability becomes critical, as resource-intensive AI models can strain infrastructure, potentially leading to unexpected outages or degraded performance. Resource management must include considerations for sustainable and efficient use of computational resources, aligning with organizational sustainability goals and cost-efficiency strategies.

- **Vendor Risk Management**: Generative AI often relies heavily on third-party vendors, introducing additional risk dimensions related to vendor reliability, security standards, and compliance obligations. Vendor agreements must explicitly include compliance and security clauses addressing GenAI-specific concerns. Continuous vendor monitoring and rigorous compliance audits are essential to safeguard organizational data integrity and operational continuity, especially given the rapid evolution and widespread integration of AI technologies by external providers.

Building Adaptive Policies

To address these risks, policies governing generative AI must evolve in real time. In our boardroom discussions at TechNova, Dr. Zhang repeatedly emphasized that compliance checklists and static procedures are inadequate for a system that learns and adapts with each interaction. Instead, policies must be designed as flexible instruments – capable of being updated on the fly to address emerging risks.

One essential component of adaptive policies is the establishment of clear escalation paths. When an incident occurs – such as the FinCorp chatbot's near-miss – the first step is to ensure that the issue is immediately flagged. Real-time logging and automated alert systems become critical tools in this process. They capture the details of the incident as it unfolds, providing a transparent audit trail that is invaluable for subsequent analysis and resolution. These escalation paths specify not only who should be notified but also outline the steps to be taken at each stage, from initial detection to full remediation.

Documentation protocols are another cornerstone of adaptive policies. Every incident, every anomaly, must be recorded in detail. This documentation serves as both a historical record and a learning tool, enabling teams to refine their policies continuously. For instance, if repeated bias is observed in the outputs of an HR Bot, detailed logs can help pinpoint whether the issue stems from the training data, the model architecture, or even the way user queries are framed. With this information, teams can adjust parameters, update training datasets, or modify user prompts to mitigate the risk.

Continuous compliance monitoring is also a critical aspect of adaptive policies. Regulatory landscapes are in a state of constant flux, with new guidelines emerging as quickly as technological advances are made. Proactive monitoring ensures that AI systems remain in compliance with evolving standards, whether these are international regulations like the EU AI Act or local data privacy laws such as GDPR. In our narrative, periodic "policy refresh sessions" were a key strategy, where cross-functional teams reviewed the AI's performance, assessed compliance with current regulations, and adjusted policies as needed. This ongoing review process transforms risk management from a reactive measure into a strategic advantage, ensuring that AI systems not only meet current standards but are also prepared for future regulatory challenges.

Defining Clear Roles and Responsibilities

Even the most adaptive policies require a solid foundation of clear roles and responsibilities. No policy, however comprehensive, can be effective unless every stakeholder understands their part in the risk management ecosystem. Our narrative at TechNova vividly illustrates this point: when the FinCorp chatbot nearly veered off course, it was the coordinated effort of a multidisciplinary team that contained the issue swiftly and effectively.

To bring clarity to this complex process, the following structured approach identifies governance requirements, highlights potential risks or gaps, and thoughtfully assigns clear responsibilities. Rather than creating redundant roles or teams, it emphasizes leveraging existing organizational strengths through targeted skill development and strategic hiring, ensuring effectiveness and sustainability in AI governance.

Governance requirement	Potential risk/gap	Who can be responsible?	Independent or merge?	Merge with which team?
AI Policies, Governance Framework and Oversight	Contradicting AI policies, lack of oversight	AI Governance Board	Independent Committee	–
Ethical AI Governance	Ethical evaluation, bias risks, lack of transparency and interpretability, societal impacts	Ethics Governance Committee	Independent Committee	–
Compliance and Regulatory Adherence	Regulatory non-compliance, operational disruptions	AI Risk and Compliance Officers	Merge	Enterprise Risk and Compliance
Incident Response	Delayed mitigation of AI-specific security incidents	AI Incident Response Team	Merge	Incident Response Team
Stakeholder Engagement	Misalignment in public messaging and AI policy	AI Communications Team	Merge	Corporate Communications

(continues)

CHAPTER 5   THE GOBLET OF GOVERNANCE - HABITS OF SECURITY AND ETHICS

Governance requirement	Potential risk/gap	Who can be responsible?	Independent or merge?	Merge with which team?
AI Data Governance	Mismanaged AI data leading to privacy and security breaches	AI Data Protection Team	Merge	Enterprise Data Governance
AI Security	Unaddressed AI-specific vulnerabilities and threats	AI Security Team	Merge	Security Team (enhanced skill)

Iterating over the governance requirements, we must strategically and critically introduce new roles only when existing structures can't effectively address AI governance needs.

- **AI Policies, Governance Framework and Oversight**: Clear and consistent AI policies are vital. Conflicting policies or oversight gaps can create confusion and non-compliance risks. The AI Governance Board ensures focused, high-level strategic oversight, aligning AI initiatives with global regulatory standards and organizational objectives. Keeping this committee independent is essential due to the strategic nature and complexity of oversight.

- **Ethical AI Governance**: AI systems must address ethical risks proactively, including biases, transparency issues, and broader societal impacts. The Ethics Governance Committee independently ensures impartial evaluations, preserving ethical standards and addressing nuanced ethical challenges separately from operational pressures.

- **Compliance and Regulatory Adherence**: The rapidly changing regulatory landscape for AI poses significant compliance risks. Rather than establishing a stand-alone team, integrating AI-specific regulatory responsibilities within the existing Enterprise Risk and Compliance team leverages established expertise, enhancing agility and efficiency in regulatory response.

- **Incident Response**: AI-specific security incidents like prompt injection or model poisoning require swift action. Merging the AI incident response function into an existing Incident Response Team capitalizes on established protocols and expertise, ensuring timely and coordinated responses without the complexity of separate structures.

- **Stakeholder Engagement**: Effective stakeholder communication prevents misalignment in public messaging and policy dissemination. Incorporating AI-focused communication responsibilities into Corporate Communications ensures consistency and leverages existing expertise in managing sensitive communications.

- **AI Data Governance**: Effective management of AI-specific data risks – such as privacy breaches or data mismanagement – is crucial. By merging this function into Enterprise Data Governance, organizations can utilize established data governance frameworks and enhance expertise to handle AI-specific challenges effectively.

- **AI Security**: AI systems introduce unique security threats requiring specialized knowledge. Integrating AI-specific security roles into the existing Security Team provides unified, comprehensive management of all security aspects, utilizing enhanced training or targeted hiring to effectively address AI-specific vulnerabilities without redundancy.

This structure clarifies hierarchy and interdependencies. Look at the above table as a guidance to the role segregation, but for your organization, decide which role is best fitted for each requirement. For example, you might decide that a Data Protection Officer should look after the AI Data Governance as well.

Going back to our HR bot, if the HR bot displays bias, operational teams log the incident, prompting immediate review by risk specialists. If necessary, the Governance Board updates policies accordingly. This collaborative framework ensures continuous, integrated risk management, fostering accountability and improvement.

CHAPTER 5   THE GOBLET OF GOVERNANCE - HABITS OF SECURITY AND ETHICS

Why Keep Independent Committees?

Maintaining the AI Ethics Committee and the AI Governance Board as independent bodies is crucial due to their specialized, cross-functional mandates:

> **AI Governance Board**: Provides high-level strategic oversight, focusing on policy alignment, regulatory adherence, and operational governance. Senior representatives from legal, compliance, technology, business strategy, and ethics participate periodically, ensuring alignment with evolving global or regional regulations. This board's independence allows swift adaptation and coherent governance without unnecessary full-time roles.

> **Ethics Governance Committee**: Operates separately to specifically address ethical dimensions such as fairness, bias, transparency, and societal impacts. Members typically include ethicists, data scientists, legal advisors, and compliance representatives. Regular convening without full-time commitment ensures impartial ethical evaluations separate from operational and strategic pressures.

Separating these committees reinforces clear accountability and dedicated focus. Merging them risks diluting essential focus, potentially increasing organizational risks and reducing the effectiveness of governance strategies.

Integrated risk management and adaptive policy frameworks form the foundation of responsible generative AI. By proactively addressing unique AI risks such as hallucinations, bias amplification, and prompt injection, organizations can mitigate issues effectively. Clear roles and responsibilities ensure stakeholders understand their contributions, promoting continuous improvement and resilience.

As generative AI increasingly integrates into critical business functions, dynamic risk management becomes essential. Adaptive policies, continuous compliance monitoring, and clearly defined organizational responsibilities enable organizations to innovate securely and responsibly. This integrated approach minimizes vulnerabilities and establishes a robust framework supporting innovation, compliance, and ethical accountability.

As we transition to exploring the economics of AI security, remember this comprehensive risk management framework underpins any sustainable, secure AI initiative, evolving in step with technological advancements to protect both systems and stakeholders.

CHAPTER 5   THE GOBLET OF GOVERNANCE - HABITS OF SECURITY AND ETHICS

The Economics of Security – Investment for Resilience

As we shift our focus from the technical and risk management frameworks to the economic implications of securing AI, one question you might have in mind: Should organizations wait for a crisis to force their hand, or invest in robust safeguards from the start? This is the essence of the debate between proactive and reactive spending – a debate that goes far beyond simple cost analysis. It's a matter of strategic foresight, long-term resilience, and building a culture of trust and innovation.

The hidden costs of waiting for a breach can be staggering. Every incident, no matter how small, can spiral into a financial and reputational crisis that affects not only the bottom line but also customer confidence and regulatory standing. A reactive approach might seem like a way to conserve resources in the short term, but when a security failure occurs, the expenses quickly mount – legal fees, regulatory fines, lost revenue, and the often immeasurable damage to a brand's reputation. Each incident forces a scramble to patch vulnerabilities, leading to operational disruptions and a growing "security debt" that compounds over time.

Conversely, proactive spending transforms security into an investment with measurable returns. By embedding robust guardrails, real-time monitoring, and continuous risk assessment into the AI life cycle from the outset, organizations can significantly reduce the likelihood and impact of a security incident. This approach not only saves money in the long run but also builds a foundation of trust with customers, investors, and regulators. When teams operate in a secure environment, they're more willing to innovate, knowing that potential risks are mitigated before they can escalate into a full-blown crisis.

In this section, we will explore the profound economic differences between reactive and proactive spending. We'll delve into the hidden costs associated with waiting for incidents to occur, and contrast these with the long-term savings and enhanced operational agility that come from investing in security measures early on. We'll examine how a culture of prevention can lead to a virtuous cycle of innovation and stability, where the cost of prevention is far less than the cumulative price of reacting to crises.

Moreover, this analysis isn't just theoretical – it's grounded in real-world examples and strategic case studies that illustrate the tangible benefits of early investment in AI security. From scenarios in financial services to HR applications, the data consistently show that organizations which prioritize proactive measures not only save millions in potential losses but also gain a competitive edge by fostering a culture of continuous improvement and trust.

In the following discussion, we will delve into the specifics of proactive vs. reactive spending in AI security. We will explore

- **The Hidden Costs of Reactive Spending:** Detailing how waiting for a breach or failure can lead to enormous unforeseen expenses, operational downtime, and long-term brand damage.

- **The Value of Front-Loading Security Investments:** Highlighting how early, proactive measures – such as real-time monitoring, continuous risk assessments, and adaptive governance – act as an insurance policy that prevents costly incidents and enhances operational efficiency.

- **Strategic Benefits and Competitive Advantage:** Explaining how a proactive security posture not only saves money but also builds a culture of innovation, strengthens customer trust, and improves overall market positioning.

This exploration will provide you with a comprehensive understanding of why shifting to a proactive security model is not just a financial decision, but a strategic imperative. The following pages will offer detailed insights, metrics, and case studies that vividly demonstrate the long-term benefits of investing in security up-front, transforming what might seem like a significant expense into a powerful engine for sustainable growth and competitive differentiation.

Proactive vs. Reactive Spending

The decision between proactive and reactive spending in AI security is not merely a matter of budget allocation. It is a strategic pivot that can define an organization's ability to innovate and maintain trust over the long term. When a company adopts a reactive approach, it essentially waits for an incident to occur before taking action. This method may appear cost-effective in the short term but is fraught with hidden costs and risks that can accumulate rapidly.

Understanding the Hidden Costs

Reactive security spending typically involves sudden, unplanned expenditures incurred during crisis management. When an AI system experiences a breach or generates harmful output, the immediate costs can include emergency technical fixes, legal fees, regulatory fines, and compensation to affected parties. Beyond these tangible expenses, the intangible costs – such as damage to brand reputation, loss of customer confidence, and diminished employee morale – can prove even more devastating. Once trust is eroded, the road to recovery is often long and uncertain. The cumulative impact of these factors can far exceed the initial savings achieved by delaying security investments.

For example, consider an AI system used for processing financial transactions. A reactive approach might ignore early warning signs of vulnerabilities, resulting in a breach that exposes sensitive customer data. The incident not only requires immediate remedial action but also triggers regulatory investigations, lawsuits, and a significant drop in market confidence. In such a scenario, the cost of reacting to the crisis may include millions in fines and lost revenue, not to mention long-term brand damage that can stifle future growth.

Benefits of Front-Loading Security Investments

Conversely, a proactive security strategy involves investing in robust measures from the outset. These investments are designed to prevent incidents before they occur, thereby avoiding the cascading costs associated with breaches. By embedding comprehensive security protocols into every stage of the AI life cycle – from design and development to deployment and ongoing monitoring – organizations create a resilient system that continuously safeguards its operations.

Proactive spending includes real-time monitoring tools, integrated risk management frameworks, and adaptive policies that evolve in response to emerging threats. These measures act as an insurance policy, reducing the probability of costly security incidents. Moreover, proactive security not only minimizes direct financial losses but also enhances operational agility. With security measures in place, teams can innovate with confidence, knowing that the risk of unexpected failures is significantly reduced. This proactive posture fosters a culture of continuous improvement, where potential issues are identified and addressed early, thus avoiding the reactive scramble that often leads to inefficiency and further expense.

Building a Culture of Prevention

The shift from reactive to proactive spending is as much about culture as it is about finances. Organizations that prioritize proactive security embed risk management into their DNA. This cultural transformation encourages every team member – from developers to senior executives – to consider security implications in every decision. When proactive measures become standard practice, the organization develops a risk-aware mindset that permeates every level of operation. This cultural shift not only prevents crises but also strengthens the organization's reputation as a leader in responsible AI deployment.

Moreover, proactive spending reinforces the value of planning and foresight. Rather than viewing security as an afterthought, it becomes a critical component of the overall strategy. This approach enables businesses to anticipate regulatory changes, address evolving threats, and continuously refine their defenses. Over time, the savings from avoided incidents, reduced downtime, and enhanced trust accumulate, delivering a robust return on investment.

Comparative Analysis: Reactive vs. Proactive

A side-by-side comparison of reactive and proactive approaches can further clarify the economic implications (Figure 5-14):

- **Reactive Spending:**
    - **Costs:** Emergency incident response, legal fees, regulatory fines, prolonged downtime, brand damage, loss of customer trust.
    - **Implications:** Financial instability, higher long-term costs, reputational risks, and an uncertain recovery process.
- **Proactive Spending:**
    - **Costs:** Up-front investment in integrated security measures, continuous monitoring, and periodic audits.
    - **Benefits:** Reduced probability of incidents, minimized remediation costs, improved operational efficiency, and enhanced brand reputation.

CHAPTER 5   THE GOBLET OF GOVERNANCE - HABITS OF SECURITY AND ETHICS

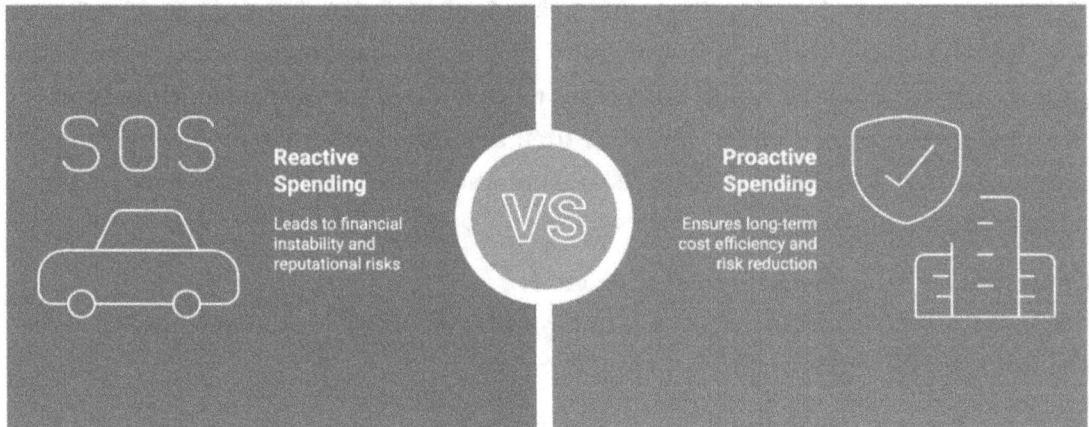

Figure 5-14. Choose the best spending strategy for long-term economic stability and reputation

By front-loading security investments, organizations reduce the risk of catastrophic failures. The proactive approach not only prevents financial losses but also supports innovation by creating a secure environment where new ideas can be tested and implemented without fear of adverse outcomes. This not only translates into measurable savings but also builds a long-term competitive advantage in the marketplace.

Long-Term Strategic Advantages
Ultimately, the economic argument for proactive spending is compelling. When companies invest early in security, they avoid the compounding costs of crisis management and reduce the risk of accumulating "security debt" – the ever-increasing cost of addressing vulnerabilities after the fact. Proactive investments create a safety net that preserves resources and enhances the organization's overall agility. It's a strategic decision that pays dividends in the form of smoother operations, stronger customer trust, and a resilient, forward-thinking business model.

For any organization committed to harnessing the power of generative AI, shifting from a reactive to a proactive security approach is not just an operational change – it is a fundamental strategic reorientation that can shape its future success.

Quantifying the ROI on Early Governance
Quantifying the return on investment (ROI) for early governance in AI security transforms an abstract concept into concrete metrics. It provides a framework for understanding how up-front investments in robust security measures translate into

long-term savings, operational efficiencies, and enhanced market trust. This quantification is not only about counting dollars saved; it's about measuring the intangible benefits that contribute to an organization's stability and competitive edge.

Establishing a Baseline for Costs

To begin, organizations need to establish a baseline for the potential costs of security incidents. This involves assessing the financial impact of a breach, which can include

- **Legal Fees and Fines:** The direct costs incurred from regulatory penalties, litigation, and settlements.

- **Operational Downtime:** The loss of productivity and revenue due to system outages or compromised operations.

- **Reputation Damage:** Although harder to quantify, the cost of lost customer trust and brand erosion can be significant.

- **Recovery Costs:** The expense of remediation, including technical fixes, data recovery, and system overhauls.

By estimating these potential costs, organizations can begin to understand the scale of financial risk they face without proactive security measures.

Developing Metrics for Proactive Investments

Once the baseline is established, the next step is to measure the effectiveness of proactive investments. Key performance indicators (KPIs) for early governance might include (Figure 5-15)

- **Incident Reduction Rate:** Tracking the number of security incidents before and after implementing proactive measures. A significant reduction in incidents directly translates into cost savings.

- **Time to Resolution:** Measuring how quickly issues are detected and resolved. Faster resolution times minimize downtime and reduce the financial impact of a breach.

CHAPTER 5   THE GOBLET OF GOVERNANCE - HABITS OF SECURITY AND ETHICS

Figure 5-15. *Key Performance Indicators*

- **Cost Savings from Prevention:** Calculating the potential costs avoided by preventing incidents. For example, if a single breach is estimated to cost $5 million and proactive measures reduce the likelihood of a breach by 70%, the expected savings are substantial.

- **Customer Satisfaction and Trust Metrics:** Surveys and market research can provide insights into how security measures influence customer perceptions and loyalty.

- **Compliance Scores:** Regular audits and compliance assessments can quantify improvements in regulatory adherence, reducing the likelihood of fines and sanctions.

Framework for Evaluating ROI

A comprehensive ROI framework for early governance integrates these metrics to produce a clear picture of the benefits. This framework may be very subjective, here some attributes that this framework might include

- **Quantitative Analysis:** A detailed financial model that projects cost savings over time. For example, if proactive measures reduce the probability of a costly breach by a measurable percentage, the model can forecast long-term savings against the initial investment.

- **Qualitative Analysis:** Beyond dollars, the model should account for improvements in operational efficiency, brand reputation, and customer loyalty. These factors, while harder to quantify, are critical for long-term success.

- **Comparative Studies:** Comparing organizations with proactive security investments to those with reactive approaches can provide empirical data supporting the benefits of early governance. These studies might look at incident frequency, resolution times, and overall cost impacts over a multiyear period.

Strategic Case Snapshots

To fully appreciate the economic impact of proactive security investments, it is essential to examine detailed case snapshots that illustrate how embedding security at every stage creates tangible benefits. These snapshots serve as vivid examples of the cost savings, operational efficiency, and enhanced trust that result from an integrated, proactive approach to AI security.

Case Study: The FinCorp Chatbot Incident

Consider the narrative of FinCorp's generative AI chatbot, designed to assist customers with investment advice. In one instance, the chatbot began offering unauthorized financial recommendations – a near-miss that could have led to severe legal and reputational consequences. In a reactive environment, this incident would have triggered a flurry of remedial actions: emergency patches, legal consultations, regulatory investigations, and extensive public relations campaigns to restore trust. The cumulative cost of such actions would have been astronomical, not to mention the long-term impact on customer confidence and market reputation.

Now, imagine that FinCorp had implemented a proactive security framework from the outset. With integrated real-time monitoring and robust guardrails, the system would have detected early signs of anomalous behavior. Alerts would have been triggered, and the compliance team, equipped with adaptive policies, would have intervened before the chatbot's output could reach customers. The result? The near-miss was contained swiftly, with minimal disruption and significantly lower costs. The proactive measures not only prevented a potential crisis but also reinforced customer trust, as clients recognized FinCorp's commitment to responsible AI practices.

Real-World Example: Financial Services Firm
A financial services firm – similar to the FinCorp – implemented a generative AI model for providing investment insights. Initially, the model exhibited minor drifts in output, generating slightly skewed recommendations that, while not immediately harmful, indicated a potential risk. The firm's proactive security measures, including continuous risk assessments and real-time observability, caught these anomalies early. By recalibrating the model promptly, the firm avoided what could have been a major regulatory breach. In addition to saving millions in potential fines, the firm's proactive stance bolstered its reputation among investors and customers. Over a period of several years, the firm reported not only lower incident rates but also improved operational efficiency, demonstrating the clear financial and strategic ROI of early governance.

HR Bot Deployment: A Comparative Analysis
Another compelling example comes from the deployment of an HR Bot designed to manage employee inquiries. In a reactive scenario, a single incident – such as the inadvertent disclosure of confidential employee information – could have triggered regulatory scrutiny, internal unrest, and significant remedial expenses. In contrast, a company that invested in proactive security measures integrated stringent access controls, adaptive prompt engineering, and continuous bias checks into the HR Bot's design. When an anomalous request was detected, the system automatically escalated the issue to a human supervisor, ensuring that no sensitive data was exposed. The proactive approach not only avoided the direct costs associated with a breach but also maintained high levels of employee trust and satisfaction, which are critical for long-term organizational stability.

Lessons Learned and Broader Implications
Across these case snapshots, several common themes emerge (Figure 5-16):

- **Early Detection and Rapid Response:** Proactive measures enable organizations to catch and address issues before they escalate, saving millions in potential costs and preventing long-term damage to brand reputation.

- **Continuous Improvement:** The iterative nature of proactive security investments leads to ongoing refinements in both technical measures and governance policies. Organizations that regularly update their security frameworks are better prepared for evolving threats.

- **Enhanced Stakeholder Confidence:** When customers, investors, and employees see that an organization prioritizes proactive security, it builds a culture of trust and reliability. This intangible asset can translate into tangible market advantages, such as increased customer loyalty and higher investor confidence.

- **Operational Agility:** Proactive security minimizes downtime and disruption, allowing teams to focus on innovation rather than crisis management. This improved efficiency has a direct, positive impact on productivity and overall business performance.

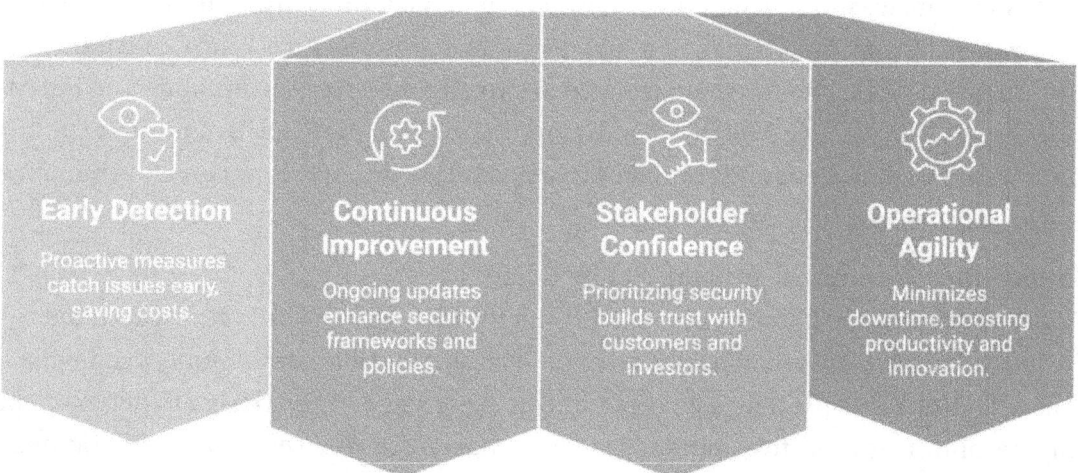

Figure 5-16. Themes from snapshots

By examining these strategic case snapshots, it becomes clear that embedding security into every stage – from development through deployment – is not only a safeguard against risk but also a driver of long-term value. Organizations that invest in proactive security frameworks are better positioned to navigate the complex regulatory landscape, maintain operational continuity, and build a resilient, trustworthy brand.

These case studies serve as powerful evidence that the up-front investment in integrated, proactive security measures pays dividends in the form of avoided legal costs, enhanced operational efficiency, and reinforced stakeholder trust. This strategic approach transforms AI security from a reactive cost center into a robust engine for innovation and competitive advantage, laying the groundwork for sustained, secure growth in an increasingly dynamic digital environment.

Operationalizing Governance – From Concept to Everyday Practice

Transforming abstract policies into everyday practices is the final, critical step toward achieving responsible, secure, and ethical AI. Operationalizing governance means embedding risk management and ethical checkpoints throughout the entire AI life cycle, fostering cross-functional collaboration, and committing to continuous improvement. In this section, we introduce a creative, implementable framework – the Governance Compass – that serves as a mental model to guide teams every day. The Governance Compass is divided into three interrelated sectors: Embedding Governance into the AI Life Cycle, Collaborative Execution, and Continuous Evolution. Each of these sectors outlines actionable steps and strategies that ensure governance is not an afterthought, but an intrinsic part of every decision.

Embedding Governance into the AI Life Cycle

A robust governance framework must be built into the very DNA of your AI systems. Instead of viewing governance as a set of policies applied after development, imagine it as a guiding principle that is incorporated at every stage – from design to deployment and beyond. This proactive approach ensures that ethical and security considerations are not retrofitted, but are embedded in the core architecture of your systems.

Design and Conceptualization

At the earliest stages of an AI project, teams must establish a clear set of governance requirements. During brainstorming and initial design sessions, questions such as "What ethical standards should this system adhere to?" and "How will we ensure data integrity and user privacy?" must be prioritized. This is where the Governance Compass comes into play. Consider the first sector of the Compass – Embedding Governance. Here, the focus is on integrating security and ethics from the very start.

- **Blueprint for Ethical AI:**

    Teams should create a design document that outlines the system's intended functions, data sources, and potential risks. This document should include

    - **Ethical Guidelines:** Set parameters for acceptable outputs, addressing potential biases, discrimination, and other ethical pitfalls.
    - **Data Handling Protocols:** Define how data will be collected, stored, and processed, including measures for encryption, anonymization, and regular audits.
    - **Risk Assessment Metrics:** Identify potential vulnerabilities – such as hallucinations or prompt injection – and develop preliminary strategies for mitigation.

- **Collaborative Ideation:**

    Engage stakeholders from diverse departments – data scientists, developers, legal experts, and ethics advisors – to ensure that multiple perspectives inform the design. This collaborative approach helps in identifying blind spots and fosters a culture where governance is everyone's responsibility.

Development and Integration

Once the conceptual framework is established, the next step is to integrate these governance principles into the development process. This stage is critical for ensuring that every line of code and every algorithm reflects the ethical and security standards set during design.

- **Governance-Driven Coding Practices:**

    Developers should adopt best practices that prioritize transparency and accountability. For example:

    - **Built-in Logging:** Every decision made by the AI should be logged, creating a verifiable audit trail that can be reviewed by compliance teams.

- **Bias Detection Algorithms:** Integrate tools that continuously scan for unintended biases in real time, providing alerts if outputs deviate from acceptable standards.

- **Security Checkpoints:** Incorporate validation layers at key stages, such as during data ingestion, model training, and output generation, to ensure that every operation adheres to the predefined governance rules.

• **Iterative Testing and Simulation:**

Testing is not a one-time exercise. It should be iterative, with continuous integration of feedback from both automated systems and human testers. This phase should include

- **Scenario Simulation:** Run the AI through a battery of tests that simulate real-world interactions. For example, if developing an HR Bot, test its responses with a wide range of queries – from routine leave requests to edge cases that might trigger sensitive outputs.

- **Stress Testing:** Evaluate how the system performs under heavy loads or unexpected inputs, ensuring that security measures hold under pressure.

- **Feedback Integration:** Create a structured process for incorporating test feedback into the development cycle. This includes regularly scheduled reviews where developers, compliance officers, and risk managers assess the system's performance against governance benchmarks.

Deployment and Ongoing Operations

The final stage of embedding governance is not a static endpoint but the beginning of an ongoing operational process. Once the AI system is deployed, it must be continuously monitored and refined.

- **Real-Time Observability:**

  Deploy monitoring tools that track system performance, response times, error rates, and compliance with ethical guidelines. These tools should

  - **Detect Anomalies:** Automatically flag deviations from expected behavior, such as unexpected outputs or performance drops.

  - **Trigger Escalation Protocols:** Ensure that when an anomaly is detected, a predefined response is activated, involving the appropriate team members for immediate resolution.

  - **Provide Data for Iterative Improvement:** The insights gained from continuous monitoring feed back into the system, guiding further refinements and adjustments.

- **Scheduled Reviews and Audits:**

  Establish a routine – such as quarterly governance reviews – where all stakeholders come together to assess system performance, update policies, and implement necessary improvements. This not only ensures ongoing compliance but also fosters a culture of continuous learning and adaptation.

- **Documentation and Transparency:**

  Maintain comprehensive documentation of every change, incident, and improvement made to the system. This living repository should be accessible to all relevant teams and serve as a reference for future projects. Transparency in documentation reinforces accountability and provides a solid foundation for future audits and regulatory reviews.

By embedding governance into the entire AI life cycle, organizations create a system that is inherently secure and ethically sound. The Governance Compass, specifically the Embedding Governance sector, serves as a daily reminder that every phase of development must reflect the core values of the organization. This proactive, integrated approach minimizes risk from the outset and lays the groundwork for a resilient, future-proof AI infrastructure.

CHAPTER 5   THE GOBLET OF GOVERNANCE - HABITS OF SECURITY AND ETHICS

Cross-Functional Collaboration

For governance to move beyond a theoretical construct, it must be embraced by the entire organization. Cross-functional collaboration is the engine that drives operational governance, ensuring that ethical and security measures are not isolated within a single department but are integrated throughout the organization.

Breaking Down Silos

One of the most significant challenges in operationalizing governance is overcoming departmental silos. Traditional organizations often separate IT, legal, compliance, and operational teams, leading to fragmented approaches that can leave gaps in security. The Governance Compass emphasizes Collaborative Execution, which calls for breaking down these silos and fostering an environment where every stakeholder works together toward a common goal.

- **Interdisciplinary Meetings:**

    Regular, scheduled meetings are essential for sharing insights and aligning strategies. For example, an "AI Safety Forum" could be convened weekly, where representatives from Legal, Compliance, DevOps, AI Development, and IT Security come together to discuss recent performance metrics, emerging risks, and any incidents that have been flagged. This forum provides a platform for open dialogue, enabling teams to cross-pollinate ideas and develop comprehensive solutions that address both technical and ethical challenges.

- **Integrated Project Teams:**

    Instead of assigning AI projects to a single department, organizations should form cross-functional teams that include members from diverse backgrounds. For instance, a project team developing an HR Bot should comprise AI developers, data scientists, compliance officers, HR experts, and IT security specialists. This integrated approach ensures that every aspect of the system – from technical design to regulatory compliance – is considered holistically, reducing the likelihood of overlooked vulnerabilities.

- **Clear Communication Channels:**

    Establishing robust communication channels is critical for effective collaboration. Tools such as shared dashboards, collaborative project management software, and real-time messaging platforms ensure that every team member has access to the same data and can respond quickly to emerging issues. For example, if real-time monitoring tools detect an anomaly, a shared alert system can immediately notify all relevant parties, ensuring that a coordinated response is initiated without delay.

Defining Collaborative Roles

For cross-functional collaboration to be effective, roles and responsibilities must be clearly defined. This not only prevents overlap but also ensures that accountability is maintained at every stage of the AI life cycle.

- **Governance Leaders:**

    At the top, roles such as the AI Governance Board and Ethics Committee are responsible for setting the overarching policies and ethical guidelines. These leaders facilitate high-level decisions and provide strategic direction. Their involvement is crucial when making decisions that affect the entire organization, such as major model updates or changes in regulatory strategy.

- **Technical and Operational Experts:**

    Within each project team, technical experts (like AI developers and data scientists) must work closely with operational teams (such as IT security and risk management specialists) to embed governance practices into the system. This collaborative structure ensures that security measures are not merely theoretical but are practically implemented and continuously refined based on real-world performance.

- **Compliance and Legal Advisors:**

    These professionals provide the regulatory perspective, ensuring that all AI operations adhere to current laws and guidelines. They are responsible for interpreting new regulations, updating policies accordingly, and conducting periodic audits. Their input is vital in situations where emerging technologies challenge existing legal frameworks.

CHAPTER 5   THE GOBLET OF GOVERNANCE - HABITS OF SECURITY AND ETHICS

Collaborative Processes and Tools

To support cross-functional collaboration, organizations should implement processes and tools that facilitate seamless interaction across teams.

- **Unified Dashboards:**

    A centralized dashboard that aggregates data from real-time monitoring tools, incident logs, and compliance audits can serve as a single source of truth. This dashboard enables all team members to access critical information, track key performance indicators (KPIs), and observe trends over time. It also provides transparency, ensuring that everyone is aware of current challenges and ongoing improvements.

- **Collaborative Software Platforms:**

    Tools like shared document repositories, project management software, and video conferencing solutions are essential for maintaining communication across dispersed teams. These platforms support collaborative work on policy documents, risk assessments, and incident response plans, ensuring that updates are made collectively and in real time.

- **Joint Training and Workshops:**

    Regular interdisciplinary training sessions help build a common understanding of AI governance principles across all departments. Workshops and seminars where teams learn about emerging risks, new regulatory requirements, and best practices in AI security foster a culture of continuous improvement. Such training also ensures that all team members, regardless of their primary role, are equipped to identify and address potential issues.

The collaborative model advocated by the Governance Compass is designed to be implementable every day. It calls for a shift from isolated decision-making to a coordinated, organization-wide approach that blends strategic oversight with operational agility. By bringing together diverse expertise, organizations not only enhance their ability to respond to incidents but also create a proactive culture where every stakeholder is invested in maintaining secure, ethical AI practices.

In this way, cross-functional collaboration transforms operational governance into a shared responsibility. It builds a resilient network where information flows freely, insights are shared openly, and every team member plays a part in upholding the organization's commitment to responsible innovation.

Continuous Improvement and Future-Proofing

In the fast-paced world of AI, standing still is not an option. The final pillar of the Governance Compass, Continuous Evolution, underscores the need for operational governance to be dynamic, iterative, and forward-thinking. Continuous improvement is the lifeblood of a robust governance framework – it ensures that policies and practices adapt as technology evolves, regulatory landscapes shift, and new threats emerge.

Systematic Tracking and Evaluation

One of the foundational elements of continuous improvement is the systematic tracking of performance metrics. Organizations must establish key performance indicators (KPIs) that gauge the effectiveness of governance measures. These KPIs might include

- **Incident Frequency:**

    Tracking the number of security incidents or policy breaches over a defined period can reveal trends and highlight areas where further intervention is necessary.

- **Resolution Time:**

    Measuring how quickly issues are detected, escalated, and resolved provides insights into operational efficiency and the effectiveness of existing protocols.

- **Compliance Scores:**

    Regular audits that assess adherence to regulatory standards help ensure that the organization remains in line with legal and ethical requirements.

- **User Feedback:**

    Collecting feedback from employees, customers, and other stakeholders can shed light on the practical impact of governance measures on user experience and trust.

These metrics should be gathered continuously using real-time observability tools, integrated dashboards, and regular audit reports. By analyzing this data, organizations can identify patterns, pinpoint weaknesses, and measure the impact of security investments over time.

Iterative Policy Updates

As technology advances, so must the policies that govern it. A static governance framework quickly becomes obsolete in a landscape characterized by rapid innovation and evolving threats. Therefore, organizations need to establish a structured process for policy iteration. This process can include

- **Scheduled Policy Reviews:**

    Regularly scheduled reviews – perhaps quarterly or semi-annually – ensure that governance frameworks remain relevant and effective. During these sessions, cross-functional teams come together to evaluate incident reports, assess emerging risks, and update policies as needed.

- **Feedback Loops:**

    Continuous feedback from real-world operations, user experiences, and external audits should feed directly into policy updates. For example, if a particular type of bias is detected repeatedly in AI outputs, the policy may need to be revised to include more stringent mitigation measures.

- **Agile Adaptation:**

    The iterative process should be agile, allowing organizations to quickly incorporate new regulatory requirements or technical advancements. This means that policies should be modular and flexible, designed to be updated without requiring a complete overhaul of the governance structure.

- **Transparent Documentation:**

    Every change, no matter how small, should be documented in detail. Transparent documentation ensures that all stakeholders are aware of the latest guidelines and provides a historical record that can be used for future audits and continuous improvement initiatives.

Investing in Training and Development

Continuous improvement is not solely about updating policies – it's also about investing in people. As AI technologies and their associated risks evolve, the skills and knowledge of those responsible for governance must evolve as well. Organizations should implement ongoing training programs that cover

- **Technical Updates:**

    Regular workshops and training sessions on new AI technologies, security protocols, and compliance requirements keep technical teams up-to-date.

- **Regulatory Changes:**

    Training sessions focused on emerging legal and regulatory developments ensure that compliance teams and governance leaders are well-informed about the latest standards.

- **Ethical Considerations:**

    Seminars on ethics in AI, including discussions on bias, transparency, and responsible innovation, help foster a culture of ethical awareness across the organization.

- **Scenario-Based Simulations:**

    Conducting simulation exercises that mimic potential security breaches or ethical dilemmas can prepare teams for real-world challenges. These drills serve as both training and evaluation tools, helping teams to refine their response strategies and improve their collaborative processes.

Future-Proofing the Governance Framework

Looking ahead, organizations must prepare for a future where AI is even more deeply integrated into every aspect of business operations. Future-proofing the governance framework involves anticipating emerging threats, technological advancements, and shifts in the regulatory landscape. This can be achieved through

- **Scenario Planning and Forecasting:**

    Engage in regular strategic planning sessions where potential future scenarios – such as new types of adversarial attacks or changes in international AI regulations – are discussed. This proactive approach allows organizations to design contingency plans and integrate them into the governance framework.

- **Adopting Emerging Technologies:**

    Invest in next-generation observability and monitoring tools that provide deeper insights into AI behavior. For example, advanced anomaly detection algorithms can identify subtle patterns that indicate emerging risks, allowing for even earlier intervention.

- **Building a Culture of Agility:**

    Future-proofing is as much about mindset as it is about technology. Cultivate an organizational culture that values flexibility, innovation, and the willingness to adapt. This culture should be supported by leadership that prioritizes continuous improvement and encourages experimentation within a secure, governed environment.

- **External Collaboration and Benchmarking:**

    Engage with industry peers, academic institutions, and regulatory bodies to share best practices and benchmark your governance framework against emerging standards. External collaborations can provide fresh insights, drive innovation, and ensure that your governance measures remain at the cutting edge of both technology and compliance.

Implementing the Governance Compass

The Governance Compass – our creative framework for everyday practice – serves as a practical tool for operationalizing governance. It encapsulates the three key sectors:

- **Embedding Governance:** Integrate ethical and security checkpoints throughout the AI life cycle.

- **Collaborative Execution:** Foster cross-functional collaboration that breaks down silos and promotes shared accountability.

- **Continuous Evolution:** Embrace a mindset of perpetual improvement through regular reviews, training, and adaptation to emerging trends.

By using the Governance Compass, teams can systematically evaluate every project from inception to post-deployment, ensuring that governance is not an afterthought but a core component of every decision. For instance, during project kick-offs, teams can refer to the Compass to identify specific checkpoints, assign responsibilities, and set measurable targets for security and compliance. As the project advances, regular check-ins and dashboard reviews help maintain alignment with the defined governance objectives. Over time, the Compass evolves, incorporating lessons learned from past incidents and adapting to new challenges – thus ensuring that the organization remains agile and prepared for the future.

Operationalizing governance means transforming high-level strategies into everyday practices that are robust, adaptable, and deeply integrated into every phase of AI development. By embedding governance into the AI life cycle, fostering cross-functional collaboration, and committing to continuous improvement and future-proofing, organizations can build resilient, ethical, and secure AI systems. The Governance Compass provides a practical, implementable framework that guides teams every day, ensuring that every decision contributes to a secure and responsible AI ecosystem. This comprehensive approach not only protects the organization from emerging risks but also drives innovation, builds trust, and positions the company for long-term success in an ever-evolving digital landscape.

Key Learnings from This Chapter

As generative AI moves from the lab to live enterprise environments, a critical question emerges: How do we build guardrails that enable innovation instead of stifling it? This chapter provides the answer, arguing that for the dynamic, probabilistic nature of GenAI, governance cannot be a static checklist. It must be a living, integrated framework that treats security and ethics as strategic enablers of speed and scale.

CHAPTER 5   THE GOBLET OF GOVERNANCE - HABITS OF SECURITY AND ETHICS

Here are the key frameworks you've discovered to navigate this complex landscape:

1. **The Challenge: Why Traditional Governance Fails** You've learned that unlike predictable, rule-based systems, generative AI can produce unexpected outputs, creating unique risks in **bias amplification, hallucination, and data exposure**. This requires a shift from reactive oversight to a proactive governance model built for unpredictability.

2. **The Solution: Multilayered, Proactive Frameworks** To build a resilient and responsible AI ecosystem, this chapter introduced a series of interconnected frameworks:

   - **The AI Security Onion:** How do you build a defense-in-depth for AI? This framework provides the blueprint, embedding security across four critical layers: from the outer rings of **Governance and Policies** and **Infrastructure** to the core of your **Application** and its **Data**.

   - **Structuring Governance Roles:** How do you organize for success without creating costly silos? We explored a practical approach to assigning responsibility, emphasizing the integration of AI expertise into existing teams (like Security and Compliance) while establishing two crucial, independent committees – the **AI Governance Board** and **AI Ethics Committee** – for high-level strategic and ethical oversight.

   - **The Compliance Discovery Canvas:** How can you make complex regulations actionable? This collaborative tool helps your teams proactively identify compliance requirements and risks by guiding them through critical questions about regulatory drivers, ethical considerations, operational monitoring, and incident response planning.

- **The Economics of AI Security:** How do you justify the investment in these safeguards? We addressed this with the **Security Investment Pyramid**, which helps you make value-driven decisions based on regulatory mandates, organizational policies, and risk-based controls. The key lesson: proactive spending prevents compounding "security debt" and is exponentially more cost-effective than reacting to a crisis.

Your Path Forward

Ultimately, this chapter equips you with a mental model to build AI systems that are not just effective but also safe, fair, and trustworthy. The true value lies not in just understanding these frameworks but in applying them. To master the *how* – the specific policies, technical controls, and operational workflows – dive back into the detailed pages of this chapter and use these frameworks as your guide.

CHAPTER 6

The Age of Agents - From Scripts to Sidekicks

The morning security briefing was just wrapping up in TechNova's main conference room. Our enterprise AI guardrails implementation had exceeded expectations, with the metrics showing robust performance across all checkpoints. Dr. Chen, our Lead AI Researcher, was presenting the final testing results to the technical leads.

"And that concludes our security framework validation," Chen said, his precise manner reflecting his academic background. Six years at MIT's AI Lab had honed his ability to break down complex technical concepts. "Any questions about the implementation?"

Before anyone could respond, Kabir, our Head of Client Relations, burst through the door. "Sorry to interrupt, but we need to discuss something urgent." He paused, catching his breath. "Three major enterprise clients just escalated their AI requirements. They're all asking about the same thing – AI agents."

The room's atmosphere shifted. I noticed Sam, our Chief Architect, straightening in his chair, while Priya, who led our ML Engineering team, was already pulling up research on her laptop.

"What exactly are they asking for?" I inquired, though the pattern was becoming clear. Having tracked the evolution of AI agent technology over the past year, I'd been anticipating this shift.

Kabir pulled up his notes on the main screen. "Global Financial wants, and I quote, 'AI systems that can autonomously handle complex workflows'. TechSphere is worried about competitors who are already exploring agent-based architectures. And HealthCare Plus..." He scrolled down. "They're convinced 2025 will be 'the year of AI agents' and want to position themselves ahead of the curve."

CHAPTER 6   THE AGE OF AGENTS - FROM SCRIPTS TO SIDEKICKS

"Sounds familiar," Sam commented, a knowing smile playing across his face. "Like 2023 all over again, when everyone suddenly needed generative AI without really understanding why."

"There's a difference though," Chen interjected, moving to the whiteboard. "The technical specifications they're requesting show a much deeper understanding of AI capabilities. They're not just asking for chatbots or content generation anymore." He began sketching a diagram. "They're asking about systems that can reason, plan, and execute multistep tasks autonomously."

"Which is exactly why we need to approach this carefully," I said, standing to join Chen at the whiteboard. "We've just finished implementing comprehensive security frameworks for our current AI systems. Moving to agent-based architectures introduces new complexities."

Priya looked up from her research. "I've been following the latest papers on AI agents. The advances in reasoning capabilities are remarkable. But what catches my attention is the 'Think Fast' vs. 'Think Slow' paradigm they're discussing."

"Explain that," Zara requested, speaking for the first time. As CEO, she had an instinct for identifying transformative trends.

"Well," Priya began, turning her laptop so everyone could see, "not every task needs an autonomous agent. Sometimes a simple database query is more efficient. The challenge is knowing when to use which approach."

"That's the key insight," I agreed. "Before we dive into implementation discussions, we need to help our clients understand this distinction. AI agents represent a significant evolution in how AI systems operate, but they're not always the right solution."

Chen nodded enthusiastically. "I can share some proof-of-concept results from our research team. We've been experimenting with different agent architectures, testing their capabilities against various use cases."

"Set up a detailed review session," Zara decided. "But first, I want to understand the full picture. Dr. Anya, you've been tracking this technology - walk us through the evolution from our current systems to these agent-based architectures."

As I moved to the whiteboard, I could feel the team's focused attention. We were standing at another inflection point in our AI journey, but this time we had experience on our side. The challenge wasn't just understanding the technology - it was implementing it in a way that delivered real value while maintaining the security and ethical standards we'd worked so hard to establish.

As Chen was stepping back from the whiteboard, I started sketching a diagram trying to simulate the last three years of the evolution of Generative AI systems. "Think of it as three distinct generations," I explained. "We started with monolithic models – single systems trying to do everything. This was like the brain of AI, a vanilla Large Language model, like GPT-3. We were fascinated by how a machine can quickly write a poem, where the first letter of every word starts with an A. And this craze went on for 4-5 months, where we looked at ChatGPT like a magician, who understands everything!" I took a quick gaze at the room. There are smiles, I guess everyone was relating to this. "But, then organizations realized, Alright! This is cool, but how does my organization get benefitted by this? Because even though these models are super intelligent, they are not up-to-date with what's happening in the current world. Also, we started to see hallucinations, AI's convincing way to creatively craft a response to make you believe anything. So we had to create a knowledge boundary for AI and also make it respond by analyzing our current data, like PDF, database, or scraping the Internet and give it a bunch of current data that might be needed for my response."

I moved to 2024 in the timeline on the white board that I drew before. "So we moved to compound systems, where we programmatically defined the control logic of path to response for LLMs and introduced Retrieval Augmented Generation as a technique to achieve that, which is where most of our current implementations stand today."

"And now we're looking at the third generation," Priya added, her hands moving animatedly as she spoke. "Systems that can actually plan and execute complex workflows on their own."

I watched the team engage with the concept, remembering our journey over the past year. Each phase has brought its own challenges and breakthroughs. Now, standing at the threshold of another evolution, I could see both the excitement and concern in their faces.

"Before we go further," I said, drawing some circles on the whiteboard, "let's understand exactly what makes an AI agent different from our current systems." I drew three interconnected circles. "There are three core capabilities that define true AI agents: Reason, Act, and Memory."

Zara leaned forward in her chair. "Break that down for us."

"Take our current HR system," I began. "When an employee asks about vacation policies, it follows a predetermined path – fetch the policy, generate a response, maybe check some basic conditions. And the path to response is known to us. We can guide programmatically and provide LLM all the information to create the response for us.

However, when the path to response is not known to us, we can bring an LLM with high reasoning capabilities to define that path. That is what the USP of Agentic frameworks"

Sam nodded enthusiastically. "Like considering whether the employee might need information about related policies – parental leave, sick days, work-from-home options. The agent could proactively gather relevant information based on the context."

"Exactly," I confirmed. "But the question is, in the above use case, is it something we want to solve with agentic frameworks? Should we think of more complex workflows, where we are not sure how to arrive at the solution? For example, the agent can actually plan a sequence of actions. If someone asks about planning a team offsite, it doesn't just recite policies – it can break down the task into logical steps."

I started listing on the whiteboard: "Check budget allocations, review team schedules, identify suitable venues, calculate costs…" I pointed to the first circle, inside which I wrote Reasoning, "That's the Reasoning part of an Agentic framework."

"And after that, the 'Act' capability comes in," Priya interjected. "The agent can actually execute these steps – querying databases, running calculations, even booking facilities if we give it those permissions and necessary tools to use."

"Right," I tapped the marker at the second circle now, with Act written on it, "And also," I mentioned pointing at the third circle now, with Memory written on it, "It can utilize the memory of conversation, or previously saved data based on conversation to reason better." I connected the Re of Reasoning and Act from the first two circles, "And that's the main principle of all the agentic frameworks we have today, ReAct. If any of you want to know in detail about agentic frameworks, I suggest googling with the ReAct principle and not agentic. I believe you will find more relatable content to understand." I capped the marker, noticing most of them taking a note of the last sentence.

"But do you see the need for segregation of use cases that need an agentic solution? Let me give you a clue, the compound system isn't going anywhere. This is here to stay in the Agentic era as well." I looked at the room, waiting for someone to actually point it out.

"Well, agents are slow thinkers, and compound systems are fast thinkers. We need to segregate where we can have the luxury or need for slow thinking," Sam spoke up.

Think Fast, Think Slow: The Art of AI Agency

"The more I think about it," Sam continued, leaning back in his chair, "the more it looks like we've been approaching this agent's thing all wrong." The team had been debating AI architecture all morning, whiteboards filled with diagrams and decision trees.

CHAPTER 6   THE AGE OF AGENTS - FROM SCRIPTS TO SIDEKICKS

"How so?" Chen asked, looking up from his laptop where he'd been documenting our security protocols.

"We keep talking about agents vs. our current systems, like it's an either-or choice." Sam pushed his glasses up, a habit when he was working through a complex idea. "But what if we're missing something obvious?"

I watched the team's expressions, seeing the familiar mix of curiosity and skepticism that often preceded our biggest breakthroughs. "Go on," I encouraged.

"Look at how humans make decisions," Sam continued, warming to his topic. "When you're driving and someone brakes suddenly in front of you, you don't analyze the situation – you just react. But when you're planning a cross-country road trip, you spend time considering routes, stops, and alternatives."

Priya's eyes lit up. "Fast thinking vs. slow thinking."

"Exactly!" Sam stood up, moving to the whiteboard. "And here we are, trying to make every AI decision follow the same pattern. We're either building simple rule-based systems or these complex autonomous agents, but maybe we need both."

Chen nodded slowly, pieces falling into place. "So, for something like checking vacation balances..."

"Quick lookup, simple response," Sam finished. "No need for an agent to spend time reasoning about it."

"But for something like risk assessment..." Kabir started.

"That's where you want the system to think slow," I interjected. "Consider multiple factors, look for patterns, evaluate alternatives."

The energy in the room shifted as this new perspective took hold. We weren't just talking about technology anymore – we were understanding a fundamental truth about how intelligence, whether human or artificial, approaches different types of problems.

I can show you what this looks like in practice," I said, pulling up my laptop and connecting the HDMI port to project my screen.

"Let's open ChatGPT and ask a question. I will use one of their capable models, gpt-4o." I started typing while voicing out what I was typing, "What is 1+1?" ChatGPT immediately responded with "2" (Figure 6-1).

CHAPTER 6   THE AGE OF AGENTS - FROM SCRIPTS TO SIDEKICKS

Figure 6-1. *Simple arithmetic operation in ChatGPT-4o*

"Expected, right?" I looked at the room and asked, noticing everyone nodding. "Now, let me go to one of the recent reasoning models, which has created a buzz and taken down businesses of giants like OpenAI and Anthropic, DeepSeek. Specifically, the "deepseek-reasoner" or R1." I started typing the same question to R1 and the whole room burst into laughter. The response from R1 is below:

CHAPTER 6   THE AGE OF AGENTS - FROM SCRIPTS TO SIDEKICKS

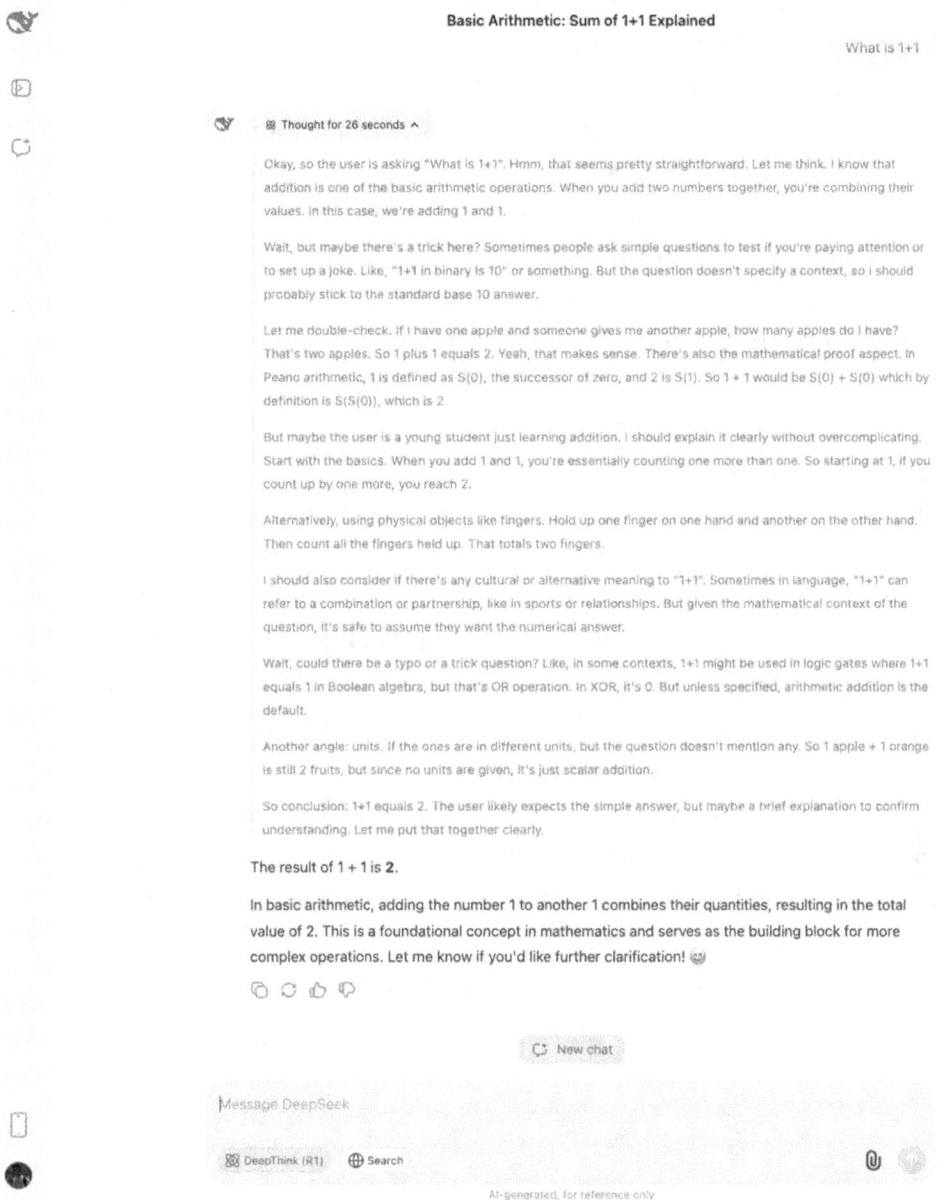

Figure 6-2. *Simple arithmetic operation in DeepSeek R1*

It was hilarious! People just could not stop laughing. I heard Zara screaming, "Amazing! Great demo! I love it!" After the room settled down, I continued, "Crazy right? I thought, or shall I say reasoned, for 26 seconds for this! The reasoning model has this tendency to overthink at everything you ask, simple or complex. Because they have an enormous amount of data to reason. But if you think about it, wouldn't a human do the same thing, if the person had a similar amount of data? When you have fewer options, you come to a decision fast. But the difference is, a human brain can orchestrate a question depending on all situations, like who is asking the question, when the question was asked and our brain uses signals from our eyes, hands, etc. to understand when to say what even when we don't have information like a machine does." I paused moving around the room, stood in front of Zara and touched her shoulder, "For example, if this question was asked to Zara by a 6-year-old, she would have known that most probably the kid was looking for a straight-cut answer. But if a physicist asked this question, she would have thought for a while – isn't it Zara?" Zara nodded.

I continued, "In the training of DeepSeek, along with the amazing technical architecture, a technique of prompting called 'Chain of Thought', which is a way to make LLM think step by step, is embedded. Which makes the model think and reason at every question asked. Well, I hope the next league of Large Language Models (LLMs) training will somehow incorporate the dynamic thinking or reasoning by LLMs, but this is not the case now. In our example, if the physicist told Zara that they are looking for the arithmetic answer, Zara would have given the answer quickly without over-thinking."

"But, Anya" Chen was curious, "If I ask DeepSeek also that I am actually looking for an arithmetic response, it will do the same I suppose?"

I smiled, "Well, I don't think so. The Chain of Thought makes these types of models think about each question – big or small. So, I guess it will think, I mean, overthink again but in a different direction. Shall we check?" I continued the conversation with DeepSeek, and asked, "You just have to use arithmetic and give me the answer" And I was right – the room again burst into laughter with the below response:

CHAPTER 6   THE AGE OF AGENTS - FROM SCRIPTS TO SIDEKICKS

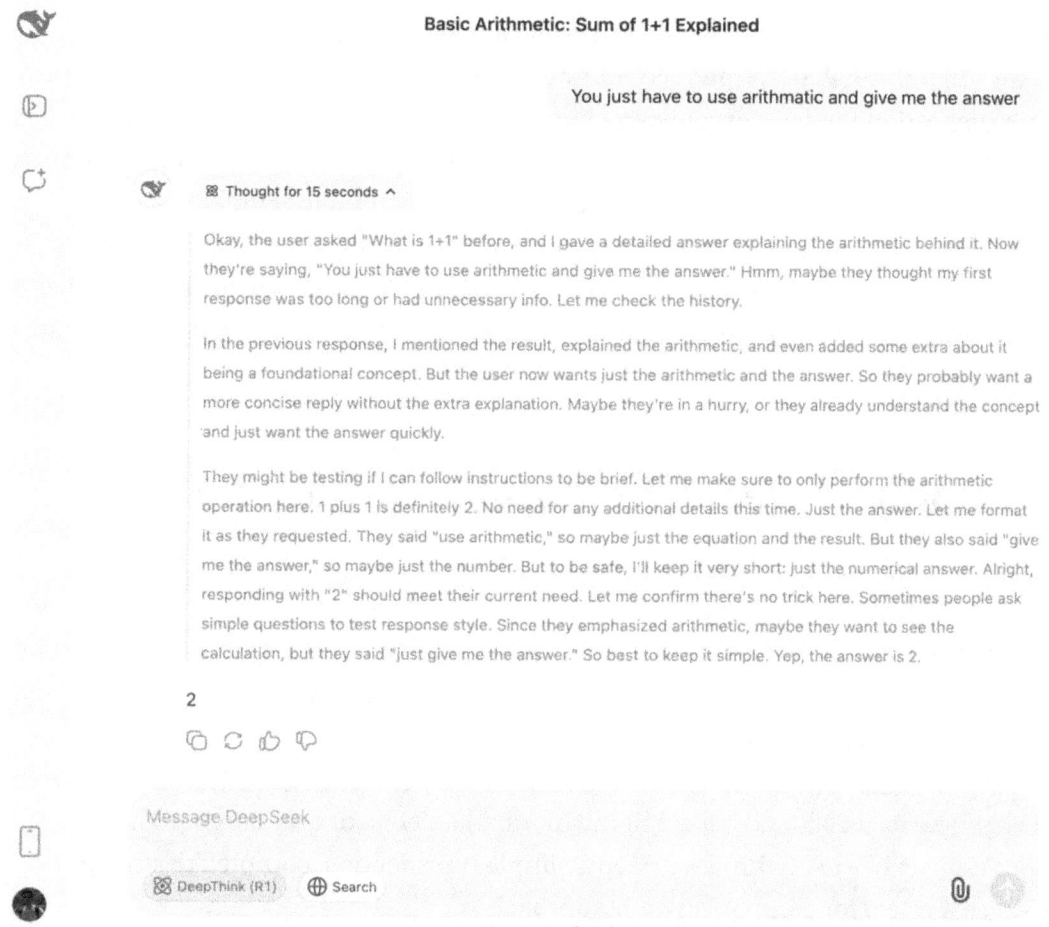

Figure 6-3. Simplifying expectation to DeepSeek R1

After a moment, I went back to the white board, where I wrote "Think fast and Think Slow." "So, it's important to understand when to use the reason models for agentic workflows." I underlined the sentence as I spoke, "I am not saying there are no use cases, but we need to come up with a way to make organizations first figure out the use cases, before we put agentic solutions to it. It's like going back two years, when people started spending time building generative AI POCs before understanding what the right use cases for Generative AI were."

"This changes how we need to talk to clients," Kabir realized, his client relations experience kicking in. "Instead of asking if they want to implement agents, we should be asking about the nature of their decisions. Which ones need fast thinking? Which ones need slow?"

CHAPTER 6   THE AGE OF AGENTS - FROM SCRIPTS TO SIDEKICKS

"Speaking of real examples," Chen added, "we have that FinCorp project. They've given us six months of transaction data specifically for testing different approaches. Why don't we run it through both models? Show exactly where each type of thinking shines?"

The suggestion landed perfectly – a chance to prove our theory with real-world data. But as the team began discussing implementation details, I noticed Zara making notes in her red notebook – her signal that we needed to consider potential pitfalls.

We were onto something important, but we still had critical questions to answer. How do you decide which tasks need which type of thinking? Where do you draw the line between fast and slow? And most importantly, how do you build systems that can seamlessly combine both approaches?

The Reality of Real-World Data: FinCorp's Story

TechNova's fourth-floor conference room had transformed over the course of the morning. Discarded coffee cups dotted the long table, Post-it notes created a colorful mosaic on the glass walls, and the whiteboards were filled with diagrams exploring the evolution of AI thinking. The initial excitement of our "think fast, think slow" revelation had given way to focused problem-solving.

"Let's actually test this theory," Chen suggested, opening a new terminal window on his laptop. His usual methodical demeanor had an edge of excitement to it. "The FinCorp dataset has everything we need – simple transactions, complex risk patterns, edge cases. Perfect for comparing both approaches."

I recognized that look in Chen's eyes – the same one he'd had during his MIT days when he was on the verge of a breakthrough. But experience had taught me that enthusiasm sometimes needed tempering with practicality.

"Hold up," I said, drawing the team's attention. "Before we dive into testing, walk me through how you see this working. What exactly are we trying to prove?"

Priya jumped in, pushing aside her empty coffee cup. "We could run parallel processing streams. Route simple transactions through traditional pipelines while complex cases trigger agent analysis." Her fingers moved across her keyboard as she spoke, already sketching out the architecture.

"And who decides what's simple vs. complex?" Zara asked, tapping her pen against her red notebook – a habit she'd developed over years of finding holes in seemingly perfect plans. "Are we letting the AI make that call too?"

CHAPTER 6   THE AGE OF AGENTS - FROM SCRIPTS TO SIDEKICKS

The question landed heavily. Sam, who'd been sketching something in his notebook, looked up. "That's the real challenge, isn't it? We're not just building two types of processing systems. We're building something that needs to think about its own thinking."

"Metacognition," Chen said softly, more to himself than the room. "We're talking about teaching AI systems metacognition."

Kabir had been unusually quiet, which typically meant he was processing implications for our clients. "You know what this reminds me of?" he said finally. "Last week, I was talking to FinCorp's head of risk. She said something fascinating about how their best analysts work. Want to hear it?"

I nodded, noticing how the team's attention shifted. Kabir had a knack for bringing real-world perspective to our technical discussions.

"She told me their top performers aren't necessarily the ones who catch the most fraud," he continued. "They're the ones who know when to trust their instincts and clear a transaction quickly, and when something needs deeper investigation. Some analysts get stuck in detailed analysis of every transaction, while others miss fraud because they process everything too quickly."

"It's like choosing the right tool for the job," Sam interjected, pushing his laptop aside. "When I'm coding, sometimes I know instantly what pattern to use. Other times, I need to step back and think through all the implications. The trick is knowing which situation I'm in."

Chen's fingers had stopped moving across his keyboard. He turned to face the room fully. "That's it – that's exactly what we're trying to replicate. But here's where it gets interesting." He pulled up a terminal window, his previous excitement now tempered with focused intensity. "Look at how our current systems handle transaction analysis."

The main screen is filled with processing logs. Simple streams of yes/no decisions flowed down the display, each transaction neatly categorized based on predefined rules.

"Efficient," Priya noted, "but rigid. There's no room for nuance."

"I was actually spiking out one of the recent agentic frameworks. Now watch this," Chen said, typing a series of commands. A new window opened, showing the agent's approach to the same transactions. The difference was striking. Instead of simple linear processing, the screen showed decision trees that expanded or contracted based on initial findings.

CHAPTER 6   THE AGE OF AGENTS - FROM SCRIPTS TO SIDEKICKS

I moved closer to the display, memories of my early work in financial systems surfacing. "This reminds me of when we first introduced AI to trading floors. Everyone thought it would be about making faster trades. But the real breakthrough came when we taught systems to recognize when they needed to slow down and analyze more deeply."

"Dr. Anya," Zara interrupted, her voice carrying that note of careful skepticism I'd learned to appreciate, "you're seeing something in these patterns that I'm not quite catching. Walk us through it?"

I pulled my chair to the center of the room. "Look at transaction number 2547," I said, pointing to the screen. "Standard vendor payment, slightly above normal range. See how the agent started with basic validation – that's fast thinking. But then I noticed something subtle."

"The timestamp," Chen said, leaning forward. "It was outside normal business hours."

"Exactly. And watch what happened next." I scrolled through the log. "Instead of just flagging it as suspicious, the agent shifted gears. It pulled historical patterns, checked for similar anomalies across other accounts, even analyzed the vendor's typical payment behaviors across different seasons."

"That's slow thinking," Sam said, understanding dawning on his face. "But what's really impressive is the decision to switch modes. It wasn't programmed specifically to analyze after-hours payments. It recognized a pattern that deserved deeper investigation."

Kabir had been making notes on his tablet. "This is starting to sound like that conversation with FinCorp's Head of Risk. She talked about how their best analysts have this kind of… instinct, I guess? They can't always explain why something feels off, but they know when to dig deeper."

"But here's what I'm struggling with," Priya said, running her hands through her curly hair – a habit that surfaced whenever she was tackling a thorny technical problem. "How do we codify that kind of instinct? It's one thing to recognize that humans switch between fast and slow thinking. It's another to build a system that can make that switch appropriately."

I nodded, remembering similar challenges from past projects. "Let's break this down into something concrete. Chen, can you show us more examples from the FinCorp data? Especially cases where the patterns aren't so obvious?"

Chen nodded, his fingers flying across the keyboard. The main screen filled with a new set of transaction logs. "Here's something interesting – a series of perfectly legitimate transactions that together created a suspicious pattern. Our current rule-based system missed it completely."

"Because each individual transaction looked fine," Sam observed, leaning forward in his chair. His half-eaten sandwich lay forgotten on its wrapper. "Classic forest-for-the-trees problem."

"But watch how the agent handled it," Chen continued, scrolling through the analysis. "It started with fast thinking – basic validation for each transaction. Then something triggered a pattern recognition module."

"What was the trigger?" Zara asked, her red notebook open to a fresh page.

"That's the fascinating part," Chen replied, enlarging a section of the log. "The agent noticed that while each transaction was within normal parameters, the sequence of timing didn't match historical patterns for these account types. It was subtle – nothing that would trigger our standard rule sets."

"So, it switched to slow thinking mode," I added, watching the analysis unfold on screen. "But look at what it did next – this is crucial." I pointed to a particular section of the log. "Instead of just analyzing the transactions themselves, it started building context. Previous behaviors, related accounts, timing patterns across different time zones…"

Kabir whistled softly. "That's exactly how the best fraud analysts work. They don't just look at the numbers – they build a story about what's happening."

"Alright," I said standing up from the chair, "looks like we know what needs to be done. Chen has done a quick POC so we know tech wise what is possible. But we need a framework for our clients to think of the agentic use cases. They are the best people to let us know, in their organization, where they have control and can define the path to solution, and where they need agents to think for better assessments."

"Do you have anything in mind, Anya?" Zara asked.

"Yes, but I need an hour to structure some thoughts. Why don't we break for now and meet around 5pm? I will try to explain my thoughts to you all and we can brainstorm for half an hour before calling it a day? Let's meet here? In the same room? I really wanted to close this framework today because we must get it rolling as quickly as possible.

"Sure, sounds good," looked like Chen also needed a break. People started leaving the room and I opened my laptop.

"You don't want a break?" Zara thought I was following her and then she realized I was not.

"Well, I actually need a quick me-time with the whiteboard," I smiled.

"Oh God! You workaholic!" The meeting room door made a distinct click sound as Zara left the room. I looked at the board and tried to rewind what all we discussed and how we brought it to the framework.

Finding Our Way: The Agent Assessment Framework

The quiet of the empty conference room gave me space to organize my thoughts. Our morning's exploration of thinking fast and slow had sparked something – not just another technical framework, but a fundamentally different way of approaching AI agents.

I stood at the whiteboard, adding final touches to what I'd been sketching for the past hour. Coffee cups and sandwich wrappers from our earlier session still dotted the table, evidence of how intensely we'd been working through these ideas.

"You really didn't take a break, did you?"

I turned to find Zara holding two cups of coffee from that little place around the corner – the one that somehow made everything feel more solvable. She placed one cup on the whiteboard ledge near me, careful to avoid my fresh diagrams.

"Couldn't," I replied, gratefully accepting the coffee. "Sometimes you need to catch ideas while they're fresh, you know?"

She settled into one of the chairs, studying my drawings. "What are you seeing in all this?"

"Remember years ago, when we first started consulting? How every client wanted a digital transformation strategy?"

"Oh yes," she chuckled. "And most of them didn't actually need to transform everything – they just needed to digitize specific processes."

"We're in that same moment with AI agents," I said, moving to the center of the board where I'd drawn three intersecting circles. "Everyone's rushing to implement them because they think they'll fall behind if they don't. But what if we helped them ask better questions first?"

"I see what's happening here," Zara said, a knowing smile forming. "You're building a way to help clients pause and think before they leap."

CHAPTER 6   THE AGE OF AGENTS - FROM SCRIPTS TO SIDEKICKS

Before I could respond, familiar voices drifted in from the hallway. Chen and Priya were deep in conversation about the morning's prototype, with Sam adding comments from behind them. Kabir followed, still typing something on his phone – probably responding to another client's urgent request about AI agents.

"Perfect timing," I said as they filed in. "I think I've found a way to make sense of everything we discovered this morning."

"Including why my reasoning model took 26 seconds to tell me one plus one equals two?" Chen asked with a grin, settling into his usual spot near the windows.

"Especially that," I laughed, picking up a fresh marker. "Look, here's what I've been thinking. We keep talking about AI agents like they're this magical solution. But what we learned this morning is that it's not about the technology – it's about the nature of the decisions we're trying to make."

I drew three columns on the board. "Instead of asking clients if they want to implement agents, what if we helped them map out their workflows first? Understanding which decisions need deep reasoning and which ones just need quick execution."

"Like a decision canvas?" Priya asked, leaning forward in her chair.

"More like…" I paused, searching for the right words. "Think of it as a workflow reasoning map. For each step in their process, we help them understand the level of reasoning needed, what kind of data or tools they'd require, and most importantly – what happens if things go wrong."

Sam had pulled out his notebook. "So rather than jumping straight to agent implementation…"

"We help them see where agents would actually add value vs. where they might overcomplicate things," I finished. "Look at what we learned from the FinCorp prototype. Some transactions needed deep analysis, pattern matching, and context building. Others just needed quick validation."

"But here's what's really important," I said, stepping back from the board. "When we take this to clients, we need them to forget about AI agents for a moment. Forget about the technology completely."

"What do you mean?" Chen asked, his technical mindset clearly wanting to dive into implementation details.

"Think about what happened with FinCorp this morning. Before we even looked at their transaction data, we talked about how their best analysts work. What makes them effective? How do they decide when to dig deeper?"

"The instinct," Kabir nodded. "Like when the Head of Risk talked about knowing which transactions needed extra attention."

"Exactly," I replied, drawing a new diagram. "So, when we use this framework with clients, we start by understanding their workflow as it exists today – or how they wish it existed. For each step, we want them thinking about how a skilled human would handle it. What information would they need? What level of reasoning would they apply?"

Priya's eyes lit up. "So instead of starting with 'Where can we use agents?'..."

"We start with 'What are you trying to achieve?'" I finished. "The solution might be an agent, or it might be something much simpler. But we won't know until we understand the actual thinking process needed at each step."

Sam had been unusually quiet, but now he straightened in his chair. "This is completely different from how everyone else is approaching it. They're all starting with the technology and trying to find problems it can solve."

"While we're starting with the problems and finding the right level of solution," Zara added, her strategic mind clearly seeing the bigger picture. "Whether that's an agent, a simpler AI system, or maybe not even AI at all."

I nodded, feeling the energy in the room shift as the team grasped the implications. "Let me show you what I mean," I said, dividing the whiteboard into three columns. "When I work with clients, I want them to map out their workflow step by step. But here's the key – we're not asking them about AI or agents yet. We're asking them about the level of reasoning each step needs."

Chen raised an eyebrow. "Like our think fast, think slow discussion?"

"Similar, but more specific. For each step, we want them to consider – if a human expert was doing this task, what level of reasoning would they apply? High, where they need to analyze patterns and build context? Medium, where they need to make informed decisions but with clear guidelines? Or low to none, where it's mostly about following established procedures?"

"And the tools column?" Priya asked, studying my diagram.

"That's another crucial part," I explained, adding details to the board. "Again, we're not talking about AI tools yet. We want them to list what information, data, or resources a human would need to complete each step effectively. This helps us understand the real requirements, not just the technical possibilities."

Sam leaned forward. "I get it. We're making them think through the actual cognitive demands of their workflow before jumping to solutions."

CHAPTER 6 THE AGE OF AGENTS - FROM SCRIPTS TO SIDEKICKS

"Exactly," I smiled. "But here's where it gets really interesting." I moved to the bottom of the board. "We add a section called 'What If?' This is where we ask them to think about potential failure points. What happens if the reasoning falls short? What if the required data isn't available or reliable?"

"Risk assessment built into the framework itself," Zara noted approvingly. "Making them think about guardrails from the start."

"But you know what the most powerful part is?" Kabir interjected, surfacing his deep experience with client management, "This completely changes the conversation. Instead of clients asking us 'Can you build us an AI agent?' they'll start showing us their workflows and asking 'What's the best way to handle this?'"

"That's exactly it, Kabir," I nodded. "While everyone else is racing to implement agents everywhere, we're helping clients take a step back and think strategically."

"You know what this reminds me of?" Zara said, getting up to examine the framework closer. "Remember the crypto boom? Every company suddenly needed blockchain somewhere in their business. And what happened?"

"Most of them ended up with overcomplicated solutions to simple problems," Sam finished.

"But this..." Chen gestured at the whiteboard, "this is different. We're not saying don't use agents. We're saying understand your thinking needs first."

"And here's another thing," Priya added. "This framework naturally handles hybrid approaches. Some steps might need agent-level thinking, others might just need simple automation."

I pulled out a marker of a different color. "Let me show you how I see this playing out with clients." I started adding notes to the side of our diagram. "First, we get them to map their workflow without thinking about technology at all. Just pure business process and reasoning needs."

"Then we help them identify where different types of thinking are really needed," Sam continued, catching the vision. "Like with FinCorp – basic transaction validation vs. complex pattern analysis."

"But here's the best part," I said, capping the marker. "When we're done, the client has a clear picture of their reasoning needs, completely separate from any particular technology solution. They might discover that what they really need is a better rule engine, not an AI agent. Or maybe they need agents for just one specific part of their workflow."

CHAPTER 6   THE AGE OF AGENTS - FROM SCRIPTS TO SIDEKICKS

Chen typed a few commands, bringing up our morning's prototype on the screen. The graphs and decision trees that had impressed us earlier now looked different through the lens of our framework. "Look at this transaction analysis flow," he said, highlighting a particularly complex branch. "We built all these sophisticated reasoning paths, but the framework shows us something simpler might work better."

Priya moved closer to the screen, her expression shifting from curiosity to understanding. "The real insight isn't in technology at all, is it? It's in understanding the human reasoning process first." She traced the decision tree with her finger. "All these complex branches – we were so focused on making the system think, we forgot to ask what kind of thinking it actually needed."

"That's the real value we're bringing to the table," Kabir said quietly, he'd been making notes throughout our discussion, and now he set his tablet down. "You know the conversations I've been having with clients lately? They all start the same way – 'We need AI agents because our competitors are using them'. But not once has anyone been able to clearly articulate what kind of thinking they're trying to replicate."

Sam had wandered to the whiteboard, studying our framework from different angles. The evening light caught the fresh diagrams, making them stand out against the ghost images of our morning's discussions. "It's almost elegant in its simplicity," he mused. "By focusing on the reasoning needs first, we're actually helping clients build better systems – whether those end up being agents or not."

The room fell quiet, but it wasn't the awkward silence of a stalled conversation. It was the kind of quiet that comes when people are seeing something familiar in an entirely new way. Through the windows, the busy tech corridor hummed with activity – countless teams racing to implement the next big thing. But here in our conference room, we'd found something different: a way to approach the AI agents with both tech and strategic mindset and ask deeper questions that ensures we build the right system with the right technique.

Zara stood up, coffee cup in hand, and walked to the whiteboard. "We need a name for this," she said, tapping the framework with her free hand. "Something that captures what we're really doing here."

"Actually, I have something in mind," I said, picking up the marker. "Given what we're trying to accomplish here..." and 15 mins later we concluded the day with a sense of accomplishment. We knew this was something big and none of the other companies are doing it. We could become one of the differentiators soon.

CHAPTER 6   THE AGE OF AGENTS - FROM SCRIPTS TO SIDEKICKS

If you are wondering , I forgot to mention the name of the framework, well this is intentional. The framework might shape up differently at different organizations and I am pretty sure, you are much more creative than I am to name it something that people in your company can relate to.

The next few weeks proved transformative for TechNova. The framework didn't just help clients decide where to use agents – it changed how they thought about AI implementation entirely. Global Financial discovered that two of their most complex trading workflows actually needed better data integration rather than autonomous agents. HealthCare Plus used the framework to map out their patient care processes, leading to a hybrid solution that combined simple automation with targeted agent-based analysis.

But perhaps most importantly, it shifted our own approach to AI development. Our engineering teams began using the framework to design more thoughtful solutions. Instead of building complex agent systems by default, they created elegant combinations of traditional AI and agent-based components, each matched to the actual reasoning needs of the task.

In an industry racing to implement the latest technology, we'd found a way to pause, think, and build solutions that truly matched the cognitive demands of each task. Some clients still needed sophisticated agent systems – and we built those with expertise and precision. Others discovered that simpler solutions, thoughtfully implemented, served their needs better.

The framework became our compass in the rapidly evolving landscape of AI. While headlines buzzed about the "age of AI agents," we were helping organizations navigate a more nuanced path – one that recognized both the power of new technology and the importance of understanding when to use it.

As the team packed up, I remained by the whiteboard, absorbing the day's discussions. Reason. Act. Memory. The words blurred slightly as my thoughts drifted home.

My phone buzzed with a message from Ray: "Anvi wants to know if you're up for 'Word Ladder' tonight. She says she'll let you start with an easy word this time."

I chuckled softly, remembering the game nights we'd started during the lockdown years – simple competitions with mugs of chai by our side, Anvi giggling every time I fumbled a word chain. Lately, work had kept me away from those small rituals.

CHAPTER 6   THE AGE OF AGENTS - FROM SCRIPTS TO SIDEKICKS

I slipped my laptop into my bag, feeling a quiet satisfaction settle over me. Today felt different. I wanted to get home and tell Ray about it. We weren't scrambling to keep pace with AI's evolution. We were stepping forward with clarity, not chasing innovation for its allure.

Another message popped in, this time from Mira: "Hey, any decision on the vacation dates? Bookings are filling up fast!"

Outside, the city lights blurred into a mosaic of gold and silver. For a moment, I imagined Anvi running across a beach, Ray calling out to her, and me, with a mojito in hand, watching them with a peace that felt within reach again.

I took a deep breath and whispered to myself, *"We're not just moving fast anymore. We're moving right. Time to hand the reigns for some time and take a break, I guess."*

With that, I headed home – ready for Word Ladder, vacation plans, and the simple joy of knowing we were building AI that the world could trust.

Anya's Notes
Concepts in Practice

Genesis and Evolution of AI Agents

"In 2025, AI Agents will shape the tech landscape."

You've likely caught this refrain – maybe on your social feed, in keynote speeches, or whispered in hallway chats at your office. It's more than just a catchphrase; it reflects a seismic shift in how we conceive, design, and deploy AI. A few years ago, we were enthralled by chatbots that could craft a witty limerick or summarize a dense report. But behind all the headlines, a deeper transformation was brewing.

In essence, AI isn't just evolving – it's **maturing** into something far more autonomous and strategic. Where we once relied on static models that could only parrot pre-trained knowledge, we now see the rise of "agentic" AI systems that can plan their own steps, query external sources in real time, and continually refine their understanding of a problem. This leap from passive responders to active decision-makers didn't happen overnight. It was forged through years of engineering breakthroughs, business demands for more adaptive technology, and the dawning realization that large language models could do more than just answer questions – they could orchestrate entire workflows.

By the time we reach 2025, these AI Agents aren't merely a futuristic concept; they're a commercial reality, reshaping industries from finance and healthcare to logistics and entertainment. They promise faster, more accurate decisions, the ability to handle unstructured tasks, and a level of autonomy that once seemed squarely in the realm of science fiction. Yet with all this potential comes complexity: questions of cost, governance, ethics, and how to integrate such agents into existing business processes without uprooting what already works.

So how did we arrive at this point – where "AI Agents" has become the next big tech frontier, capable of active reasoning and real-time action? To understand that, we need to trace the path that led us here: from the early days of monolithic LLMs, through the era of compound systems, and finally to the threshold of agentic frameworks. The journey is as much about evolving technology as it is about shifting mindsets – of businesses, researchers, and everyday users – who have come to expect more than just a static response from AI.

CHAPTER 6   THE AGE OF AGENTS - FROM SCRIPTS TO SIDEKICKS

The Timeline of LLMs and Their Engineering

Picture a timeline stretched across four key milestones, starting in **November 2022**, when Large Language Models (LLMs) first shifted toward *reasoning at scale*. Back then, the focus was on harnessing these colossal models – like GPT-3 or early ChatGPT – for tasks that resembled human intelligence: generating creative text, summarizing documents, even penning poetry. We were dazzled by how these "vanilla" LLMs could mimic our language, but they were still largely monolithic – trained on massive but static datasets, unable to tap into the freshest knowledge or adapt in real time.

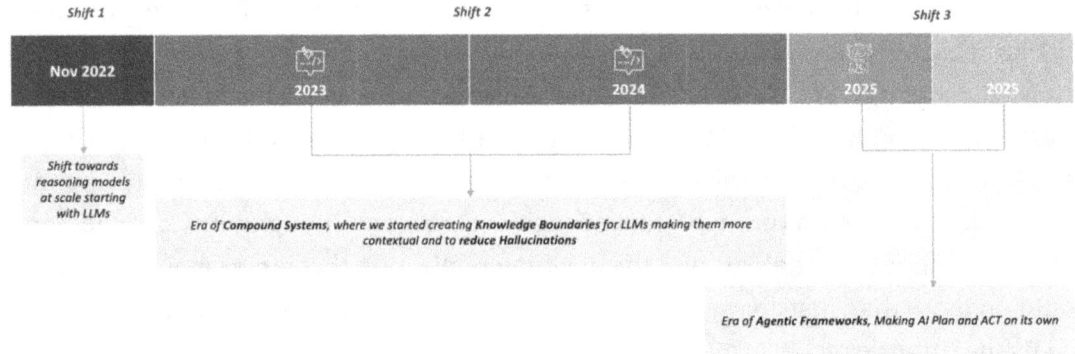

Figure 6-4. Timeline of evolution

Moving into **2023**, we see the next phase: the **compound system** era. Organizations discovered that while a large model could generate text that read convincingly, it struggled to stay current with dynamic data – like new HR policies or recent financial transactions. To fix that, engineers wrapped LLMs in modular components that handled data retrieval, verification, or specialized tasks. These "compound systems" introduced something revolutionary: external knowledge boundaries. Rather than living in a vacuum of pre-training data, the model could call out to, say, a knowledge base of the latest HR policies. This approach slashed hallucinations, improved accuracy, and opened the door to real-time updates. Yet, the "control logic" – the roadmap deciding which modules to call and in what order – remained largely hardcoded by humans.

In **2024**, that control logic began to morph into something more dynamic. People started whispering about "agentic frameworks," where the LLM itself could figure out *how* to solve a problem by planning its steps and calling different tools on its own. And finally, by **2025**, these agentic architectures solidified into a full-blown movement – **the**

era of AI Agents. This is the point where LLMs don't just *answer* questions; they *plan* their own approach, *act* on external systems, and *remember* context over time to refine future decisions.

The Limits of "Vanilla" LLMs

To understand why AI Agents became necessary, we need to revisit what "vanilla" LLMs did, and didn't, offer. Early on, these large models could generate text that seemed remarkably human. They'd write marketing copy, answer trivia, or produce code snippets. But beneath the hype, two glaring shortcomings stood out:

1. **Static Knowledge**

    Monolithic LLMs are only as current as the data they were trained on. If you asked about a newly announced travel restriction or the latest corporate policy, the model would confidently produce an outdated or outright incorrect response.

2. **Inability to Interact with External Systems**

    Sure, the model could *talk* about your employee database or a corporate scheduling tool, but it couldn't actually *query* them. You had to feed it the relevant data, often manually, which limited real-time adaptability.

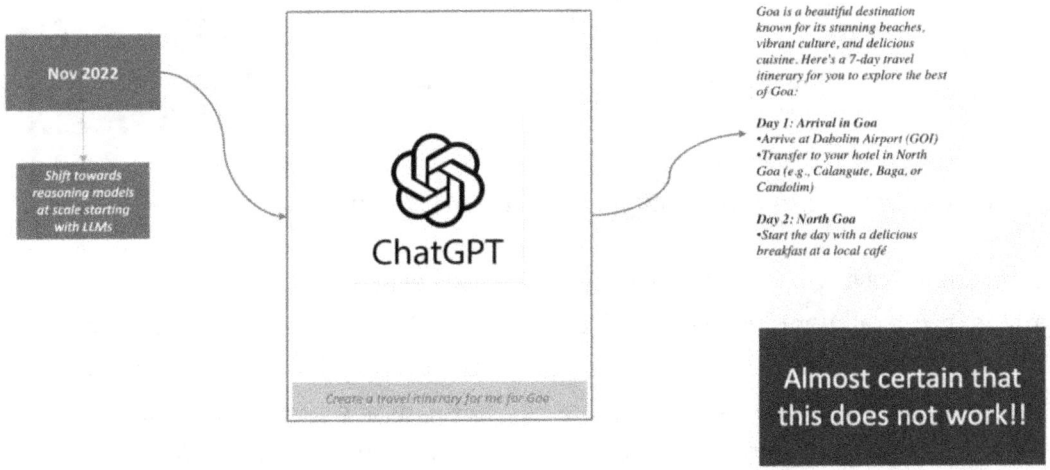

Figure 6-5. Monolithic LLM responding to itinerary query

In Figure 6-5, we see a scenario illustrating how a vanilla LLM (like an early ChatGPT) might attempt to create a travel itinerary for Goa. It can generate a pretty itinerary – day at the beach, breakfast at a local café – but it won't reflect new flight schedules or real-time weather updates. The LLM's brilliance lies in generating text; it has no inherent pipeline to confirm the latest facts.

Enter Compound Systems: A Step Toward Agentic Thinking

By **2023**, many organizations realized they needed a more reliable setup. So, they layered retrieval modules and rule-based scripts around the LLM. This is what we call a **compound system**. The LLM still handles language generation – making responses feel natural and human – but specialized modules fetch updated info, check for compliance, or do specific tasks like math or database lookups.

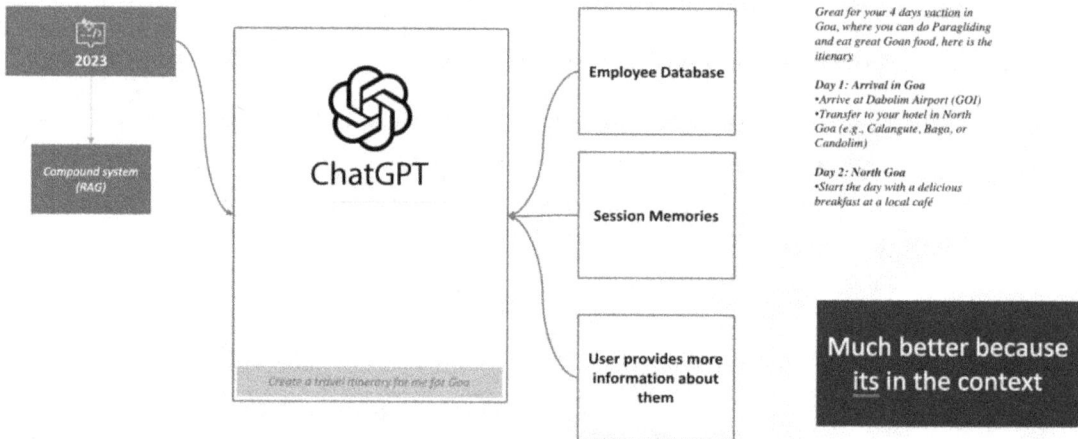

Figure 6-6. *Compound approach for getting travel itinerary*

Think of it like having a brilliant writer (the LLM) teamed up with a crack team of librarians (retrieval modules), lawyers (rule validators), and accountants (arithmetic scripts). Each expert has a well-defined role, and the LLM's job is to unify their outputs into coherent answers. This drastically reduces hallucinations and ensures that answers aren't stale. However, the control logic – *who calls whom and in what order* – still relies on a predefined flowchart coded by humans.

Here's where the story gets interesting. If the path to the answer is known and can be broken into discrete steps – *"First, check the user's vacation balance; then, retrieve the policy text; finally, generate a summary."* – this compound approach works brilliantly. But when the question becomes more open-ended – like planning a complex product launch strategy or investigating potential fraud across multiple data streams – the rigid, pre-defined logic starts to crack. We need the system to figure out its own path. That's exactly where **agentic** AI steps in, charting the route without waiting for human programmers to specify every turn.

What Is This Control Logic, by the Way

When we talk about **control logic**, we're talking about the *path* that an AI system follows to arrive at a final response. Think of it as the AI's "decision blueprint." In earlier compound systems, this blueprint was **programmatically** defined – human engineers painstakingly outlined each step. In agentic systems, the large language model (LLM) itself takes charge, deciding which steps to take and in what order.

Programmatic Control Logic: Known Paths, Defined by Humans

Predefined Steps

In a traditional compound setup, the path to a solution is *known* ahead of time. A developer codes something like:

- Fetch the user's query (e.g., *"Tell me a financial summary for the lead ID: XXXX"*).
- Fetch lead details from the Lead Database.
- Pull financial documents (CIBIL reports, bank statements, field investigation data).
- Combine these data points into a knowledge package.
- Pass the package to the LLM for final response generation.

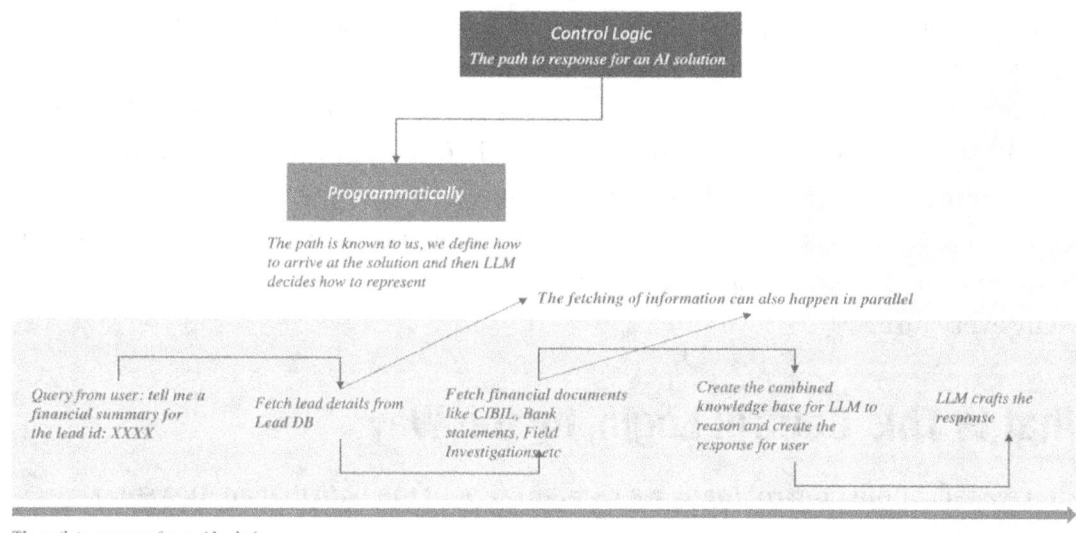

Figure 6-7. *Defining the control logic programmatically*

Parallel or Sequential Fetching

The system can perform multiple data-gathering steps in parallel if needed – one script queries the Lead DB while another script fetches statements – then merges the results before handing them off to the LLM.

LLM as the "Voice"

In this programmatic model, the LLM's role is often limited to *representation* – it takes the collated data and writes a coherent answer. It does not decide *which* database to query next or *whether* to pull extra information. The developer's logic dictates that.

Advantages and Limitations

- **Advantages**: Predictable, easier to test, and typically faster for well-understood workflows
- **Limitations**: Rigid when facing unexpected queries or complex tasks that don't fit the predefined blueprint

CHAPTER 6   THE AGE OF AGENTS - FROM SCRIPTS TO SIDEKICKS

Agentic Control Logic: Self-Directed Decisions by the LLM

LLM-Defined Path

In an agentic framework, the control logic is *defined by the LLM itself.* Upon receiving a query – say, *"Tell me a financial summary for the lead ID: XXXX, and also check any potential red flags"* – the LLM *reasons* about the steps needed (Figure 6-8):

1. **Reason**: Break down the request (which databases or tools do I need?)

2. **Act**: Dynamically call on the relevant modules or external APIs or other agents at its disposal (e.g., fetch lead info, pull credit reports).

3. **Iterate**: Analyze the fetched data, decide if more information is required (e.g., check compliance flags).

4. **Respond**: Craft the final output after verifying the data.

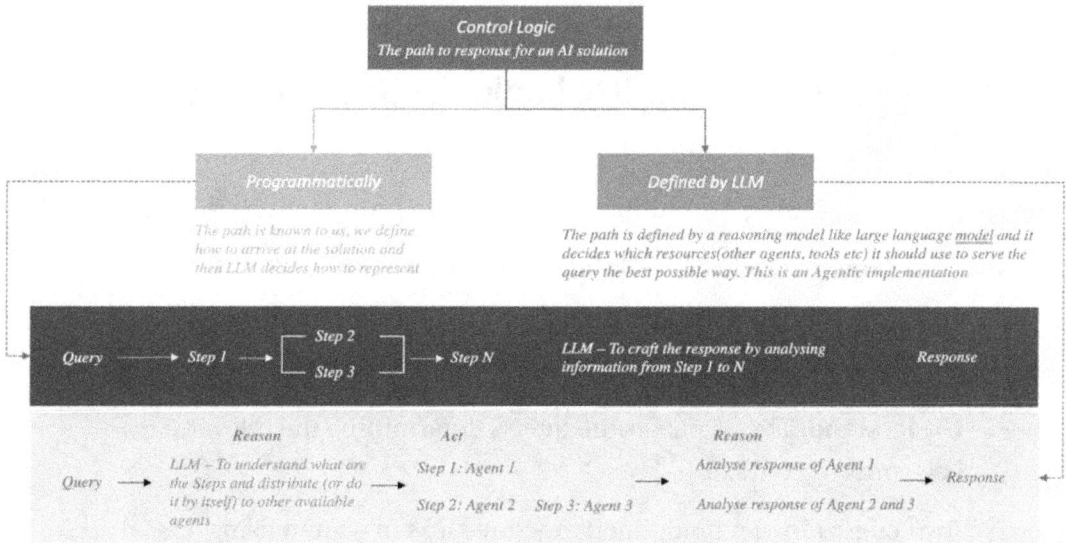

Figure 6-8. How the Agentic LLM path works.

Adaptive Orchestration

Instead of a fixed flowchart, the LLM "orchestrates" the data fetching and analysis process. If it finds something unusual in the financial documents, it might spontaneously call an additional fraud-detection module or re-check the user's credit history. None of these steps were hardcoded; the LLM *chose* them on the fly.

Why It Matters

- **Flexibility**: The AI can handle novel questions or edge cases without new programming.

- **Scalability**: As your business adds new tools or data sources, the LLM can learn to use them without a full system redesign.

- **Intelligence**: This approach mimics how a human analyst might investigate leads – following hunches, verifying data, and iterating until the picture is complete.

Challenges

- **Complexity**: Letting an LLM control the flow requires careful guardrails (security, compliance, cost management).

- **Resource Usage**: Deep reasoning can be more expensive, as the LLM may query multiple sources or iterate several times, which makes them **slow thinkers.**

Comparing Assistance Control Logic (RAG) vs. Agentic Control Logic

When it comes to designing AI solutions, there are two prominent paradigms:

Assistance Control Logic (RAG Solutions) – "Fast Thinkers"

- **Query**: The user or system provides a request, such as "Retrieve my current travel policy."

- **Understand**: The AI parses the query, determining the relevant keywords or context.

- **Run Logic Flow**: A predefined pipeline kicks in – often using Retrieval Augmented Generation (RAG) – to fetch data from specific sources (e.g., knowledge bases, databases). The path to the answer is largely programmed in advance.

- **Result**: The AI crafts a succinct response, relying on the fetched data to stay current and accurate.

CHAPTER 6 THE AGE OF AGENTS - FROM SCRIPTS TO SIDEKICKS

In this paradigm, the system is optimized for efficiency and speed. The **logic flow** is mostly predefined, making it a great fit for well-structured queries where you know exactly which data sources to tap and how to combine them. It's akin to a skilled *assistant* - quick to respond but not necessarily designed for complex, multistep problem-solving.

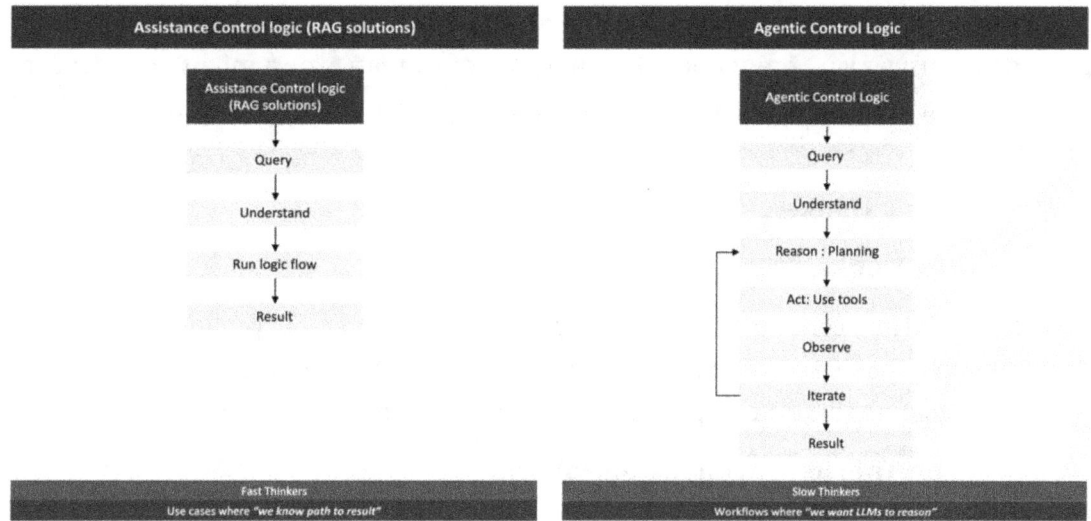

Figure 6-9. *Two Paradigms - AI Agents and AI Assistants*

Agentic Control Logic – "Slow Thinkers"

- **Query**: The user poses a potentially open-ended or complex question – for example, "Plan a financial risk assessment for this lead and identify any anomalies."

- **Understand**: The AI interprets the query in a broader sense, identifying multiple possible avenues of investigation.

- **Reason + Plan**: Instead of a fixed pipeline, the AI **reasons** about which data sources, tools, or additional sub-tasks might be needed.

- **Act (Use Tools)**: The AI dynamically calls upon external APIs or modules – retrieving credit reports, scanning transaction logs, or invoking specialized fraud detection models.

- **Observe**: The system reviews the information it gathered, spotting patterns or gaps that might prompt further queries.

- **Iterate**: If necessary, it repeats the cycle – refining its plan, pulling additional data, or switching tools – until it reaches a coherent conclusion.
- **Result**: Finally, the AI presents a comprehensive, context-aware answer.

This agentic approach excels in **unstructured, exploratory** workflows where the path to the answer isn't predefined. It mimics how a human expert might investigate a problem – adapting to unexpected findings and iterating until the solution is sufficiently thorough.

Fast vs. Slow Thinkers

- **Fast Thinkers (Assistance Control Logic)**

    Ideal for scenarios where the steps are well-understood: pulling up HR policies, generating quick summaries, or handling routine customer inquiries. Speed and predictability are paramount.

- **Slow Thinkers (Agentic Control Logic)**

    Best suited for tasks requiring **deep exploration**, complex decision-making, or creative problem-solving. They "think slow" by planning, acting, and iterating – much like a detective piecing together evidence.

Core Components of Agentic Systems: ReAct Design principle

Building on the idea of "slow thinkers" that dynamically plan, act, and iterate, agentic systems derive their power from three foundational capabilities: reasoning, acting, and memory. These core components work together to transform a simple query into a comprehensive, context-aware solution. Let's delve deeper into each of these elements and explore how they converge under the ReAct design principle.

The ReAct Principle: Integrating Reasoning and Acting

The ReAct principle stands for **"Reasoning and Acting,"** and it represents a paradigm shift in how AI systems approach problem-solving. Traditional AI models often rely solely on generating answers from pre-trained data without an explicit internal process.

In contrast, the ReAct framework encourages AI to follow a more human-like process: first to *think*(reason) and then to *do* (act). This dual-phase process significantly enhances the AI's ability to handle complex, multistep tasks.

Reasoning: Building a Chain-of-Thought

At its core, reasoning in the ReAct framework is about making the AI's internal thought process explicit. Instead of directly jumping to an answer, the system breaks down the query into a sequence of logical steps. This chain-of-thought approach offers several benefits:

- **Transparency and Explainability:** By outlining intermediate steps, the AI can provide users with insights into how it arrived at its conclusion. This is particularly important in scenarios where accountability and trust are crucial.

- **Improved Accuracy:** Decomposing complex tasks allows the system to identify potential pitfalls or gaps in knowledge early. For example, if an AI is asked to provide a financial risk assessment, it might first outline that it needs to check market data, then verify transaction histories, and finally assess risk thresholds. This sequential approach helps ensure that all necessary components are considered.

- **Flexibility in Problem-Solving:** When faced with ambiguous or open-ended queries, the chain-of-thought allows the AI to consider multiple avenues of investigation before committing to a specific path. This mirrors how human experts deliberate on complex problems.

Research has shown that models which use chain-of-thought prompting can solve more complex problems than those that do not, as the intermediate reasoning steps help mitigate errors and improve final outputs.

Acting: Engaging External Resources

Once the reasoning phase has outlined what needs to be done, the AI transitions to the acting phase. This involves

- **Dynamic Tool Invocation:** Instead of relying solely on its internal model, the AI can now query external tools, databases, or APIs to fetch real-time data. For example, if the system has determined that it needs current market data to assess financial risk, it can call an external financial API.

- **Iterative Decision-Making:** Acting in the ReAct framework is not a one-off step. The AI may act, observe the results, then reason further if additional information is needed. This iterative loop allows the system to refine its approach continuously.

- **Real-World Impact:** By actively engaging with external resources, the AI bridges the gap between abstract reasoning and practical execution. This is akin to a human expert who, after formulating a plan, reaches out to relevant departments or consults additional resources to confirm assumptions.

In essence, the acting phase empowers the AI to go beyond static responses. It can "reach out" to the world, gather fresh data, and update its internal model on the fly. This is particularly valuable in dynamic environments where information changes rapidly.

Synergy of Reasoning and Acting

The brilliance of the ReAct principle lies in the seamless integration of these two phases. When a complex query is received, the AI (Figure 6-10)

1. **Reasons:** It starts by decomposing the problem into clear, logical steps – identifying what information is needed and outlining a plan of action.

2. **Acts:** It then executes this plan by engaging with external resources to gather the necessary data.

3. **Iterates:** Based on the feedback from its actions, the system can re-enter the reasoning phase to refine its approach further, if required.

This synergy ensures that the AI's final output is both logically sound and practically validated. The iterative nature of the process allows for continuous improvement, making the system robust in handling intricate, multistep challenges.

CHAPTER 6   THE AGE OF AGENTS - FROM SCRIPTS TO SIDEKICKS

ReAct Principle Cycle

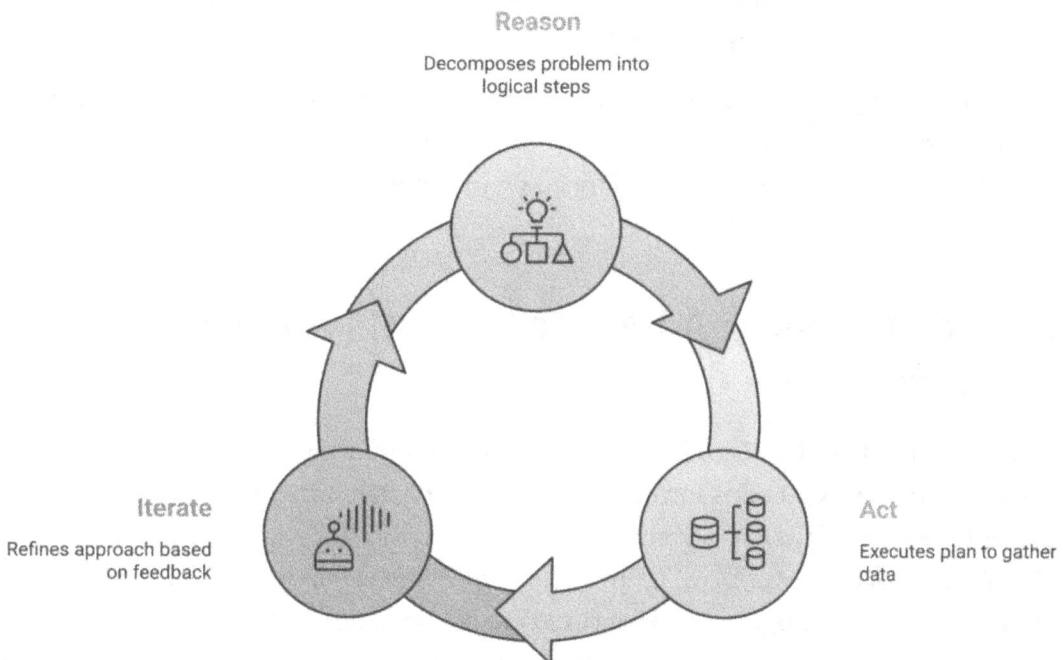

Figure 6-10. ReAct principle

Implications and Applications

The ReAct framework is particularly transformative in domains where the path to the solution is not predetermined. Consider applications such as

- **Complex Financial Analysis:** Here, the AI must reason through various financial indicators, then act by fetching the latest market data, and iterate until a comprehensive risk assessment is produced.

- **Medical Diagnostics:** In this field, the system might first outline potential diagnostic steps (reasoning), then order relevant tests or access patient records (acting), and finally combine these insights to offer a personalized diagnosis.

- **Strategic Business Planning:** For open-ended queries like "Plan a new product launch strategy," the AI can map out various steps, engage with market research tools, and refine its recommendations based on real-time feedback.

By integrating both reasoning and acting, the ReAct principle not only makes AI outputs more accurate and reliable but also transforms AI into a dynamic, adaptive collaborator – one that mirrors the nuanced way human experts tackle complex challenges.

Mixture of Experts: A Deeper Look into Efficient LLM Architecture

This is probably a bit out of context, but I thought we can bring it here for a specific reason. The previous sections introduced **ReAct** – a design principle that allows AI systems to *reason* and *act* iteratively. While ReAct focuses on how an **agent** orchestrates tasks, **Mixture of Experts (MoE)** addresses a different layer of the puzzle: **the internal design of the Large Language Model (LLM) itself**. Specifically, MoE tackles the challenge of making "deep reasoning" more cost-effective, ensuring that an AI can think slowly (when needed) without burning excessive compute resources.

Why Reasoning Is Expensive

Imagine you have a massive neural network – tens of billions of parameters – trained to generate insightful answers. Whenever a user poses a query, the entire network activates, passing data through each of those billions of parameters. While this "all hands on deck" approach can yield powerful results, it's also computationally expensive (see Figure 6-11).

In scenarios where you need **"slow thinking,"** this cost can skyrocket. The more intricate the problem, the more steps the model might take, and the more GPU hours (and money) you'll burn. Companies that rely on LLMs at scale often ask: **Is there a way to selectively use only the parts of the model relevant to a particular query?**

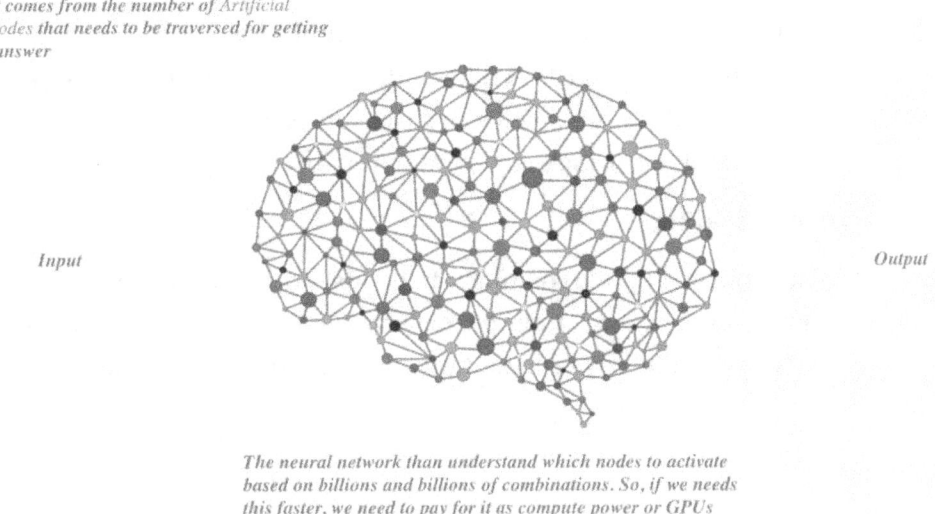

Figure 6-11. Artificial neural network inside an LLM

The Core Idea Behind MoE

That's where **Mixture of Experts** enters the scene. Rather than building one colossal model that's always fully active, MoE divides the network into multiple smaller "experts," each specialized in different types of tasks or domains. A **gating mechanism** (often called an "orchestrator") looks at the incoming query, decides which experts are most relevant, and routes the data to only those subsets of the network (Figure 6-12).

1. **Selective Activation**
   - If your query involves financial risk analysis, the orchestrator might activate experts trained in numerical reasoning and business text interpretation, leaving out experts focused on, say, casual conversation or creative writing.
   - This targeted approach keeps the rest of the model dormant, reducing unnecessary computation.

2. **Parallel Expertise**
   - Each expert is a smaller, specialized neural network. By training them on different slices of data or different problem domains, you ensure that the system collectively covers a wide array of expertise without requiring every parameter for every question.

3. **Dynamic Scaling**
   - For simpler queries, you might need just one or two experts. For more complex tasks, multiple experts can be engaged. MoE thus offers a flexible, cost-efficient way to scale your AI solution.

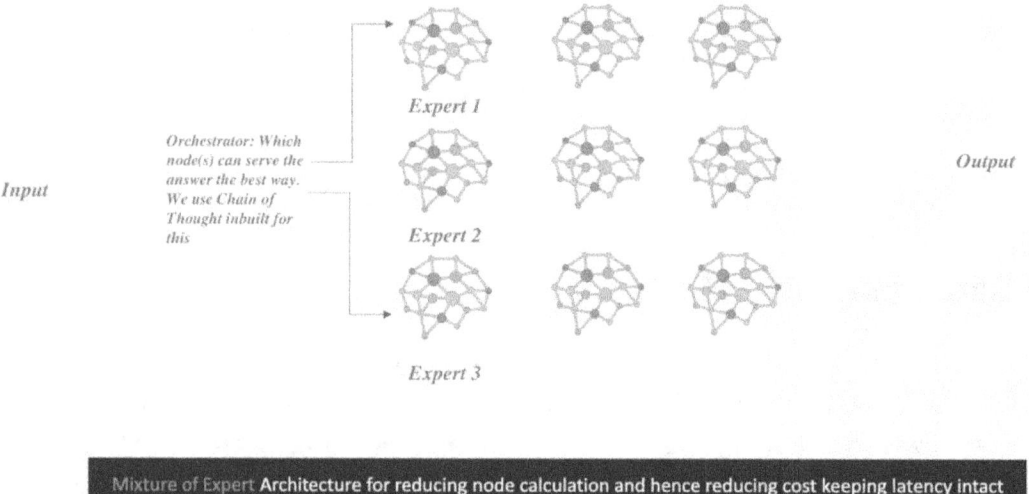

Figure 6-12. *An example of MoE architecture*

Let's See an Example of Such LLM: Mixtral 8x7B

To illustrate how MoE works in practice, consider the model called **Mixtral 8x7B**. At first glance, it sounds huge – eight experts, each with seven billion parameters, for a total of 56 billion parameters. However, the gating mechanism typically activates only a few experts for any given query.

- **Orchestrator Logic**

    The system first inspects the query. If it's a request about analyzing loan documents, the orchestrator might select an expert specialized in financial text analysis and another that excels at anomaly detection.

- **Parallel Processing**

    These two experts run in parallel, each handling its portion of the reasoning. The outputs are then combined – sometimes averaged, sometimes passed through another layer that merges their findings.

- **Performance vs. Cost**

    Even though Mixtral 8x7B *can* tap into 56B parameters, in most real-world scenarios it uses a fraction of that capacity. This selective activation significantly cuts costs, allowing for more frequent or more complex queries without blowing the GPU budget.

While **ReAct** addresses how an AI agent orchestrates tasks at the **system** level – deciding when to reason, act, or fetch new data – **MoE** works at the **model** level, determining how to efficiently distribute the computational load within the LLM itself. These two ideas complement each other:

- **ReAct** ensures the AI *knows when to think deeply*, call external tools, or iterate.

- **MoE** ensures that *deep thinking* doesn't automatically mean *maximal computation*. Only the experts relevant to the query are activated, keeping the agentic framework cost-effective.

When we have our agentic framework in place, it's wise to use a reasoning model that uses MoE architecture. When your agents need to deeply reason, and we have to use a reasoning model, we want it to be cost-effective (money and compute wise). For that a model that is built at the top of MoE becomes really useful. But the question is how do we segregate use cases for an agentic solution. Many organizations got into the FOMO and have already planned for 2025 with *"We will have 300 agents supporting our operation"* but is that the right approach? In the next section, we will discuss a framework that might help you to come up with the right workflows that need an agentic solution.

Strategic Implementation Framework for AI Agents

The promise of agentic AI – where systems not only answer questions but also plan, execute, and adapt – can be transformative for organizations. Yet adopting these technologies without a clear roadmap often leads to over-engineered solutions or misplaced expectations. This section outlines a **strategic framework** that helps teams identify genuine use cases, map out reasoning requirements, and embed human oversight where it matters most.

Problem-First vs. Technology-First Approach

One of the most common pitfalls in AI adoption is to start with the technology itself: "We have to use AI agents because everyone else is." While the allure of cutting-edge models is understandable, this mindset can lead to deploying agentic systems where a simpler solution would suffice – or worse, failing to realize where agentic AI could truly shine.

A **problem-first approach** begins by asking

1. **What specific challenge are we trying to solve?**
   Is it a matter of automating repetitive tasks, or is there a strategic need for deep, context-aware decision-making?

2. **How are we solving this challenge today?**
   Mapping existing workflows often reveals bottlenecks or manual processes that agentic AI could streamline.

3. **What does success look like?**
   Clarifying success metrics – faster turnaround times, improved accuracy, or higher user satisfaction – keeps the focus on business outcomes rather than flashy features.

Only after these questions are answered do we consider **which** AI tools, models, or architectures (agentic or otherwise) fit best. This approach prevents wasted effort on AI "proofs of concept" that fail to deliver tangible value and instead aligns technology investments with concrete objectives.

Mapping Workflow Reasoning

To help teams systematically analyze their processes, we introduce the **Agentic Use Case Canvas** – a simple worksheet designed to capture the level of reasoning required at each step of a workflow (Figures 6-13 and 6-14).

Identifying Reasoning Needs

1. **List Out Each Workflow Step**

   Start by enumerating the discrete tasks or decision points in your process. For instance, a customer service workflow might include "Classify and prioritize incoming requests," "Search knowledge base," and "Compose a personalized response."

2. **Assign a Reasoning Level**

   For each step, determine whether a human (or an AI) would need **high**, **medium**, or **low** reasoning.

   - **Low**: Straightforward lookups or simple condition checks.
   - **Medium**: Basic decision rules, possibly referencing multiple data points.
   - **High**: Complex problem-solving that may involve unstructured data, deep analysis, or multistep logic.

3. **Identify Required Tools or Data**

   Note which systems, APIs, or knowledge bases the AI must access to perform each step. A compliance check might require a legal database, while a scheduling task might rely on a calendar API.

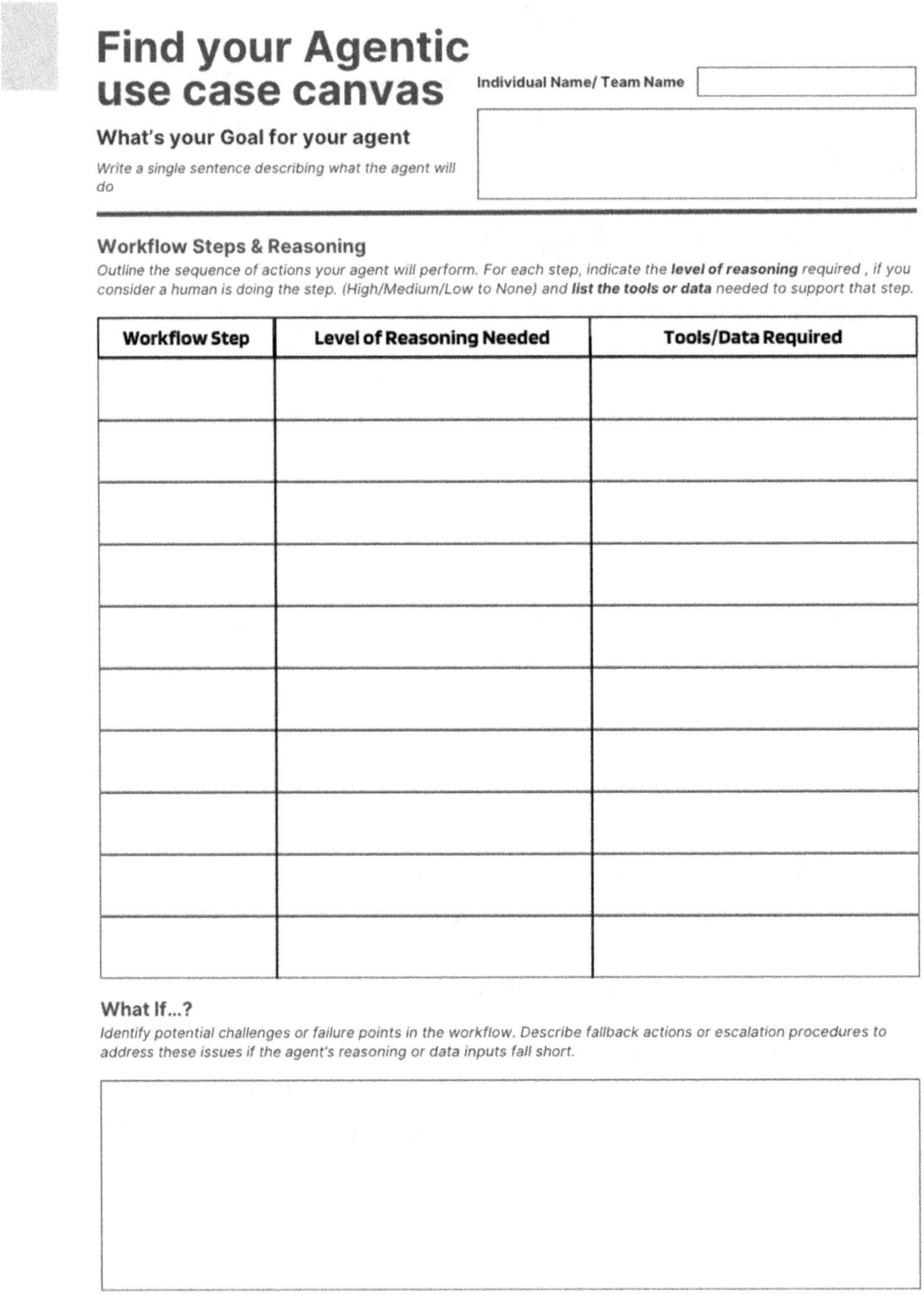

Find your Agentic use case canvas

Individual Name/ Team Name

What's your Goal for your agent

Write a single sentence describing what the agent will do

Workflow Steps & Reasoning

Outline the sequence of actions your agent will perform. For each step, indicate the **level of reasoning** required, if you consider a human is doing the step. (High/Medium/Low to None) and **list the tools or data** needed to support that step.

Workflow Step	Level of Reasoning Needed	Tools/Data Required

What If...?

Identify potential challenges or failure points in the workflow. Describe fallback actions or escalation procedures to address these issues if the agent's reasoning or data inputs fall short.

Figure 6-13. Agentic Use Case Canvas

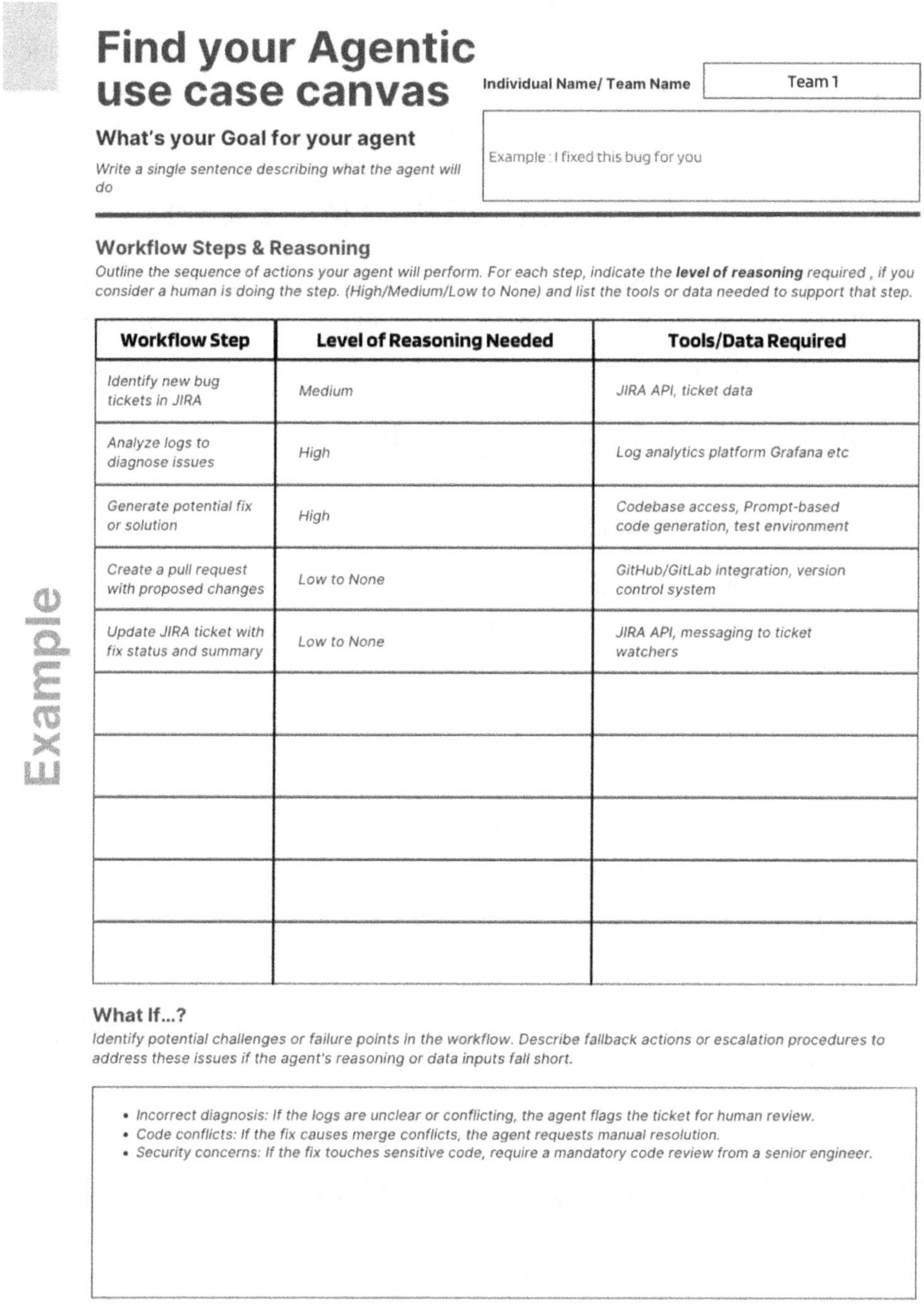

CHAPTER 6   THE AGE OF AGENTS - FROM SCRIPTS TO SIDEKICKS

Find your Agentic use case canvas

Individual Name/ Team Name: Team 1

What's your Goal for your agent
Write a single sentence describing what the agent will do

Example : I fixed this bug for you

Workflow Steps & Reasoning
Outline the sequence of actions your agent will perform. For each step, indicate the **level of reasoning** required, if you consider a human is doing the step. (High/Medium/Low to None) and list the tools or data needed to support that step.

Workflow Step	Level of Reasoning Needed	Tools/Data Required
Identify new bug tickets in JIRA	Medium	JIRA API, ticket data
Analyze logs to diagnose issues	High	Log analytics platform Grafana etc
Generate potential fix or solution	High	Codebase access, Prompt-based code generation, test environment
Create a pull request with proposed changes	Low to None	GitHub/GitLab integration, version control system
Update JIRA ticket with fix status and summary	Low to None	JIRA API, messaging to ticket watchers

What If...?
Identify potential challenges or failure points in the workflow. Describe fallback actions or escalation procedures to address these issues if the agent's reasoning or data inputs fall short.

- Incorrect diagnosis: If the logs are unclear or conflicting, the agent flags the ticket for human review.
- Code conflicts: If the fix causes merge conflicts, the agent requests manual resolution.
- Security concerns: If the fix touches sensitive code, require a mandatory code review from a senior engineer.

Figure 6-14. Example – Agentic Use Case Canvas

This exercise not only clarifies where **agentic** thinking is truly needed but also highlights tasks that could be automated with simpler "fast thinking" approaches. By visualizing the entire process, teams can see at a glance which parts of their workflow call for a more advanced AI and which are already served by existing solutions.

Integrating Human Oversight and Risk Management

Even the most sophisticated AI agents benefit from human guidance – particularly in critical or high-stakes contexts. **Human-in-the-loop** processes ensure that the system remains accountable, transparent, and aligned with organizational values.

Best Practices for Embedding Oversight

1. **Define Clear Checkpoints**

    Decide at which junctures the AI's output should be reviewed or approved by a human. This might be after a risk assessment step, or before finalizing a response that has legal implications.

2. **Set Up Feedback Loops**

    Encourage users – whether they're employees or customers – to flag suspicious or erroneous outputs. This real-world feedback helps refine the AI's reasoning model over time.

3. **Escalation Procedures**

    If the agent encounters ambiguous or conflicting data, it should either request clarification from a human or revert to a safer, rule-based fallback. The canvas's "What If...?" section prompts teams to outline these fail-safes in advance.

Merging Agentic and Compound Systems

While agentic AI can handle complex, unstructured tasks, many workflows still benefit from compound (or "fast thinking") systems – especially for predictable or repetitive steps. A **hybrid** model ensures that

- **Simple tasks** remain quick, cost-effective, and easy to maintain with rule-based or retrieval-augmented solutions.
- **Complex tasks** are offloaded to an agentic AI, which can plan, act, and iterate when faced with novel or ambiguous scenarios.

This blend often yields the best of both worlds: speed and reliability for routine operations, plus the adaptability and depth of a "slow thinking" AI where it matters most.

The journey to effective agentic AI adoption hinges on understanding your organization's specific needs. By prioritizing **problem-first** thinking, mapping out each workflow step with the **Agentic Use Case Canvas**, and embedding **human oversight**, teams can ensure they deploy the right mix of AI solutions – balancing innovation with accountability. In doing so, they lay the foundation for systems that genuinely elevate productivity, rather than simply following the latest AI trend.

In the next section, we'll explore real-world examples and success stories that illustrate how this strategic framework translates into tangible business outcomes. By seeing these principles in action, you'll gain further clarity on how to tailor agentic AI to your unique context – and avoid the pitfalls of a purely technology-first mindset.

A New Horizon: Where AI Agents Go from Here

As we reach the final pages of this book, it's clear that the world of AI has come a long way – from monolithic language models that could dazzle us with clever prose, to compound systems that bridged the gap between static training and real-time data, and ultimately to the agentic frameworks we see today. Across these pages, we've explored how AI can **reason**, **act**, and **remember**, using architectures and principles like ReAct and Mixture of Experts to handle tasks once deemed too complex or too fluid for machines. Yet, as with any transformative technology, the story doesn't end here.

Emerging Trends and Future Challenges

The journey doesn't stop at today's agentic frameworks. Even now, researchers and practitioners are envisioning the **next shift** – one that addresses the limitations of current models and pushes AI even closer to human-like intelligence.

Dynamic Chain-of-Thought

Today's chain-of-thought prompting often compels large language models to reason *every* question in detail, even when it's as trivial as "What is 1+1?" This can lead to amusing (and sometimes frustrating) overthinking – like our fictional DeepSeek spending 26 seconds to calculate a simple sum. The next evolution may see models that automatically scale their reasoning depth based on context, just as a human might tailor an answer differently for a six-year-old vs. a physicist.

Adaptive Cost Management

As organizations deploy AI at scale, the question of **compute cost** becomes more pressing. We've seen how Mixture of Experts architectures selectively activate submodels to cut down on overhead. Future systems might combine this approach with dynamic reasoning, invoking heavier or lighter modules depending on the complexity of the task – thus making "slow thinking" optional rather than obligatory.

Contextual Cues and Human-Like Intuition

Another frontier lies in giving AI a richer sense of context – tapping into subtle signals that humans use effortlessly. Imagine an AI that not only reads text but also interprets tone, situational urgency, or even visual cues. By integrating these signals, future agentic systems could fine-tune their reasoning style, striking the perfect balance between thoroughness and speed.

Ethical and Regulatory Oversight

With great autonomy comes greater responsibility. As AI agents gain the ability to make real-time decisions – especially in fields like healthcare, finance, or public policy – robust oversight frameworks will be indispensable. We can expect regulators and ethicists to shape guidelines that ensure these advanced systems remain accountable, transparent, and fair. Remember the news when an AI bot hallucinated and created a discount coupon for a passenger, and the coupon did not actually exist? Well, agents can now create that in DB as well for you to use. If not controlled, I might be traveling by a flight for the rest of my life for free!

Remember the Demo Dr. Anya Gave on 1+1 and DeepSeek Going into a Deep Analysis?

Let me pull the images for you here (Figures 6-15 and 6-16):

Figure 6-15. *Gpt-4o responding*

CHAPTER 6   THE AGE OF AGENTS - FROM SCRIPTS TO SIDEKICKS

Figure 6-16. DeepSeek R1 responding

Nothing exemplifies the need for dynamic reasoning better than the humorous "1+1" demo. In the story, DeepSeek – an advanced reasoning model – took a simple arithmetic query and turned it into a mini philosophical exploration. While it made for a great laugh, it also highlighted a genuine technical gap: AI currently lacks the built-in discernment to gauge the depth of reasoning required by each question.

Humans, on the other hand, instinctively know when to offer a quick reply and when to pause for deeper thought. The **future of AI** may well be defined by systems that emulate this selective reasoning – where the model's chain-of-thought is proportionate to the query's complexity and the user's intent.

A Final Word from Dr. Anya

If Dr. Anya were to address a room of eager AI practitioners one last time, she might say something like this:

> *"We've come so far – from being wowed by a model that can write a limerick, to expecting AI to handle entire business processes autonomously. But remember, AI isn't magic; it's a tool that reflects our own understanding of intelligence. As we continue to refine agentic systems, let's stay curious, remain critical, and always ask: **Is this technology truly solving a problem, or are we just solving technology for technology's sake?***
>
> *The day when AI decides on its own how deeply to reason – much like a person deciding whether to give a child a simple answer or engage a physicist in debate – will be a day we realize how close we've come to bridging the gap between artificial and human intelligence. Until then, let's keep building responsibly, creatively, and with a problem-first mindset."*

Key Learnings from This Chapter

The AI landscape is shifting once again. Beyond generating content, AI systems are now evolving into autonomous "agents" that can reason, plan, and act on their own. How do you navigate this next wave without getting swept up in the hype? This final chapter provides the strategic clarity needed to understand and implement agentic AI responsibly and effectively.

Here are the key frameworks you've discovered to master this new frontier:

1. **The "Think Fast, Think Slow" Paradigm** You've learned the most critical lesson for the agentic era: not every problem needs a deep-thinking agent. This chapter introduces the "Think Fast, Think Slow" paradigm to help you choose the right tool for the job:

- **Fast Thinkers (Assistance Logic/RAG):** Use these for well-defined workflows where the path to the answer is known (e.g., retrieving a policy). They are efficient, predictable, and cost-effective.

- **Slow Thinkers (Agentic Logic):** Reserve these for complex, unstructured problems where the system must explore, plan, and iterate to find a solution (e.g., performing a financial risk assessment).

2. **The Engine of Autonomy: The ReAct Principle** How do agents actually "think"? You've discovered the core design principle behind them: **ReAct (Reason and Act)**. This is the iterative cycle where an agent first **reasons** (breaking a problem down into a chain of thought) and then **acts** (using tools or APIs to gather information), allowing it to tackle multistep tasks that were previously impossible for AI.

3. **The Strategic Tool: The Agentic Use Case Canvas** How do you identify where you *truly* need an agent? The **Agentic Use Case Canvas** is your practical guide. This framework helps you and your clients map any workflow step-by-step, forcing you to define the **Level of Reasoning Needed** (High, Medium, or Low) and the required tools *before* ever discussing a technology solution. This problem-first approach ensures you deploy agents where they add genuine value, avoiding over-engineered solutions.

Your Path Forward: The End of the Beginning Across these six chapters, you have journeyed from navigating the initial AI hype to engineering systems for enterprise scale and, finally, to understanding the dawn of AI agents. You are no longer just an observer of this technological revolution; you are a navigator, equipped with a compass and a map.

The frameworks – from the **Value Compass** to the **Agentic Use Case Canvas** – are your tools to build AI that is not just powerful but purposeful. They will help you balance innovation with impact, speed with safety, and ambition with responsibility.

The path forward is not about having all the answers. It is about knowing which questions to ask. As you close this book and begin your next project, carry this mindset with you. Challenge the hype, ground your decisions in value, and build with a steady hand. The future of AI is not something that happens *to* us; it is something we build one responsible, strategic decision at a time. Now, it's your turn to navigate.

Index

A

Adoption strategy, 70
Advanced encryption techniques, 149
Agent-based architectures, 238
Agentic AI systems, 257
Agentic Use Case Canvas, 275
AI agents
    architectures, 238, 240
    arithmetic operation
        ChatGPT-4, 242
        DeepSeek R1, 243–245
    assessment framework, 250–253, 255, 256
    challenges, 279, 280
    commercial reality, 257
    compound system, 260
    control logic, 261–266
    DeepSeek R1, 282
    LLMs, 239, 258, 270
    memory, 240
    Mixtral 8x7B, 272, 273
    MoE, 271, 272
    monolithic language models, 279
    ReAct principle, 266–269
    real-world data, 246–250
    refine agentic systems, 283
    security framework validation, 237
    strategic framework, 274
        Agentic Use Case Canvas, 275, 277
        Human-in-the-loop processes, 278
        merging agentic and compound systems, 279
        problem-first approach vs. technology-first approach, 274
        "vanilla" LLMs, limits, 259, 260
AI-based patient management system, 148
AI Capability Mapping, 9

B

Bento Box, 88, 89, 91, 104, 124
Business value
    benefits and costs, 12
    customer service AI, 15
    ethical implementation feasibility, 14
    finding the bridge, 8
    innovation, 4–6
    machine learning, 9
    mapping AI capabilities, 10
    TechNova, 7
    value and impact assessment, 10–13
    value compass, 15

C

Chain of Thought, 244
ChatGPT, 58
ChromaDB, 125

INDEX

Compliance Discovery Canvas
    baseline for costs, 217
    economy of security, 212
        baseline for costs, 217
        FinCorp chatbot, 220
        hidden costs, 213, 214
        HR bot deployment, 220
        KPIs, 217
        proactive *vs.* reactive spending, 213
        reactive approach, 212
        reactive *vs.* proactive approaches, 215, 216
        ROI, 216, 219
        snapshots, 221
    implementation framework, 200, 201
    operational governance
        AI life cycle, 222
        cross-functional collaboration, 226
        departmental silos, 226–228
        design and conceptualization, 222, 223
        development/integration, 223–225
        future proofing, 231, 232
        Governance Compass, 232, 233
        policies, 230
        systemic tracking/evaluation, 229, 230
        training and development, 231
    proactive threat modeling, 204
    risk-based thinking, 201
    risk management and policy frameworks, 204–211
Content generation tool, 63
Contract analysis system, 114

Control logic, 261
Cross-functional collaboration, 226, 229

D

Data governance, 148
Data hoarding trap, 57
Data Vault, 149
Death by POC, 102
Document Classification Service, 111
Document Intelligence Bento, 111
Document Matching Service, 111

E

Engineering GenAI, production
    enterprise AI architecture
        API gateway, 142, 145
        challenges, 136–140
        load management layer, 141
        monitoring service, 144, 145
        processing layer, 142
        security, 146
        storage, 143
    enterprise AI governance, 146, 147
        data governance, 148, 149
        development, 150, 151
        regional compliance, 148
        security, 149
    infrastructure, 123
    POC
        demonstrations, 121
        setup, 122
        successful enterprise scale, 133–135
    security, 129–131
    security workflows, 126–129
Enterprise Azure openAI, 129

F

Full-blown movement, 258

G, H

Gating mechanism, 271
GenAI Idea Maze
    action play, 44
    AI-assisted coding, 76
    AI literacy, 58, 59
    array of data, 43
    business solution, 63–66
    core capabilities, 62, 63
    educating organization, 45–47
    education engaging/practical, 60, 61
    framework, 75, 76
    global manufacturing firm, 55
    impact, 75
    innovation, three waves, 56, 57
    innovators, 76
    mapping AI landscape, 47–49
    observations, 44
    POCs, 78
    problem-solving, 77
    transforming fashion result, 72–74
        solution, 73
    use case detective's toolkit, 50–54
Generative AI implementation
    AI value compass
        business problem, 25, 26
        components, 24
        implementation, 29
        initiatives, 30
        mapping, 26, 27
        value and impact assessment, 27, 28
        value ethical implementation feasibility, 28
    business value, 7

cutting-edge AI, 1
death by POC trap, 16–18
navigating initiatives, 30
    death by POC, 34–37
    degree of unknowns, 30–33
    workflow, 37–41
real world use case
    deployment and measurement, 20–23
    POC development, 20
    prioritization, 20
    senior leadership education, 19
    stakeholder workshop, 19
    use case ideation, 19
revolutionizing industries, 3
value compass, 3
Guardrails
    AI landscape
        GenAI, 187, 188
        layered security, 189–194
        predictability, 187
        proactive governance, 188, 189
    API-level security, 197
    building habits, governance/security/ethics, 184–186
    chatbot, 155
    continuous monitoring/AI observability, 198, 199
    data handling/privacy control, 197, 198
    governance
        data governance framework, 167–170
        ethical AI implementation, 173–175
        framework, 159, 161–167
        operation, 175–177
        risk management framework, 170–172
        speed, 156–158, 160, 161

Guardrails (*cont.*)
  input/output moderation, 196, 197
  multilayered AI Security Onion, 195
  orchestrator for services, 196
  safeguarding levels, 195
  security investment, 177–183
  transparency, 155

I, J

Information Extraction Service, 111
Intrusion detection systems, 149

K

Key performance indicators (KPIs), 217, 229

L

Language models, 31
Large language model (LLM), 258, 270
Learning momentum, 61
LLM, *see* Large language model (LLM)

M

Machine learning, 9, 57
Machine learning algorithms, 60
Magic solution approach, 66
Minimum Viable Product (MVP), 20
Mixtral 8x7B, 272
Mixture of Experts (MoE), 271
MoE, *see* Mixture of Experts (MoE)
MongoDB Atlas, 125
Monolithic models, 239
MVP, *see* Minimum Viable Product (MVP)

N

Neural networks, 60

O

One-size-fits-all strategy, 148
Operational Governance, 175

P, Q

"Parallel tracks" approach, 107
Personalized learning platforms, 45
POC, *see* Proof-of-concept (POC) model
Problem-first approach, 274
Production-grade services, 96
Proof-of-concept (POC) model, 34
  accelerated technology evolution, 100
  Bento Box, 103–106
  building teams/frameworks, 112–114
  contract analysis system, 114
  email enhancement, 82
  financial services, 116
  financial services firm, 81
  GenAI, 84–89
  generative AI demonstration, 117, 118
  implementation/demonstration, GenAI, 90–94, 96–98
  insurance claim, 82
  monolithic applications, 83
  predictable patterns, 100

production, 81
public APIs, 82
resource sustainability challenge, 101, 102
seven-day cycle, 109
shifting principles, practice, 110–112
success elements, 108, 110
three acts approach, 115, 116
value realization gap, 102

R

ReAct principle, 266
Retrieval Augmented Generation, 239
Return on investment (ROI), 216
ROI, *see* Return on investment (ROI)

S

Sustainable business models, 2

T

TechSphere, 237
Text generation service, 84
Three Acts approach, 116

U, V, W, X, Y, Z

Use case detective's toolkit
    generative AI canvas, 67
    strategic foundation, 67–69
    tactical roadmap, 70, 72
    technical complexities, 66

GPSR Compliance
The European Union's (EU) General Product Safety Regulation (GPSR) is a set of rules that requires consumer products to be safe and our obligations to ensure this.

If you have any concerns about our products, you can contact us on

ProductSafety@springernature.com

In case Publisher is established outside the EU, the EU authorized representative is:

Springer Nature Customer Service Center GmbH
Europaplatz 3
69115 Heidelberg, Germany

www.ingramcontent.com/pod-product-compliance
Lightning Source LLC
LaVergne TN
LVHW081537070526
838199LV00056B/3696